T WAY AND THE POWER

THE
WAY
AND THE
POWER

Secrets of
Japanese Strategy

Fredrick J. Lovret

PALADIN PRESS
BOULDER, COLORADO

The Way and the Power:
  Secrets of Japanese Strategy
by Frederick J. Lovret

Copyright © 1987 by Frederick J. Lovret

ISBN 0-87364-409-3
Printed in the United States of America

Published by Paladin Press, a division of
Paladin Enterprises, Inc., P.O. Box 1307,
Boulder, Colorado 80306, USA.
(303) 443-7250

Direct inquiries and/or orders to the above address.

The photographs in this text were provided courtesy of Sandia
Budokan (Albuquerque, NM), Dallas Budokan (Duncanville,
TX), Maryland Budokan (Beltsville, MD), and Seattle Budokan
(Mountlake Terrace, WA).

Visit our Web site at www.paladin-press.com

Contents

BOOK II: THE POWER

Dedication

Dedicated to my *makideshi:* Tart, Rajguru, Reafsnyder, Ostrowski, Weiss, Corley, Gaudin, and Knight. They maintained.

A special note of thanks to the people of the National Diet Library of Tokyo, Japan. They were fast and courteous in supplying me with invaluable research materials.

Introduction

The essence of life is struggle and its goal is domination. There are higher goals and deeper meanings, but they exist only within the mind of man. The reality of life is war.

While walking through the woods you may discover a tree growing through a slab of granite. It started as a delicate seedling—but even a seed has a dream. Day after day, year after year, it drove ever upward, taking advantage of every weak spot in its monolithic opponent. The tree lived and the rock began its degradation into sand. The seedling did not seek the confrontation; neither did it surrender and die. It only obeyed the first law of nature: Win!

A man, like a tree, begins as a seed. As with a tree, his birth is a time of struggle. From that day forward, he exists in a constant state of war with his environment. To live he must eat and to eat he must kill. He kills the tree to make his shelter. He kills the seed to make his bread. He kills other animals for their meat. Even when taking a sip of water, he kills countless microscopic forms of life.

Physically, man is a weakling. There are many other animals that are stronger, faster, or better armed. But man had a dream, a dream of winning. His lust for victory drove him to develop the only weapon he had: his brain. This development allowed him to win, but the process did not stop there. His large brain allowed him to dream of even greater things. Man became the beast which is always hungry.

In some long-forgotten cave, a nameless hominoid discovered he could control more territory by throwing stones than he could by fighting with his bare fists—and modern war was born. Since that rudimentary beginning, the human race has devoted much of its energy and intellect to the development of warfare into an exact science. With ever greater weapons, the race of man dominated more and more territory. But he could never capture his dream. Even when he had all the food he could eat and all the land he could use, he lusted for more.

Finally, when he had defeated nature, man looked to his only remaining worthy opponent: himself. When there was no more food, he took his neighbor's food. When there was no more land, he took his neighbor's land. Along the way he developed civilization.

"Civilized man"—a nice-sounding phrase. However, all too often the promise of this phrase is but a dream. Civilized man does not believe in reality; he believes in believing. He believes that his intellect has become so great as to place him above nature. The civilized man does not believe in violence; he believes his society should shield him from violence. He closes his eyes to a fact that society does this by violent means. A civilized man does not believe in killing; he has other civilized men do his killing for him. The civilized man believes in the sanctity of all life; he does not let this interfere with his enjoyment of a good steak.

The technical term for such behavior is schizophrenia: a retreat from reality. This is a characteristic disorder of civilized man. The higher the degree of civilization, the greater the retreat from reality will be. The result is predictable. A man concentrates so intently on the ideals and accomplishments of his civilization that he forgets he is a man. There would be no great harm in this if the degree of civilization was constant throughout the world. However, it is not—there are still wolves.

The first step toward a cure for civilization's schizophrenia must be an awareness and understanding of the wolves. Along

with this must come an understanding of the fact that the
sheep are only safe when the wolves are not hungry. The first
great truth of nature is that violence exists. It always has and
always will. A modern society does not protect the individual
from this violence. The best it can manage is an occasional
punishment of the wrongdoer. That the vast majority of a
society's members find this sufficient is truly terrifying.

The root of the problem is the reversal of roles between
man and his civilization. Civilization is a tool. It is a tool
created by man, for the good of man. Its purpose is to allow
a large group of individuals to live within a small area without
undue conflict. In return for the benefits derived from such a
grouping, the individual must give up certain rights. In a
limited civilization the cost is small and contributions are
voluntary. However, as the society grows a role reversal
occurs. Man no longer shapes his society; the society shapes
the man. It is as if, upon reaching a certain size, the civilization becomes a living thing. No longer just a tool, it struggles
for its own survival.

Realizing there is less conflict within a herd of sheep than
in a pack of wolves, the society attempts to render sheep-
like the greatest killer the world has ever known: man.
Beginning at birth, the individual is conditioned to abhor
violence and conform to the group. Each stage of his life
serves to further isolate him from any other reality. If the
process is carried to its ultimate extreme, the individual lives
in a completely socialized world. Dealing with rational
men, he solves all conflicts with reasonable methods.

Sometimes, however, the plan does not work. When the
cry is "havoc"[1] and the dogs of war are set loose, the modern
individual discovers he no longer has the temperament for
war. Suddenly slapped in the face with reality, he finds that
generations of social conditioning have taken their toll.
Instead of greeting the cry "To arms! To arms!" with a leap
of the heart as did his ancestors, he hears it with a shiver of
apprehension. By adopting the mannerisms of a sheep, he
has become a sheep. No longer the hunter, he is now only
food.

All living things can be placed in one of two categories:

the eaters and the eaten. By conditioning its members to abhor violence a society can suppress the lust for combat, but in so doing it also sows the seeds of its own destruction. By isolating its members from the reality of war, civilization renders many of them incapable of waging it. Elimination of war is a lofty ideal—someday the lion may lie down with the lamb—but, for the foreseeable future, this must remain only a dream. There are just too many people in the world who still prefer the thrill of the chase to the security of the flock.

It is not that the wolves of the human race love the act of war itself—that is madness. What they find terribly addictive is the result of war. Winning, achieving a glorious victory, satisfies a primal urge. This instinct is so deeply buried within a man's psyche that he may not even be aware of its existence. In the words of Genghis Khan, as orally passed down in Oriental schools of war: "There is no joy a man can feel which is greater than when he destroys his enemies and drives them before him." A society can suppress this urge but will never eliminate it. To do so might make men more than human, but it would also make them less than alive.

Any civilization that wishes to advance must give its members a goal. However, if it wants to survive, it must never allow its dreams for the future to obscure the reality of the past. The individual must be taught that he is first an animal and only secondly of the genus *Homo*. The civilization he holds so dear must be appreciated for what it is: an artificial shell. Only by understanding his true nature can a man live with the flock while retaining his abilities for war. Such a man, while he may dream of peace, will never forget Thomas Jefferson's statement: "The tree of liberty must be refreshed from time to time with the blood of patriots and tyrants."[2]

Realistic societies have always accepted that it is impossible to reason with irrational men. Because of this, warfare became "a continuation of national policy by other means."[3] This required the creation of the profession of arms; the common man, because of his conditioning, was no longer strong enough for war. The act of violence now required specialists. These specialists ranged from policemen to soldiers, but, whatever their task, their essential nature remained constant. In one form or another, they were charged with the application of controlled violence.

Because conflict is an inherent part of life itself, the profession of arms necessitates a two-class society. Those who are required to go in harm's way must be only semi-domesticated if they are to have any hope of survival on the field of battle. Such men may then easily shed the restrictions of civilization and set free the beast within.

In feudal Europe the two-class system consisted of the gentle and the simple. The simple were the commoners. They lived under the restrictions of (and received protection from) the gentle. The gentle were the property owners. They were men of noble birth who bore arms.[4] This was a very logical and just system, for those who had the most to lose bore the brunt of the fighting.

However, as time went on the structure of society changed—while the gentlemen were fighting, the commoners were breeding. Eventually the commoners achieved by numbers what they could not win earlier: control. This led to the creation of the democratic state. Such a system is never seen in nature—all other forms of life only accept leadership from those strong enough to enforce it. The commoners immediately set about disarming the nobility and bringing it into the fold of society. They succeeded, perhaps too well.

Modern man has become trapped by his own society in a dichotomy of philosophies. Because the traditional relationships—the relationship between a man and his society and between commoner and noble—have been inverted, he finds himself in a difficult situation. A civilized man is forced to fight all-too-real nightmares from his past with insubstantial dreams of the future. The idealistic teachings of his society ill prepare him for the reality of war.

The composition of a modern army is a reflection of modern civilization. In the past, an army was led by the king. He was followed by his princes and barons. These professional warriors formed the spearhead of an attack, and the commoners followed along with the baggage carts. In such an army, a man's social status during peacetime was directly proportional to his nearness to the enemy in time of war. A nobleman might have been born into his position, but, when the trumpets sounded, he was expected to prove his merit. Now, however, like the structure of civilization, the structure of the army has changed. Those with the most to lose are furthest from the battle; those with the least to lose do the actual fighting. Unfortunately, modern society provides such men with little incentive to fight.

In modern warfare, those who direct the armies have little or no experience in combat. The men who do the actual fighting have little reason to fight—their lives would not be greatly changed by either victory or defeat.

Herein lies the great flaw in all modern governments. The feudal serf expected his king to lead the army into battle; the modern citizen should demand it. However, such is not the case. Because those with the most to lose are allowed to position themselves the furthest from the field of battle, millions of lives are needlessly lost—it is always easier to declare a war if someone else is doing the fighting. On the battlefield and in the city streets, men who are forced to experience the reality of violence are both governed and conditioned by people who are isolated from it. True, there are a few of the Old Guard left—men who are the product of generations of warriors—but, more often than not, such specialists in the profession of arms are forced to fight under rules created by men who have never seen war.

A worker must know his tools. This should be an obvious truth. However, it is a truth rarely heeded by society. Any society, if it is to work well, should consider the military a tool. It is imperative that the citizen of any modern society understand the differences between the professional warrior and himself. It is only after the physical and psychological requirements of the fighting man are understood that he may be used effectively.

Wu Ch'i said, "Men generally die when they cannot help it."[5] This is the way of the civilian. The warrior is different because he selects the manner of his own death. Every man who dons a uniform accepts, as an unwritten part of his contract, the possible requirement of being called upon to die in battle. It is this single item which makes the profession of arms unique—in no other job is a worker expected to voluntarily sacrifice his life. In any other job, if a man feels the situation is becoming too dangerous, he can always quit. Even if this forces him to break a contract, it is only a civil matter. However, when a soldier signs a contract, he gives up his civil rights. To default brings criminal charges; in time of war, desertion is a serious crime. The men who are willing to accept such a contract are very few in number, usually less than 1 percent of the population. Such men are very, very special—not better or worse than others, just special.

A civilian can never empathize with a warrior; his fundamental philosophy is just too different. However, he should at least understand enough about the motivations and value structure of the soldier to make optimum use of his services.

When the civilian understands the warrior, he will appreciate him for what he is, a specialist in violence, and treat him accordingly. He will also realize that the concept of citizen-soldier is a contradiction in terms—the soldier will never be a good citizen because the basic teachings of society are in direct conflict with the requirements of his profession. Because the warrior's shell of civilization must be thin, about the best that can be hoped for is he will learn not to bite the hand that feeds him.

By understanding the nature of war, the civilian will be prepared if it intrudes into his world. No matter how secure the environment, violence can erupt with little warning. While it would be pleasant to be able to call in a specialist every time violence occurs, this is not always possible. More often than most people care to admit, a peaceful man must put down the pen and pick up the sword in order to survive. If he knows the way of war he can do this; if not, he becomes a sheep being led to slaughter.

By understanding the warrior, the civilian protects and preserves him for future use; by understanding the nature of war, the civilian protects and preserves himself for future existence.

The profession of arms deals with the reality of violence. Because of this, true professionals are, without exception, pragmatists. (A rare idealist may be seen in a military role during peacetime, but he never survives the first war.) Although senior officers may talk about God and country, this is only a sham—it lets the civilian population sleep easier. In reality, the warrior is a relic from the past. He does not fight for God or country, he fights to win. He will endure great personal hardship in order to stand on a hill, howl at the moon, and proclaim his dominion over all he surveys. Although his uniform and equipment are much different from that of the Viking berserker, his instincts are the same. The major difference between the modern soldier and his ancient counterpart is that the modern warrior has learned to pull in his claws a bit and settle for a medal instead of the pleasures of rape and pillage.

Circumstances may force the civilian to act like a soldier. However, he always views this as only a temporary situation. As soon as the war is over he tries to flush from his consciousness all memories of both the horrors and the lessons of war. It has been often said that those who do not learn from the past are doomed to repeat it. Because the civilian does not like to think about war, he condemns himself to endless repetitions of the same battles. However, the warrior remembers.

A professional soldier is always at work. As soon as he finishes one war he begins preparations for the next. A pragmatist to the end, he knows that there will *always* be another. Objectively, he looks back at his performance in combat and works to improve this before the next battle.

Combat is a matter of conditioned reflexes. When swords are drawn there is simply no time for rational thought, and any soldier who has survived a battle understands this. Therefore, the professional fighting man is always busy creating new sets of conditioned reflexes for new situations. These reflexes are the techniques of combat. In Japanese they are called either *gihō* or *waza,* both words having approximately the same meaning.[6]

This procedure—the creation of new techniques for war—has been going on since the dawn of man. Starting with a man huddled in a cave attaching a pointed stone to a stick, it has progressed into modern times with little change. Now other men huddle in air-conditioned caverns and attach radioactive rocks to flaming shafts. Although the form has changed, the fundamental theory remains the same. Both the spear and the ICBM obey the same laws of motion. Both weapons also have the same objective: to kill the enemy.

Tools of war change from year to year. While this is very frustrating for military planners, it cannot be avoided. Because the tools change, the techniques for their use must also change. The modern rifleman uses a completely different set of muscles than those the caveman conditioned for hurling a spear. However, even though the waza are different, there are still many common factors. Both men allow for windage and elevation, both consider cover and concealment. The understanding and use of these common factors is defined as strategy, known as *heihō* in Japanese. The difference between giho and heiho is the distribution. A technique is limited to a specific weapon and/or situation. However, because a strategy is based on general principles, it is not so limited. A strategy remains the same throughout the centuries and is independent of both weapon and situation.

The process of study, design, and experimentation is known as science. In any science, and military science is no exception, the eyes turn outward. With all thought and effort directed toward some external goal, in this case the goal of overcoming an enemy, there is little time for introspection. Despite this pressure, man has occasionally found the time to look not just at, but into, war. It was this study, looking inward instead of outward, that led to the rarefied world of pure strategy.

A technique is a method of applying a tool. (The size of the tool is irrelevant. It can be a single bullet or an entire army.) A strategy, however, is a level above this. Strategy deals with the application of techniques. While the technician is limited by his tools and training, the strategist is constrained only by the limits of his imagination. This fundamental difference between technique and strategy is rarely understood, even by those who are supposed to be masters of the art of war. More often than not, the science of strategy is confused with that of tactics. In fact, many of the world's most famous generals were not strategists. They were tremendously talented technicians, masters of the art of logistics.

There are many places in the world where you may encounter an advanced science of war. Occasionally you may even see this science raised to an art form. But, in order to see a mature science of strategy, you must look to the East. To see the science of strategy elevated to an art form, you must look specifically to Japan.

The Japanese warrior was not more talented than his Western counterpart. Neither was he more suited to war in any other way. However, a unique set of circumstances provided the swordsmen of that country with both the time and the stimuli for a deep and thorough study of their art. Compared to such men, strategists of other nations were little more than gifted amateurs.

While the age of the great swordsmen is long past, the strategies they developed are still viable. Now we have armies instead of legions and riflemen instead of archers. However, the act of war itself has little changed. No matter what form it takes, war is still a matter of one man dominating another. The tools may be different, but the men who use the tools are still men. The strategist deals with ideas, ideas for the control of men, and men do not change. Neither do ideas. There are rarely new ideas, only new words to describe old ones.

THE SAMURAI

Although the warriors of feudal Japan are frequently compared to the knights of Europe, the similarities are only superficial. In Europe, both the techniques and weapons of war underwent constant change due to frequent clashes between different cultures. However, in Japan war was, with but few exceptions, an internal matter. Isolated from the rest of the world, Japanese weaponry and enemy remained the same for centuries.

The golden age of the swordsman was during the beginning of the seventeenth century. After generations of civil strife,

The samurai.

the country was unified by Ieyasu[7] and a rigid military dictatorship was imposed. Now known as samurai, warriors who had survived the battlefield became garrison troops. Instead of being a group that anyone could fight his way into, they came to constitute a caste that you had to be born into. Easily identifiable by their two swords,[8] the samurai became creatures of both privilege and obligation. Legally entitled to kill any commoner who acted in a disrespectful manner, a samurai strode through life with the knowledge that he too might one day fall by the sword. Forced to live in a violent world of sudden death, he took the only option available other than insanity; he transformed violence into an art form. The techniques of swordsmanship became the Way of the Sword.

In the words of Ieyasu, as taught to every student of the sword, "The girded sword is the living soul of the samurai." To a samurai, his sword was not just a tool for killing. Instead, it had become the symbol of everything he lived for and everything he was willing to die for. The Japanese sword[9] had always been a thing of great beauty and quality, making the finest blade of any other country seem little more than a pointed stick in comparison. It became a religious icon. The sword and the man who wore it were treated accordingly. To accidentally brush against a man's sword on a crowded street became an act of instant suicide. The offended swordsman would pivot, draw, and kill in one blinding flow of motion. Then he would walk away, as if nothing had happened.

The Japanese sword is the greatest cutting weapon ever devised by man.[10] For decades, master swordsmen researched every possible variation in its use. With only an edge and a point limiting them to varieties of cuts and thrusts, the gamut of possible techniques was soon exhausted. They soon progressed to strategic uses of the weapon. These men were not obscure theorists; they were battle-hardened veterans and their strategies reflected this. For decades they had fought, and then for decades they studied. Knowing what had worked on the battlefield, they asked themselves why it had worked and what they could do to make it even better. In some cases the answer was found to be a simple, physical manipulation of the sword. In other cases, however, they discovered that an actual change in their way of thinking was required.

(The mental shift that then took place should not be confused with what is commonly called the Code of Bushidō. Bushido, the Way of the Warrior, is a relatively modern set of ethics. It was created by those who were in authority in order to maintain their control over their subjects. The people in power never got there by adhering to bushido; neither did the great swordsmen pay much attention to it.)

Whereas the soldiers of the other nations studied how to adapt their techniques to their weaponry, the Japanese swordsman learned to adapt himself to his techniques. He treated his spirit in much the same way as the swordsmith treated a lump of iron. The samurai pounded and polished until the strength of his will matched the strength of his blade. The sword did not think about killing, neither did it feel remorse. The samurai was no different. Killing or not killing, living or dying, he strode through life not preferring it to death.

A samurai was a butcher. He could kill or die on command, without an instant of hesitation. Because he studied both acts so deeply, either could be done with great elegance. He trained himself not just to accept death but to lust for it. He did not fight with a goal of self-defense; he sought glory. Occasionally denied this in battle, he devised the most painful form of suicide possible, the ritual disembowelment of *seppuku*.[11] He turned the performance of even this into an art. To such a man, the words death and beauty were synonymous. A poet with bloody hands, he lived with death and beauty and loved them equally.

This was the swordsman: a violent man who lived in a deadly era. Knowing he could die at any moment, he trained relentlessly. He did this not just to survive, but to take as many of his enemies down with him as possible. He trained himself to fight well; he also trained to fight beautifully. To such a man, the thought of living in obscurity was infinitely worse than that of dying gloriously.

Samurai liked to compare their lives to that of the cherry

blossom. Living for but a moment in the timespan of the world, it quickly blossoms into a thing of great beauty and then falls to the earth. A swordsman knew that it was his destiny to die by the sword. He accepted this. The only thing he could do was to try and die well.

Having developed this ability himself, he attempted to pass it along to his children. When doing this, he was *not* training them for life, but for death. He regularly took his youngest children to cemetaries and execution grounds, advising them to think about death every minute of their lives. By doing this they gradually lost all fear of death. It was left to the sheep of the land, the farmers and other commoners, to live as long as they could and die when they had to. The destiny of a samurai was to live when he had to and die at a time of his own choice. To this ideal he devoted all his energy. The various methods were carefully researched, practiced, and then passed on to the succeeding generations.

The method was the *ryu;* the means was the dōjō.

THE DOJO

Throughout the world there are numerous training facilities for the Asian martial arts. However, very few of these places rate the title of dojo. The more commonly used terms of studio or gymnasium are, in general, much more appropriate. These institutions teach only the shell of an art and neither understand nor attempt to transmit its heart. There is no great harm in this, for the average customer at such a school is only interested in changing his body. He has no desire to alter his personality.

The word *dojo* may be literally translated as "way-place." The word implies that this is a place where the students will attempt to realize the ultimate reality of their chosen art. A school teaches techniques, as does a dojo. However, in a dojo, techniques are viewed as only a means to an end. The techniques must be mastered, but that is only the beginning, not the end, of study. The goal of a school is to teach a person new things; the goal of a dojo is to transform the person into something new. A school teaches how to kill; a dojo

A typical class in a modern dojo, in which the assistant instructor demonstrates a technique as the sensei observes.

teaches how to die. The member of a dojo does not think about fighting. Neither does he think about not fighting. He tries to go beyond this level and comprehend the very essence of conflict.

Although the initial training in a school and a dojo is identical, the goals are entirely different. So are the methods. A school will have a teacher and his students; a dojo will have a master and his disciples. The student attends classes to acquire new knowledge; the disciple, known as a *deshi,* attends classes to undergo a spiritual transformation. The act of becoming a deshi is the first stage in this process. A prospective deshi, before being accepted, must demonstrate a proper attitude of *nyunanshin.* This means having a flexible spirit and being capable of being molded by the dojo. Becoming a deshi requires that a person surrender his ego to the headmaster, the *sensei.* In effect, he says, "Here I am. Do with me what you will."

Physically, a proper dojo will have a rather stark and functional appearance. Reflecting a definite Zen influence, in a dojo beauty is achieved not with things but with the absence of things. A dojo is not a church, but it has many of the characteristics of a religious institution. It is not a gymnasium, but, at first glance, physical exercise will appear to be the primary activity. It is not a military barracks, but the discipline is similar to military discipline.

Discipline is perhaps the most distinctive difference between a modern school and a traditional dojo. Modern schools make many concessions in their curricula and training methods to suit the requirements of their students. On the other hand, the dojo is inflexible—the deshi does all the adapting. Rigid discipline makes this process both inevitable and impersonal.

Each square inch of the dojo floor has a certain seniority relative to every other square inch and it must be treated with the proper respect. A deshi is not allowed to use a section of the dojo which does not correspond to his grade. This carries over to the relationships between deshi, with no two ever having the same rank. A disciple would never consider sitting in some spot in the dojo that was not appropriate to his rank. He takes the same care in selecting where he sits in relationship to other deshi. He looks toward his senior and selects a spot on the mat which is junior to that man's location.

Both dress and attitude are spotlessly correct, inside and outside the dojo. An immaculate uniform for training and a conservative suit on the street is the norm. Anything less is considered a sign of a sloppy and undisciplined spirit. Training uniforms are just that: uniforms. Wearing a personalized uniform or one which is more ornate than necessary is a sign of ego; and ego is something the disciple tries to destroy.

The sensei is not so much a teacher as he is a guide. The word *sensei* is literally translated "born earlier." This indicates that the sensei has already been to the place the students are trying to reach. It is his task as the *kanchō,* headmaster, of the dojo to ensure that the disciples are proceeding in the proper direction. He merely indicates the proper path; the actual journey is left to the deshi. A good sensei will not impress by what he does as much as by what he could do. Radiating a frightening intensity of will, he is never treated casually. Although he will never, under any circumstances, request that he be treated with respect, his senior disciples will insist upon it. They regard any trace of familiarity toward their sensei as a personal insult and react accordingly. They do not do this to honor the man—more often than not a good sensei would prefer that everyone loosen up and be a bit more casual. However, the senior deshi understand the value of discipline. They know that bowing to the sensei is a spiritual exercise for one's own personal benefit. They also know that relaxed discipline will weaken the whole dojo. (This is the only instance in a traditional dojo where the wishes of the sensei may be disregarded. When he commands that there be no more bowing, the deshi should reply "Yes, Sir!" and bow deeply.)

Even the sensei will take a secondary position to the dojo shrine, the *shinza.* Be it large or small, simple or ornate, the shrine occupies the most senior spot in the dojo. Without exception, every dojo has a shrine, and it is always treated with great respect. Like the sword of the samurai, it is more than just a thing—the shinza represents the very soul of the dojo. No matter how great an individual, the shinza is a constant reminder of just how far he has yet to go.

When you combine all of this—the disciplined attitude of the deshi, the sensei, and the physical characteristics of the dojo—you have a very, very special place. Terrifying to the neophyte, for the senior it is more addictive than the strongest narcotic. For these disciples, the dojo is all things. It is a place of great serenity and great violence. There will be abject humility and tremendous authority. You may see such things in other places; however, it is only in a dojo that you will see them all simultaneously, in one person. For several hours each week, the disciple of a traditional dojo lives a fraction of an inch from crippling injury or death. During a typical training session the psychological tension is thick enough to feel. It is as if there were electricity in the air, an electricity that burns out the individual ego and transforms the deshi into something else, something both frightening and beautiful.

What manner of men are these disciples? They are hard men. There are no children in a traditional dojo—the study of death is not for the immature. Neither will you see the dilettante or dreamer there. What you will find is a broad spectrum of adults from all walks of life, with an abundance of professionals. Military officers and engineers, business executives and policemen, they are all men who live with power and understand its value.

It is not that the disciple does different things than the student; he does things differently. A student in a self-defense school learns techniques for combat. The disciple of a dojo goes far beyond this. He immerses himself so deeply within his art that his ego is drowned. While the student is busy collecting things, the deshi is busy giving them up. He gives and he gives and he gives until there is nothing left but an empty shell. At that point, fighting and not fighting are the same. Then, without having noticed the transformation, he too becomes a sensei, the master of his own dojo. Then he can sit—do nothing, just sit. But with a strange and terrible beauty.

THE RYU

The dojo transforms the disciples by its mere existence; the ryu does this in a more active manner. A ryu is both a method of teaching and a method of preserving an art. In conjunction with the dojo, a ryu can turn a raw beginner into a master of his craft. The word *ryu,* when analyzed, has a definite feeling of flowing. (The same term is frequently used as a part of Japanese compound words to describe the movement of water.) As the river flows downhill, the ryu flows through time.

A ryu is a style of fighting, which, by definition, has been passed down for several generations. To the expert eye, members of a particular ryu are instantly recognizable by minor variations in their posture or technique. However, a ryu is much more than just a style. It is a complete methodology for the transmission and preservation of a system. Its durability has proven its viability. A new system, technically, does not become a ryu until the second generation of disciples.

A traditional ryu is a family enterprise: it is created by the founder for his sons. Although outsiders may be admitted, the ryu is traditionally headed by a direct descendant of the founder. (The Japanese have always been quite pragmatic about such matters. If a suitable blood relative is not available, the best disciple is adopted into the family.)

The founder of a ryu achieved renown by acting and/or thinking in a certain way. The ryu is an attempt to pass the method of the founder along to his descendants. Its goal is not to teach, but actually to change the individual. In both body and spirit, the disciple is hammered into a fixed pattern. It is for this reason that the entire concept of the ryu is so unpalatable for many modern people. Raised on a philosophy stressing individual worth, they are unable to surrender to something greater. And that is exactly what the ryu demands. As was previously mentioned, the proper attitude for a beginner is called nyunanshin, the pliability of the spirit that allows him to be easily molded. A disciple with nyunanshin enters a dojo fully prepared to surrender his ego to the ryu. He leaves, not as a man with new knowledge, but as a completely new person.

As in all things, value is proportional to cost. The person who is prepared to give everything to the ryu receives everything from it. Others, not able to make this ultimate surrender, are doomed to remain on the sidelines. They lust for the product but not enough to pay the price. However, sometimes even the willingness to surrender the ego is not enough.

In many places combat supremacy has been a matter of survival. In feudal Japan it was more than that. There, a man's swordsmanship could also determine his social status— rank as given only to those who had earned it. Assuming that a swordsman did manage to achieve greatness, he first wanted to retain this status and, secondly, wished to choose his successor. This second item was taken care of by the ryu. A typical ryu, in addition to providing a program of instruction, also contains methods for judging and filtering the disciples. Only the most trustworthy disciples are taught the founder's methods; only the very best one inherits the ryu.

A typical ryu is divided into several layers. A triple-tiered system composed of *shoden, chūden,* and *hiden* is perhaps the most common. A new disciple begins with the shoden, the "beginning teachings," which physically prepare him for serious training. After he is capable of executing all these techniques properly, he is allowed to advance to the chuden, "middle teachings." These techniques form the heart of any style and are what give each ryu its distinctive character. Successful completion of this stage of training creates a solid, skillful technician. The men who have completed it are the ones who form the main body of a ryu.

A disciple can spend years or even decades mastering these techniques. During this time he is carefully observed by the sensei. Then if, and only if, the master thinks him worthy, will the disciple be introduced to the hiden, the "secret teachings." This initiation into the inner mysteries of a system has always been reserved for the very few, for it is these techniques that give mastery over other men. No sensei would consider imparting such information to a man he does not trust with his life. (Many old ryu have been lost because the headmaster died prior to transmitting the hiden to a successor.)

What are these hiden? Sometimes they are truly deep and complex mental principles. In other cases, they are quite simple physical actions. For example, a ryu of flower arranging could have a secret method of cutting the stems of flowers that would allow the blossoms to remain fresh a little longer. While this might not seem very important, it is enough to ensure that the arrangements from this school are always in high demand and to permit the ryu to charge accordingly. At the other extreme, a hiden can be a mental principle so esoteric as to be incomprehensible to the layman, even when explained in clear language. That is all right, for the ryu specializes in teaching things which the average man can neither see nor understand. An indication of this is the common practice of some ryu of dividing their teachings into two categories: *omote* and *oku*. The omote is the front, the things which can be seen, and the oku is the hidden, things which are not readily apparent.

This is the source of some confusion in the West. Numerous instructors have trained in a traditional Japanese ryu, but few have progressed to the oku level—they may not even be aware of the existence of such a thing. Thinking they know all of their ryu, when in fact they have only been shown the surface of it, they are prone to making statements and judgments that are not entirely correct. While they may be excellent technicians, in many cases even better than their instructors, they have no conception of what the *gokui,* the "essence," of their ryu is. Even worse are the men who pass judgment on a style after only seeing the shoden.

The traditional ryu ensures that advanced techniques and strategies are transmitted only to those deemed worthy to receive them; it also provides the method of transmission. Whereas, in Western training centers, mental principles for teaching physical techniques were developed, in Japan the physical techniques for teaching mental principles were studied. Western psychologists may debate the validity of behaviorism, but the Japanese invented the system, turned it into an exact science, and proved its worth hundreds of years ago. Both the dojo and the ryu are based on the use of applied behavioral psychology.

The dojo and the ryu constitute the fascinating difference between the Japanese Way of Strategy and other arts. In other arts you may frequently hear talk of mental principles and philosophies, but that is as far as it goes—they remain no more than ideas and words. For example, a man may say that by sitting in a certain position and breathing in a certain manner he can talk to God. How can you prove or disprove this? However, such is not the case with the Way of Strategy. It is different, different from anything else you may ever encounter.

The Way of Strategy is composed of mental principles. Not thoughts, but ways of thinking. These are taught physically and then they are physically tested. You will have, in all cases, an instant physical feedback to tell you whether or not you were actually doing the correct thing with your mind. The key word here is *instantly.* While other ways may promise some future benefit, to be achieved after sufficient training, the Way of Strategy offers it now. While more practice will obviously bring greater results, the raw beginner should achieve a measurable increase in ability with his first attempt. That is an important point to remember as you study this book. If you try something and it does not work, do not assume that you need more practice. If a measurable physical improvement is not discernible on the first try, you should change what you are doing, for there is something fundamentally wrong. Also, do not become confused if it seems too easy. It is supposed to be easy! That is the mark of all fundamental truths. The most common reaction upon executing a strategy properly is to think, "How stupid of me! I should have discovered this myself, years ago." As an overall principle of the universe may be expressed by the simple equation of $E = MC^2$, so, too, may the principles of conflict be simply stated. Things only become seemingly complex and difficult when the viewpoint is restricted.

THE WAY AND THE POWER

There are always those who wish to run before they can walk. Then, when they fall, they blame the art of running for their failure instead of blaming themselves. As you study, you should remember this and not allow contemplation of the esoteric to interfere with consideration of the practical. All of the strategies discussed in this book have real, physical, and practical applications. While acquisition of academic knowledge may be an interesting mental exercise, to bring the knowledge alive you must apply it. And that means getting your hands dirty.

The application of a strategy means you must have a tool. This can be a group of soldiers, a business, or a set of judo techniques. Whatever the method is, you must be proficient in its use. You cannot free your mind for the study of strategy if you are still forced to think about how to do the techniques involved.

While frequent mention will be made of the application of strategy to the art of *kenjutsu*, Japanese swordsmanship, you should not come to regard the strategies as simply fencing techniques. They were developed as fencing techniques and, in most cases, are still taught that way. But, this is simply because that is the fastest and easiest way to learn them. Feel free to substitute another art if you wish. Just do not expect to achieve a clear understanding quite as fast.

In Japan, the use of the term *swordsman* to describe a man with a sword is of recent vintage. The classical term for many centuries was *heihōjin,* a "strategist." It has only been in modern times that the techniques of the sword have been so stressed that the concept of strategy has been forgotten.

The art of fencing may seem rather archaic in this age of missiles and guns. It can even seem a bit comical at first glance. A group of adults, dressed in strange outfits and playing with swords, appears to have little contact with the real world. However, all trace of humor disappears the first time you hear a swordblade talk. The distinctive hiss of a razor-

The student of kenjutsu will learn strategy much faster than the student of another art.

sharp blade, missing your body by a fraction of an inch and moving so fast it is only a blur, changes everything. Your heart races and every cell in your body seems to come intensely alive. Even if your mind does not understand what is happening, the animal within knows it is standing close to a sudden and violent death.

Even *bokken,* "wooden swords," are not treated as toys. They are not used for the safety of students because, in many cases, they are even more dangerous than *shinken,* a "real sword." (A bokken shatters bone, while a shinken only cuts it.) Senior students may have invested several thousand dollars in a fine antique blade and, with polishing costs running upward of $100 per inch, they take no chances on damaging it. It is because of this, and not out of concern for personal safety, that they use a bokken for any exercise where the blades could clash.

Even solo practice cannot be treated lightly. The scabbard of a Japanese sword is made of a very soft wood and the part over the edge of the blade is almost paper thin. Draw the sword incorrectly and it will slice through the wood and amputate a few fingers in the process. Returning the sword to the scabbard is no safer. If the angle is slightly wrong, the blade will thrust through the side of the scabbard and into your body. To compound this danger, you are required both to draw and sheath the sword at high speed without looking.

All of these factors, when combined, create a very nerve-wracking situation. The typical beginner's exercise in a kenjutsu class contains far more inherent danger than do the advanced techniques of many other martial arts. The modern sport of kendo, a form of kenjutsu which uses bamboo swords and body armor, was created specifically to halt the great number of crippling and fatal accidents that have occurred in kenjutsu schools. It is this danger that makes the art of the sword such an esteemed training method.

In no other art is the concentration of a student so quickly focused with so little effort—danger has a way of focusing the mind as nothing else can. If you remove this danger, as in the sport of kendo, a student can have a good physical workout but his attention may drift. This is never seen in a kenjutsu class. As soon as the blades are drawn every student is 100 percent involved and remains that way for the duration of the class. For the study of strategy, an art that is almost totally mental, this is a basic requirement.

The advantages of fencing as a training method are more mental than physical. If you wish, you can use your hand instead of a sword for most of the exercises in this book. This will give you a physical feel for the strategy, but it will not create much spiritual development. Shape your arm and open hand into a smooth curve, slightly tense the muscles, and use it just like a sword. This is called a *tegatana,* "hand-blade."

In Book I, "The Way," some basic principles are discussed. These are the fundamental factors of combat and the background of Oriental thought. While too cursory an examination of this section may not totally disable you from further study, it will definitely complicate matters. Any difficulty in understanding a particular strategy should trigger an immediate return to the applicable section(s) of Book I. Remember, the Way of Strategy is not a set of thoughts, it is a way of thinking. If you do not understand the essence of Japanese thought, you can never hope to understand Japanese training methods.

In Book II, "The Power," you will be introduced to some actual strategies. These have been handed down for generations in the form of *kuden,* "oral teachings." They are from a variety of different ryu, including the Ittō-ryu, Shinkage-ryu, Nitenichi-ryu, and the Daitō-ryu, among others. You will also be introduced to methods of practicing these strategies and a few modern applications. You should study each strategy intellectually and then, when you think you understand it, practice it physically.

This will be a fascinating experience. To try thinking in a new pattern and then to be able to see an immediate and measurable advantage is a unique experience. There is an old saying, often heard in the dojo, that states: "Hear and forget. See and remember. Do and understand." This is the reason for the stress on physical training methods. Without such physical training the strategies are only academic exercises. They will be knowledge in your mind instead of conditioned reflexes. And you will be a man who has read a book about strategy, not a strategist.

NOTES

1. Havoc is an ancient military command meaning to give no quarter.

2. Letter to William Stevens Smith (November 13, 1787).

3. Carl von Clausewitz (1780–1831), *Vom Kriege (On War)* [1833].

4. This is the original definition of a gentleman.

5. Wu Ch'i: Chinese general (d. 381 B.C.), in *The Art of War,* by Sun Tzu, translated by S.D. Griffith, Oxford University Press, 1963.

6. These terms are an excellent example of why selective use of Japanese terminology is made in this book. The word *technique* can imply rational thought (e.g., mathematical techniques). However, a waza is by definition a conditioned reflex. Use of Japanese terms prevents the reader from inserting any preconceived ideas into the text.

7. Tokugawa (Matsudaira) Ieyasu (1542–1616) became the first Tokugawa Shōgun in 1603.

8. Certain other classes were allowed to wear a short sword. Only the samurai were allowed to wear both long and short blades. The combination is called *daishō*.

9. The Japanese name is *nippon-tō*. Calling it a samurai sword is equivalent to calling a Colt single-action army revolver a cowboy gun.

10. The classic test for cutting ability was to cut a human body in half through the pelvis.

11. This is the same as *harakiri*. Harakiri is considered a rather vulgar word.

Book I

The Way

Chapter One

In-Yo:
Positive and Negative

Western philosophies, especially those based on Judeo-Christian religions, tend to adopt a me-it view of the universe. This can be referred to as the duality approach. By contrast, in much of Asia the universe is seen as a single entity. It is believed to contain a balance of positive and negative forces, with both forces being of equal importance. In Japan, these forces are called *in* and *yō* (yin and yang in Chinese).

The fundamental concept of in-yo states that there is total balance in the universe. There is a positive and a negative force at work in each and every situation and, universally, these two forces are in perfect balance. It is only when there is a local imbalance of forces that conflict occurs. By correcting this imbalance, the conflict can be resolved.

For the scientist, this is very logical. He is used to thinking in terms of action and reaction, cause and effect. The Christian who is not a scientist has a more difficult time with it. In-yo requires that he accept that both God and Satan are of equal stature and importance in the overall scheme of the universe. This can be a hard lump for him to swallow.

Whether you accept this theory or not, you must be aware of the fact that the concept of in-yo colors all aspects of Eastern thought. Its effects are seen even in language.

Philosophers have long debated whether a culture creates a language or a language creates a culture. No matter which of these views you support, there is little room for argument that a culture and its language are very closely related. There is an even closer relationship between how an individual thinks and how he speaks. This is of vital importance to the student of the Way of Strategy.

The Japanese language is unique and, either because of or in spite of that, the Japanese art of war is also unique. Because of this it is an inescapable fact that, in order to understand Japanese strategy, you must understand at least the basic structure of the Japanese language. You do not have to become fluent in it, but you must understand enough about the language to comprehend the Japanese way of thinking. Like the Way of Strategy, it is different from what you are used to. Very different.

In English, the normal word order is subject-verb-object: "You read the book." In Japanese the word order is subject-object-verb: "You, the book, read." Note that in English the subject and the object are separated by the verb while in Japanese they seem to be pushed together by it. The result is that in English, or any related language, there is always a very subtle feeling of, *We* are doing this to *that*. Japanese, on the other hand, gives more of a feeling of, *We and that* are experiencing this together. There is a much greater sense of unity between subject and object in Japanese than there is in English. This is the primary source of many mystical sounding statements from Japan. When a master swordsman says, "When you cut the target you are really cutting yourself," he is not trying to sound esoteric. All he is trying to get across is an example of in-yo. He is saying that you and your opponent, the two opposing forces in a conflict, are unified by the technique. His statement sounds much stranger in English than it does in Japanese.

Another key factor in the Japanese language is the absence of gender or plural. For example, the verb *suwaru* can mean "I/you/they sit," "he/she/it sits," or "we sit." This gives the language a very vague grammar. While this may seem quite confusing at first, it ties in with the theory of in-yo. It tends

In-yo: Motion on the outside; stillness within.

to play down the importance of the individual and view the matter under discussion from a more universal perspective.

Finally, the tenses of Japanese verbs are a little different from those of English. In Japanese there is a sense of utter finality to the past tense. When you state (in Japanese) that something has happened, it means it is over and done with, nothing you can do will ever change it. The future tense is replaced by the possible. In English you say, "I will do this," and it has a very definite sound. However, in Japanese you would say, "I may do this." In Japanese, the present tense has a much broader time frame than in English. In English, the present refers to a specific instant of time. On the other hand, the Japanese present tense contains elements of both the past and the future. As you can see, this also results in a vague quality which further reduces the importance of the individual.

There are numerous other examples of the effect of in-yo on Japanese language and thought. What you should, and must, do is keep this sense of nonduality constantly active. You should watch what you say and how you say it until the proper thought patterns become automatic. For example, instead of thinking, "I am going to do this," you should think, "This is probably going to happen." This will require considerable time, but it is an important step toward a deep understanding of strategy.

A superb example of a physical application of this philosophy may be seen in the fencing exercise of *kiri gaeshi,* as practiced by the Tenshin-ryu. Kiri gaeshi means "cut and return," and it clearly illustrates in-yo in action. In this two-man exercise, two students stand facing each other with their swords in middle-level position. Alternately advancing and retreating, each student takes two steps, synchronized with a cut. On the first step, each raises his sword to an upper-level position. On the second step, both strike firmly, stopping their swords at the original middle-level position. The student who is advancing, yō no tachi, sets the pace. The man who is retreating, in no tachi, must present a mirror image of this.

Although in the beginning yo no tachi will set an easy pace, this soon changes. When his partner has mastered the basic stroke and footwork, the attacker will try to confuse him. On one turn yo no tachi may advance very, very slowly and take over a minute to complete his cut. The next time he may blast in with all the speed and power he can muster. He may also combine these in any manner he wishes, such as starting very fast and finishing very slowly. Whatever the attack, in no tachi is required to match it perfectly in all respects. Speed, timing, and distance must be identical. The students start with the tips of their swords touching and they finish at exactly the same instant and in exactly the same position.

Such perfect synchronization is rarely seen among beginners. By observing closely, you will note that the tip of the attacker's blade has usually moved as much as one-half inch before the defender's sword even starts. Among seniors it is a different story. There you will see no detectable difference between attack and defense. In no tachi retreats and yo no tachi advances. Other than that, either man could be a mirror image of the other. No matter what subterfuge the attacker attempts, the defender should always match the move with perfect precision. Among the very senior, it will almost seem as if their hearts were beating in synchronization.

Only among beginners do two individuals practice kiri gaeshi. Among seniors it is more a case of a pair of swordsmen experiencing kiri gaeshi. It is as if, instead of the men doing the exercise, the exercise was doing the men. This is a perfect example of in-yo, because, to do it properly, a swordsman is required to surrender his ego. As long as he is conscious of himself and tries to react to his partner, he will always be a fraction of a second too late. It is only when he forgets himself and views the exercise as a totality that a proper state of balance can occur.

For the strategist, in-yo is a very valuable concept. It allows him to treat his opponent, himself, the conflict, and the strategy used to resolve the conflict as a single, cosmic event. All factors are of equal importance, and the result must be a balanced whole. Such a strategist will view a war not as a violent event of destruction, but as an act of bringing the world into balance. For such a strategist, there is no right and wrong or good and evil; there is only balance and imbalance. He approaches the battlefield with the same impersonal objectivity as the surgeon approaches the operating table.

Understanding in-yo and its place within combat makes the difference between a junior and senior strategist readily apparent, even to the neophyte. Careful observation will reveal that the beginner always responds *to* a situation with a technique. The more experienced man, however, creates an entirely different impression. He uses a technique to react *with* a situation. He is not even aware of the situation; there is only a great *it* which encompasses everything. This difference is subtle but very important. The beginner rushes through life, reacting *to* situations; the senior strolls at a more leisurely pace, calmly adjusting the balance of in and yo as he goes. When the junior strategist must resort to violence in order to solve a problem, it will invariably have an ugly and unfinished look to it. By contrast, even when the senior causes great destruction, there will be beauty and balance—his violence does not disrupt the situation, it equalizes it.

To observe a fight between two beginners is to be repelled by the ugliness. Conflict between masters is altogether different. When they fight, the conflict becomes a work of art. It may not be pretty, but it will be glorious.

There is a key philosophical point here that merits further study. Where the typical Westerner views conflict as something inherently evil, Eastern thought is more prone to see it as a natural balancing process. This does not mean war is to be liked. Instead, it is to be viewed as little different than a surgeon removing diseased tissue with a scalpel. Such a viewpoint is mandatory for a warrior. It is only by accepting combat as a natural part of life that you can live with it. By adopting such an attitude you are victim neither to apprehension before the battle nor to self-condemnation after it. You merely do what is required when necessary, and accept it.

Another key element of the in-yo concept is so obvious as to be trite. If you accept that the normal state of the universe is one of perfect balance, then any imbalance must have a cause. To rectify the situation, you must work on this cause. One wonders how many lives would have been saved in recent wars if governments had obeyed this simple dictum. (Attacking the German heartland during World War II was a proper way to balance in-yo; the strategy used in Korea and Vietnam was not.)

Chapter Two

Michi: The Way

In the Japanese language, there are two suffixes which are commonly used with the names of a variety of arts: *dō* and *jutsu*. *Jutsu* may be roughly translated as "science" or "art." *Do,* which is read as *michi* when used as a noun, means "road" or "path." From these you get such names as kenjutsu, the art of swordsmanship, and kendo, the Way of the Sword. The suffix *jutsu* gives a feeling of primarily technical use (e.g., the science of engineering or the art of bricklaying). This does not mean that it is a purely physical art. A *jutsu* may be entirely mental, such as the game of chess. *Do,* on the other hand, implies a much more spiritual context—it gives the feeling that the art is followed as a way of life and has deep philosophical goals.

It has been a common statement for some years now that *bujutsu,* the art of war, is for self-protection and *budō,* the Way of War, is for self-perfection. This is a very limiting, and not entirely correct, oversimplification. A slightly better definition might be that you learn a bujutsu, but you do budo. However, even this manner of distinguishing *jutsu* and *do* leaves much to be desired.

If you join a dojo and learn the physical and mental techniques of a ryu, you are studying a bujutsu. You do not have to use this for self-protection. There are many other possible applications. You might use the techniques in a purely offensive manner, as would a soldier. As many students do, you could treat the ryu as merely a cultural exercise, a method for preserving an interesting facet of an ancient society. A third popular option is to view the ryu as purely a method of physical fitness.

The problem is that many ryu use the suffixes of *jutsu* or *do* as a part of their trade name and not in the generic sense. A good case in point is modern judo. When the art is practiced as a competitive sport, students of judo are technically doing jujutsu. Conversely, disciples of a classical jūjutsu ryu are really doing judo. This can make things quite confusing for a beginner. Moreover, examining these distinctions does not really answer the question: "What is The Way?" For that we must look much deeper.

Do is the Japanese pronunciation of the Chinese word *tao*. As stated previously, this means a road or a path. As used in the philosophy of Lao Tsu, this term is used to describe the ultimate reality. Lao Tsu (c. 600 B.C.) was a famous Chinese philosopher who wrote the *Tao Te Ching,* "The Book of the Way." This is one of the most influential books ever written—it forms the cornerstone of many Asian philosophies. For our needs, the first of its eighty-one sayings is the important one. In this, Lao Tsu states, "The word that can be spoken is not the ultimate word." What he means is that the ultimate reality, the true essence of anything, is beyond conceptual definition. Like Heisenberg's uncertainty principle,[1] but stated 2,500 years earlier, this means you can state a part of the truth but never its totality.

Although it is impossible to define ultimate reality, an analogy will help to understand it. The use of analogies is not very scientific. Because of the nature of ultimate reality, however, in this case it is necessary.

For an example, if you study tables you will find there are a great many different types. You could have a coffee table, an end table, or a dining table, to name but a few. Another type of table is commonly referred to as a desk and, again here, there are many variations. There are typing desks, student desks, and executive desks. Expand the field even further and you find varieties of shelves and benches that are also some form of tables.

When you look at all of these as a group, you find that they have little in common. The number of legs can vary from none to many. The shape can be a perfect square, free-form, or anything in between. A drafting table is not horizontal and certain kinds of typing tables are not even flat. And yet there is always a certain *something* that makes a thing a table. It is this essential something, this *tableness,*

The kendoka, unlike the kenjutsuka, is able to create new techniques for new situations because of his broader understanding of strategy.

that is the *tao* of tables. You can never define it because, as soon as you apply a word, you restrict yourself to a particular type of table.

This gives us, albeit only by analogy, a workable definition of *michi*, The Way. Kenjutsu becomes a definite science, something which can be taught. Kendo, on the other hand, is the Way of the Sword. It may be understood but never communicated verbally—knowledge of it comes from within. Understanding kendo means you understand the intangibles, things which are beyond the restrictions of a particular ryu or waza. The acquisition of this understanding is called a *satori*, "enlightenment." It is an awareness of the formless, indefinable something which lies beyond all things.

So, why bother? While the definition is esoteric, the reason for bothering is practical. The *kenjutsuka*[2] is limited to the techniques he has learned. The *kendōka* has no such restriction. Because he understands the essence of technique, he can freely create new ones for new situations. Also, because these new techniques are born from the essence of his ryu, they will blend perfectly with the style of previously existing techniques.

Though the suffixes of *jutsu* or *do* are not used with the word *heihō,* the principle is the same. Heiho is the art of strategy. It is composed of techniques for the application of techniques. Heiho is beyond giho (conditioned technique), but this is not the end. Deeper study will reveal the final layer, *heiho no michi,* the tao of strategy.

HEIHO NO MICHI

If you try to see the nature of conflict in the image of a tree, you will see that the techniques for resolving conflict are the leaves and the strategies are the branches. You must have both. The branch has no purpose without the leaf, and the leaf has no support without the branch.

A ryu should be viewed as a living thing. Its leaves are the work of the technician; its branches are the work of the strategist. However, the goal of the senior strategist is in neither of these areas. To follow the Way of Strategy means to get to the very roots of the tree of war. The person who has mastered the Way of Strategy is then free to travel along any branch to any leaf desired—his world is without limit. The technician, constrained by his teachings, lives in a very small world—he cannot handle new situations unless he has trained for them. This may be sufficient for his needs, but only if he is a small man. Greatness demands space.

One of the sadly comical things about bujutsu and budo in the West is the phenomenon of the young man who has created a new ryu because he was not good enough (or patient enough) to achieve any status in an existing school. The catchphrase to watch for is, "I am taking the best techniques from all styles and combining them into one art." The sad part is that the young man has never seen these best techniques. These would be the hiden, which are only revealed to the disciple of a ryu after many years of training. (The transmission of such knowledge is accompanied by an appropriate certificate.)

What the young man is actually doing is taking some warm-up exercises from the shoden of several ryu, usually out of context, and shuffling them into a new pattern. Because he does not understand the role of strategy as a unifying force in a ryu, his new style has no life. It is a tree of sorts, but it is a very strange tree. It is as if he took a stick and glued a variety of leaves from different plants to it. The leaves soon wither and fall. So do ryu created in this manner.

There are, of course, many Westerners who do not fall into this category. They have started their own ryu, for either political or philosophical reasons; but they have paid their dues. They are the product of decades of training in an established style. Without exception, these are the type of men whom you would automatically address as "sir" if you met them socially.

Every ryu has its heiho. Sometimes these have formal names and are listed in the school curriculum. In other cases, the strategy is only implied. Whatever the system, heiho is a fundamental part of every ryu. It gives the ryu life and durability to survive for centuries in a rapidly changing world.

In the beginning of your training you will study giho, the various techniques of your ryu. Starting with the simple, you progress to advanced techniques that will stretch your mind and body to their limits. It is only after a sufficient number of techniques have been mastered that you may begin the study of strategy; all strategy is concerned with the application of technique.

Even after you have mastered many strategies and are actively involved in the pursuit of the Way of Strategy, your training must remain physical. This is because words can never describe the Way—it is something that is to be felt more than understood. You can undoubtedly recall, vividly, your first sexual experience. Compare these memories with those of your first encounter with the multiplication tables. Physical training produces physical memories. By training in the correct manner, your knowledge will become instinctive instead of intellectual. This is imperative if you desire to be a person who uses strategy instead of just a person who knows about it.

"From one comes two and from two come ten thousand." This is an ancient saying which illustrates the goal of training. The Way of Strategy is the one from which springs ten thousand. With sufficient training you will see the one and you will be changed by it.

A soldier sees each battle as unique; but to the strategist, war is war. A strategist sees no difference between the corporate board meeting, a barroom brawl, or conflict between nations. To such a man there are no unique events; there are only varied applications of a central strategy. He approaches a naval battle or an advertising campaign with the same feeling. The strategy is the same in both cases; only the tools are different.

This simple fact, that strategy is beyond technique just as technique is beyond the tool, cannot be stressed enough. There may be many different tools in a mechanic's kit, but the physical actions involved in their use are few. A single motion can be used to manipulate a wide range of different tools; a single strategy can be used to manipulate an even wider range of motions.

One enemy is the same as many enemies. Your opponent may be an individual, a corporation, or an army. It does not matter. The Way of Strategy treats them all the same, for heiho no michi is the Way of Winning.

NOTES

1. Werner Heisenberg (1901-1976). His uncertainty principle of quantum mechanics says complete measurements of small particles is impossible.

2. The suffix *ka* means "a student of."

Chapter Three

Ki: The Life Force

For both traditional and technical reasons, the occidental student of bujutsu will use many Japanese words during training. Aside from the fact that Japanese serves as the international language of bujutsu, there are many Japanese terms which simply cannot be directly translated into English. Of all these words and phrases, *ki* is probably the most misused and the least understood.

There have been so many outlandish claims made about some mysterious "ki power" that it borders on the ridiculous. The vast majority of these statements are made simply because the speaker has a weak Japanese technical vocabulary. This weakness is frequently compounded by a matching lack of understanding of the basic mechanics of a particular technique or strategy. Because of this, ki is commonly used to designate almost any aspect of combat which is not easy to explain.

In reality, ki is but the life force of any living thing. It is what makes the difference between something that is alive and something that is dead. Every living organism, from an amoeba to a man, has it.

A discussion of ki can become very philosophical, too philosophical. That is because ki cannot be detected by any physical means; it merely exists. While some may choose to call it the soul, that implies a religious context. Therefore, the word *ki* is preferable. It is not a thing; it is a state of being and has no more physical existence than a magnetic field.[1]

Ki is a very popular word in Japanese. It is used as a component of many compound terms. For example, to be sick is referred to as having "weak ki," and lightning is the "*ki* of the sky." There are hundreds of other examples of such compounds, and they, at least to the Japanese, do not have any mystical connotations. It is only in the West, where the language barrier comes into play, that more is made of the word than it deserves. This problem is complicated by the fact that in a dojo there are some forms of verbal shorthand which use the word in a nonliteral sense. One of the most common of these is the command "extend ki." Extending ki is a complex blending of psychological, philosophical, and physical actions. When an instructor gives this command, it is merely an instruction to do a variety of interrelated things at once. While a student may, in fact, feel that he is extending *something,* there is no flow of some mysterious energy involved.

Ki, like a magnetic field, can have varying degrees of intensity. A man has more ki than a blade of grass, and a healthy person has more ki than a sick person. The level of ki in any living thing depends upon two factors: the being's degree of complexity and its level of organization.

Ki is the life force. To increase your life force merely means that you become more alive. This is very desirable, because the more alive you become the harder it will be to kill you. While there is nothing you can do to increase the complexity of your body, you can increase its organization. To organize something means to give it coherent form—in other words, to coordinate it. Coordination means all parts of your body are working together, toward a common goal. This is very rare in an average person—at least one part of his body is fighting the other parts. (When this lack of coordination happens on a cellular level it is called disease; when it afflicts the whole body it is called clumsiness. They are both basically the same thing. The difference is merely in scale.)

There is nothing esoteric about ki or its development. The development of ki simply requires better physical and mental health, making your mind and body work in harmony.

There is a wide range of exercises that may be used to increase your coordination. The exact nature of the exercise you select is relatively unimportant. As long as you pick enough different ones to cover the entire range of body motions, improvement will occur. As your body learns to work properly, your life force will increase; instead of struggling to exist you will begin to enjoy living.

A major advantage of certain forms of bujutsu over more familiar Western sports is their use of unique training exercises known as *kata*. A kata is a series of movements done according to *seitei*, "standard form." Some kata are designed for solo practice while others require one or more partners. The use of kata as the primary training method is a characteristic of all traditional ryu.

The beauty of kata as a training method is that, in the beginning stages, a kata forces you to turn your mind inward. This is quite different from most Western sports, where the focus is on some external goal: hit the ball, jump over the bar, run faster than the man in the next lane, and so forth. A kata is different; it has no goal of winning. Even if it is done with a partner, the outcome is fixed. Its only aim is the perfection of form. Each move is performed according to seitei and it must be perfect.

As you practice a kata your instructor will constantly point out mistakes in postures or execution. This forces you constantly to think about yourself. The result is a rapid increase in your kinesthetic sense—you become aware of what each muscle in your body is doing. This awareness, in turn, will result in a corresponding increase in your overall physical and mental coordination.

Because you study yourself in such detail, you soon become aware of imperfections and start to correct them. If a muscle is too weak, you do exercises to strengthen it. If a joint is too stiff, you stretch to loosen it. If posture is incorrect, you straighten it. You gradually become more and more coordinated. This is a surprisingly easy project. It is

Kenjutsu students practicing a kata, in which technical perfection is empha-sized over combat realism.

so easy that the vast majority of people do not bother with it. These same people also frequently bump into things or fall down.

The greatest obstacle in this development of physical coordination is not knowing how to relax. The average man, especially if he has a sedentary occupation, is unbelievably tense at all times. There is a simple way for you to prove this to yourself and, at the same time, start to correct the problem.

First, stretch out on the floor. Lie on your right side with your right arm extended at a comfortable angle in front of you. Straighten your right leg and bend your left knee, placing your left foot against your right kneecap. Press your left knee firmly against the floor. Now, straighten your left arm and extend it, with the palm upward, behind you at a right angle to your torso. Relax completely.

You will probably find your left hand is suspended a foot or more above the floor. This is caused by tension in your left shoulder. To correct the situation, take a very deep breath and then slowly exhale. Continuing to exhale for as long as possible, concentrate on trying to relax your left shoulder. Focus all of your attention on your left shoulder and, as you breathe out slowly, will it to relax. Take care that you do not allow your left knee to lift off the floor. As you repeat this, you will find that your left hand is sagging downward, approaching closer and closer to the floor. Do not force it down or help it by changing your posture. Just continue the long, slow exhalations and concentrate on relaxing your shoulder muscles, allowing your hand to gradually sink of its own weight. For many people, it will take ten or fifteen minutes before their hand touches the floor. In extreme cases, several practice sessions over a number of days may be required.

Once you have achieved the required state of relaxation and the back of your left hand is resting firmly against the floor, quietly stand up and look at yourself in a mirror. You will probably find your left shoulder is now as much as three inches below your right! You may have thought that both your shoulders were equally relaxed but, before your eyes, you have graphic evidence to the contrary. You should repeat this exercise for both shoulders until the truly relaxed state is the norm.[2]

Study the rest of your body in a similar manner. Look at each area and be sure that it is relaxed, flexible, and strong. You will find that this process is accompanied by a radical improvement in posture and balance. (If you visit a dojo, you will observe that all seniors have superb posture. This is the first requirement for physical and mental coordination.)

Once physical training is well underway, you may begin the mental exercises for ki development. No! You cannot bypass the physical training. This is the first great pitfall, the place where beginners make the mistake of trying to run before they can walk. Instructors are constantly deluged with requests for classes on ki development. However, it always seems as if the students who request these classes expect some sort of magic word that will instantly unleash great powers. Sorry, there is no magic. There is only hard work and the physical part is the easiest.

Your mind is but another muscle and you should treat it accordingly. With hard and sometimes painful exercises, you make your body strong, flexible, and relaxed. You must now do the same with your brain. This viewpoint is a unique characteristic of the ryu. While a school treats intellectual activities as something quite different from physical ones, the ryu sees them both as the same thing. Accepting this philosophy and learning to subject your mind to the same rigorous discipline you enforce on your body is a key step in the development of ki.

The development of mental strength is the easiest task, so start there. One simple and very practical exercise you should constantly practice involves understanding your surroundings. Stop for a moment and look around. Just how much of what you see do you really understand? There is undoubtedly an electrical outlet in your room. Do you really understand how this works? Can you define a coulomb, a volt, or an ampere? If you do not know, find out. How was this book printed and why are the number of pages in any publication usually a multiple of eight? What is the difference between AM and FM radio? Constantly look for small intellectual problems such as these and then solve them. In addition to strengthening your mind, this process has a secondary benefit of increasing your spatial awareness. This is of tremendous value in any form of combat, especially when you face multiple opponents.

To achieve mental strength requires thinking about things; mental flexibility requires thinking about different things. A good way to start is by reading an encyclopedia—read the whole thing. Augment this by reading magazines and newspapers from various parts of the country and around the world. Such projects will force you to consider a vast array of topics from a wide range of viewpoints.

Mental exercises such as these will result in a significant increase in the power and flexibility of your mind. An excellent test is the art of debate. Given any controversial topic, you should be able to win debates with some consistency. It does not matter whether or not you agree with the views you are espousing. If you are good enough you do not even have to understand what you are talking about. But, by means of logical and concise thought, you should be able to convince others of the validity of your argument.

Now comes the problem of mental relaxation. This is by far the most difficult task that the vast majority of students are ever confronted with. For years many people even doubted the existence of such a state. However, by use of such modern electronic devices such as the EEG (electroencephalograph), this state can be demonstrated.

The purpose of mental relaxation is twofold. First, from a purely physical point of view, it results in a significant increase in your athletic abilities. By turning off the logical areas of your brain, you will operate intuitively. This has been proven most effective in a wide variety of sports—all great athletes do it automatically.

The second result of mental relaxation is of primary importance to the strategist. When you are mentally relaxed, you can shift from one thought pattern to another with ease. As a strategist, this allows you to change strategies rapidly.

Although modern biofeedback machines may eventually

make the method obsolete, the classical exercise for developing mental tranquility is *zazen,* "seated meditation." Technically, what you are doing is suppressing the rational side of
your brain by increasing its production of alpha waves. This
results in a state known as *mushin,* "no-mind."

ZAZEN

You should think of zazen as push-ups for the brain. It is
a rather simple exercise, but one that will require years to
perfect.

To practice zazen you merely sit, doing nothing. Because
this is impossible for most people, beginners are usually given
some small task to occupy their minds. They are told, for
example, to count their breaths or to focus their gaze on
some object. By doing this, they develop the ability to sit in
one place, motionless, for long periods of time.

When practicing zazen, what you choose to concentrate on is immaterial. So, too, is your method of sitting—
as long as your posture is good, any position will work. In
a dojo you will usually sit in a position known as *seiza,*
with both legs folded beneath you in a full kneeling position. Because this position is used for many other activities
in a dojo, the sensei can kill two birds with one stone by
making it the standard position for zazen. The position of
seiza allows proper meditation and the initial pain is good
for discipline. (Beginners find this position agonizing but,
after a few years, it becomes quite comfortable.) The reason
for using seiza is that proper seated posture requires your
hips to be slightly higher than your knees. This allows your
back to assume a slightly concave position. The common
practice, in many schools, of allowing students to sit tailor
fashion, with their legs crossed in front of them, should be
avoided. In such a position it is almost impossible to keep
your back from curving outward and destroying your posture. When your posture is bad, it is impossible to relax
completely. (While it is true that in a Zen monastery monks
sit in a variation of this "tailor" posture, known as the lotus
position, they sit on special pillows to raise their hips to the

Zazen.

proper height.)

As soon as you have developed the ability to sit in one position and remain motionless, even if it is just for a few minutes, you should drop your mental crutches. Do not try any longer to concentrate on anything in particular. Just sit. After a while, and this time will vary widely from student to student, you will find that the flow of your random thoughts is gradually slowing to a trickle. Finally, you will just sit there in a timeless state, empty of all thought. Although we call zazen seated meditation, it is really seated nonmeditation. True zazen consists of merely sitting, doing and thinking nothing.

When you can hold the proper mental state while sitting, slowly and quietly shift to a standing position. Follow this with some slow walking and then attempt actual techniques. The average person will require several years of practice before he can achieve this level of ability. Although you should feel a difference in yourself after only a few minutes of practice, making this applicable to real-life situations is much more difficult. As the philosopher Lao Tsu said, "The stillness within stillness is not the true stillness. The true stillness is stillness within motion." Your ultimate goal is to be able to engage in violent physical activity while maintaining mushin, no-mind.

MUSHIN

The mental state of mushin is a tool with many applications. It is axiomatic that in order to work at maximum efficiency you must be able to do one thing at a time, devoting 100 percent of your energy to it. What most people never consider, however, is that you will never be able to do *one* thing until you are able to do *no* thing. Anyone without this ability will always have some small part of his mind thinking about something else, no matter how hard he tries to concentrate.

Mushin is not just an element in combat arts; it can be seen in all Japanese art forms. Practitioners of tea ceremony, flower arranging, and calligraphy will have it. This is one reason why senior Japanese instructors rarely take Westerners very seriously at advanced levels of training. They may well admire a man's physical ability but will sense that something is missing. The thing that is not there is the nothingness.

If there is any single area in which the difference between the Occidental and the Oriental stands out, mushin is it. When you observe a demonstration by an Oriental student who has practiced zazen for a number of years, you will note a great stillness about him. He will execute a technique and then just stop, timeless and motionless. The Occidental student, on the other hand, will rarely have the patience for prolonged study of zazen. He focuses his attention on the external physical aspects of his art and this is very evident in his demonstration. While he may pause after a technique, there will never be a feeling of deathly stillness. He will always have a busy look, even when he is trying to do nothing. (The odds are he is actually counting the seconds until it is time to move again.) This is unfortunate because without mushin he will never develop strong ki.

Although it takes considerable time and effort to develop it properly, mushin is actually a natural state. Almost everyone has experienced it at one time or another. The problem is that before training any such occurrence is likely purely accidental. To develop strong ki, you must teach yourself how to achieve mushin at will. After many years of training, you will find it difficult to remember what it was like to be without this ability. You will go through life not thinking, but reacting.

The standard response to a statement such as this is a cry of, "How can I do anything if I make myself empty? All physical action is directed by the brain and you must think about something before you do it!" This is a typical beginner's misconception. Do you think about recoiling when you touch something hot? No. You just do it. This is the purpose of mushin. You do not think, you just react instinctively to a situation. For, in combat, to think is to die. Obviously, while certain reactions are built in, others have to be developed. This is why physical training must always go along with mental exercises.

There is a very simple and elegant exercise to demonstrate the value of mushin in combat that almost anyone can do. All that is required is an average ability to relax and concentrate.

Stand with your left foot a little forward and your left forearm raised to about chest level. Bend your knees slightly and get ready to move very fast. Now have your training

The samurai learns to quiet his mind so that he may perform his strategies without hesitation.

partner stand in front of you with his right hand poised a couple of feet in front of your forehead. Striking as fast as he can, he will attempt to slap the top of your head with his open hand. Poised and ready, you will attempt to bring your left forearm up fast enough to block his strike. You will find this very difficult.

Now, to demonstrate mushin, repeat the exercise. This time instead of getting ready, just stand in a natural position with your left arm hanging loosely by your side. Relax completely and look off into the distance. When your partner steps in front of you do not look at him or think about blocking his strike, just continue to look through him and off into the distance. Now, when his hand moves, you will find it much easier to flip your left arm up in plenty of time to block his attack. The interesting thing is that, although your arm is actually traveling a much greater distance, there is much less effort. The trick is complete physical and mental relaxation. If there is the slightest bit of tension or the smallest thought of getting ready, this exercise will not work.

The achievement of a solid and usable state of mushin is an integral part of ki development. As you train to achieve this state, take care not to be misled by those who would make it something mystical. Mushin is just a tool and is no more (and no less) important than strong muscles and flexible joints.

KI NO NAGASHI

When you have a properly trained mind and body, it leads to a state known as *ki no nagashi,* the "flow of ki." No, the ki does not really flow. This is only an expression used to describe the feeling.

Ki no nagashi is a state of exaltation. It feels as if every cell in your body is intensely alive. (You will never see a senior student of any bujutsu using stimulants. They do not need them.) An analogy that perhaps comes close to giving an impression of this feeling is that of an automobile engine that has been blueprinted—it has been disassembled and all of its parts are polished to exact blueprint specifications. When there is a state of ki no nagashi your body feels like such an engine. It is purring along and operating exactly the way it is supposed to. There is no deep and mysterious force involved, unless you call life itself mysterious. Because you are operating very efficiently, there is no wasted motion or thought. Your body moves gracefully and smoothly. So does your mind. This is why this state is called a "flow of ki"—you feel as if you are flowing through life instead of being bounced from one situation to the next.

By being very alive you become very, very hard to kill. You move smoothly and strongly because your body has become a well-tuned machine. You move rapidly because you operate intuitively instead of wasting time thinking. This results in total and coordinated power. Even when you are not doing anything it is there, available at an instant's notice. It is this coordination of mind and body that allows the ki both to grow and flow. While a maniac may radiate great energy, the energy is erratic and uncontrolled. It is only when your life force becomes deep, quiet, and powerful, like a great river, that it is referred to as ki no nagashi.

Do not think of ki as something you acquire; it is something you release. By proper training you can enhance it but you can never create it. Ki is normal, and so are the training methods for developing it. There is nothing esoteric about either the process or the results. Also, do not confuse ki with strength or health. While both of these are of great importance to its development, they are only stepping-stones. After you know what strong ki feels like, it becomes self-perpetuating through constant mental feedback. This is why you can see a weak old man with strong ki and a strong young man with weak ki.

Leave the esoteric discussion of ki to philosophers. A strategist does not waste his time talking about ki; he uses it. Men have long debated the question of what life really is and they are not a bit closer to the answer now than they were ten thousand years ago. As a strategist, you should not be worrying about the definition of life; you should think only about control of it.

KIME

When you have developed ki no nagashi, you can flow from target to target during a battle. As you apply your technique to each of these targets, you focus your entire effort on one small point to ensure maximum destruction. This momentary concentration is called *kime,* "spiritual focus." The purpose of kime is pure and simple: power. By focusing your strength on one point, you greatly increase effective power. One pound of pressure spread out over a wide area is of little importance, but a needle driven by one pound of force will penetrate deeply.

When you focus your entire being on a task, there must be no conflict. All parts of your mind and body must work toward the same goal. This can be much more difficult than it might seem. For a simple demonstration of this, place your fingertips beneath the edge of a desk and try to lift it. As you apply pressure, reach across with your other hand and feel the triceps muscle of your lifting arm. In this particular case, the biceps is the working muscle and the triceps is not being used—it should be completely relaxed. However, you will probably find that your triceps is slightly tensed. In other words, it is actually fighting against the lifting action. It is this sort of physical conflict, and similar mental conflicts, that you must eliminate in order to develop kime. Doing this is not too hard. It is just time consuming.

To achieve physical kime, take each of your techniques and practice it very slowly, as in the Chinese art of t'ai chi ch'uan. As you do this, study each muscle in your body to be sure that it is helping the action and not hindering it. By a slow process of self-examination, concentration, and practice, you will achieve a state of near-perfect physical efficiency. All of your muscles not in actual use will remain relaxed so as not to interfere with the ones doing the work. In addition, your joints will be at the proper angles for optimum leverage.

This does not result in an actual increase in your physical strength; you are only using what is available with maximum efficiency. Keeping in mind the fact that muscles only pull—

In business and in battle, the strategist requires much contemplation to efficiently train in the physical and mental techniques of strategy.

all power comes from contraction, not expansion—you should be able to test the training process in a variety of ways. As you do so, strive for a feeling of naturalness and fluidity. You are not trying to do something special, you only want to direct your body into its most normal and efficient path.

In addition to the purely physical, there is mental kime to consider. This begins with mushin. First you clear your mind of all thoughts and then you fill it, completely, with the target. There is an ancient and often told dojo story which illustrates this.

It seems that once, many years ago in Japan, there was an archery contest. For the target, a paper *koi*[3] was used. The bull's-eye was to be the eye of the fish. With the koi fluttering in the wind, this was almost impossible to hit. After the contest, the participants were questioned about what they saw when they shot at the target. The typical reply was, "A brightly colored *koi* fluttering against a clear blue sky." However, the winner, the only man to score a bull's-eye, replied, "An eye!"

An eye—that was *all* the winner saw. He did not see the rest of the fish or even the sky. He only saw the target. A Japanese philosopher would note that because this man only saw the eye, that was all that existed in the universe. So, how could he miss?

In the Japanese language, hitting a target in this manner is called *atari*. To hit while being aware of other things is *uchi*. This illustrates a significant difference between Eastern and Western thought. In the West, a marksman who misses a target would blame it on some physical factor. However, in Japan, a miss would more likely be seen as a mental problem. Where a coach might say, "Your right elbow was too high," the sensei would be prone to exhort, "More concentration!"

Total kime is a fusion of physical efficiency and mental discipline. For an instant, you focus your mind and body so intensely on a task that the outside world disappears. For development of the mental half of this momentary focus, nothing works quite as well as a constant program of self-denial. If you are thirsty, delay getting a drink. If you are tired, stay awake for another hour. You treat your mind as if it were a puppy. You handle it firmly until it has been taught to sit, heel, and fetch. If this is properly done, your spirit gradually becomes like supple leather.

The ultimate state of kime is that in which your entire being is working toward a specific goal at 100 percent efficiency. You will never achieve such perfect efficiency, but what you do achieve will be far above the average person's ability. This is not some superhuman state of existence; it is perfectly normal. It only seems strange because the majority of people operate at only a tiny fraction of their true potential. To have perfect kime is nothing more than doing only what you are doing.

The only difference between a master swordsman and a beginner is that the master does not do anything else but be a master. The beginner, however, has not forgotten himself. Instead of focusing his entire attention on the job, part of his mind is always worrying about his own safety. On the other hand, the master simply does what is required, nothing more and nothing less. He does not strive (which is what gives his techniques their characteristically effortless look). He operates at such a level of efficiency that striving is unnecessary.

Kime is an expression of ki. It is not the only expression, because sometimes it is necessary to apply force along a line or over a surface rather than on a point. However, even in arts such as jujutsu or aikido, where your focus is primarily along lines rather than on points, there will be ample use made of kime.

The physical applications of kime are the most obvious ones. This is especially true for the use of kime in the art of karate. A senior student of that art can generate unbelievable power by properly focusing his mind and body. However, a teaching such as this is meant to be applied to every facet of your existence, not just to special situations. For example, consider your posture at this very moment. It is easier (and more efficient) to sit with a good posture than with a poor one. And, the better your posture the better you can move. Miyamoto Musashi[4] said, "You should make your normal stance your fighting stance and your fighting stance your normal stance." When he said this he was referring to your mental posture as well as your physical attitude. Every minute of every day, you adjust both to ensure a flow and focus to your life. This is the true meaning of kime.

In days gone by, young ladies of breeding were sent to finishing schools. There a young girl learned such things as how to walk up and down a flight of stairs with a glass of water balanced on her head. She studied how to approach every situation with a sense of style and poise. A master swordsman from feudal Japan would have felt perfectly at home with such training. Although they did not use these words, the actual goal of these finishing schools was the development of ki and kime.

NOTES

1. A field is a mathematical abstraction that denotes an effect distributed over an area. You can measure the effect but not the field itself.

2. This exercise has an awesome effect on a baseball player's batting average.

3. This is a brightly colored paper fish flown from a tall pole above a Japanese home on Boy's Day. There is one fish, appropriately sized, for each son in the family.

4. Shinmen Musashi No Kami Fujiwara No Genshin, popularly known as Miyamoto Musashi (1584-1645) was a famous swordsman and the author of *Go Rin No Sho* (A Book of Five Rings), a famous book on strategy (1645).

Chapter Four

Kokyu Chikara: Breath Power

There are two types of physical strength: *tai chikara* and *kokyū chikara*.[1] Tai chikara, usually referred to as external power, is normal physical strength. It is developed by such standard exercises as weight lifting. Compared to this, kokyu chikara, commonly referred to as internal power, seems quite different to the beginner. This difference has given rise to many extravagant tales of invincibility caused by kokyu chikara. It is usually said to derive from some mysterious power, usually called ki. If this were true, you would see many more Olympic athletes using it. In reality, the only difference between tai chikara and kokyu chikara is the muscles involved.

When you use tai chikara, it is with a feeling of compression. Even when you lift a weight over your head it is with a feeling of compressing your body. The use of kokyu chikara, however, goes with a feeling of expansion. One widely used analogy is that of a balloon—when you apply internal strength you pretend that your entire body is expanding. This is the key difference between internal and external strength. When you use tai chikara, you can use only one muscle group and relax the rest of your body. However, when you use kokyu chikara, it must be done with every part of your body working equally.

Most physical actions are done with a "get ready . . . go!" count. You inhale as you get ready and exhale as you apply power. The purpose of kokyu chikara is to allow you to get to the ready position with strength. The technique was invented by a swordsman seeking a way out of the disadvantageous position of having his swordarm held by an opponent.[2] In such a position, if you exhale while forcing your sword upward as in weight lifting, you will have no air remaining in your lungs when it is time to cut. Kokyu chikara allows you to apply power on both cycles of your breath. If you inhale with a feeling of drawing in power as you raise your sword, you can overcome your opponent's grasp. This leaves you with your lungs full of air for the cut.

As you can see, by using a combination of internal and external power, you can reduce the time required for a technique by half. Normally, you would follow a four-count pattern: first, inhale and get ready; second, exhale and lift your sword; third, inhale and get ready; fourth, exhale and cut. However, by using both tai and kokyu chikara, you reduce this to two counts: first, inhale and raise your sword; second, exhale and cut.

The purely physical advantages of kokyu chikara are only the tip of the iceberg. When this method is used properly it results in a peculiar psychological phenomenon.

When you use external power your mind tends to turn inward, matching the compression of your body. In such a case you are always aware of the limitations of your physical strength. However, when you use kokyu chikara, your mind turns outward. Because you are not concentrating on your body—in most cases you are not even aware of it—you have a feeling of effortless strength. Although you are accomplishing work, it seems as if the energy requirements are only a fraction of what would normally be needed. This is, of course, impossible. But it is a very, very useful attitude. By feeling your power is not limited to the muscular strength of your body, you do not act as if it is. Instead of thinking you may not be strong enough to do something, you come to believe you can do anything. As we'll see later, this positive spirit has many important ramifications in the art of war.

One of the most widely used examples of internal power is the so-called unbendable arm. The way this is normally taught, it is actually little more than a parlor trick. A volunteer is told to extend his arm and make a tight fist. Then another man will attempt to bend the arm, finding it not too difficult. Next, the volunteer is instructed to extend his arm, relax, and concentrate on a flow of ki shooting out of his fingers. Now when someone attempts to bend his arm it seems as solid as an iron bar. This test is often used to demonstrate the existence of ki by those who do not understand what ki really is.

The unbendable-arm demonstration actually has nothing to do with either ki or kokyu chikara. All that is really happening is that the volunteer is using different sets of muscles in the two halves of the test. When he made a tight fist, he instinctively tightened all the muscles in his arm. This meant his biceps was acting against his triceps. In other words, the biceps was actually helping to bend his arm. However, when he was relaxed and thinking about a flow of ki, he was only tensing those muscles used for pointing; his biceps was relaxed. This effectively made his arm much stronger because he was no longer fighting himself. The same results could have been achieved by instructing the volunteer to point at a particular point on the wall. He could have also been told to relax completely and concentrate on tightening his triceps. Either of these methods will result in an unbendable arm, but they do not illustrate a use of kokyu chikara.

The proper way to demonstrate an unbendable arm is to do it with internal power. Stand tall and extend your arm with a feeling of stretching and yawning. Do not think about your arm; concentrate on trying to expand your entire body. As you inhale you should feel that even your hair is expanding! If you do this properly you will find that it is almost impossible for anyone to bend your arm. Even if a person seizes your arm before it is fully extended, you should have more than enough power to complete your stretching motion. If you examine this move carefully, you will find it is extremely powerful.

Kokyu chikara may be used in any technique that has an up-and-down motion. The only problem encountered by beginners when they try to use it is that they find they do not have enough time for a normal breath cycle when fighting. This is because, at their level, they are still reacting to their enemy instead of forcing their enemy to do the reacting. The objective in any form of combat is to force your enemy to do the running around; you should work calmly and slowly. If your enemy is always hurrying to catch up with you, you will find there is ample time for proper breathing.

The technique of *kokyū-hō,* "breath-method," which results in kokyu chikara, is, in its initial stages, purely a physical action. It does not increase physical strength, it only prolongs it. Because power is applied on both cycles of the breath, it can seem mystical to the neophyte. Since he does not understand the mechanics of the action, he may attribute the extra strength to ki or some other mysterious force. The result is that, instead of viewing this new strength as something anyone can develop with proper training, he sees it as some type of magic.

Kokyu chikara is not magic. It is a simple, physical act, and anyone can develop it.

KOKYU DOSA

The classical exercise for developing kokyu chikara is called *kokyū dōsa.* To practice this, sit in seiza facing your partner. He grasps both your wrists firmly and you attempt to tip him over, toward either side or to his rear. As you raise your hands, inhale deeply and then, as you exhale, tip him over with a feeling of cutting down. This is a very popular exercise and is seen in most schools of aikido. However, because most students do not understand kokyu chikara, it is invariably done incorrectly.

If you use only tai chikara, it is almost impossible to lift your hands when they are held firmly. Therefore, many students tend to resort to the use of jujutsu. Instead of cutting upward directly against their opponent's strength, they circle around it. By making small adjustments in his hand position, a student can find a groove, a particular line of weakness. In this particular direction, his opponent, even though he is holding with maximum strength, cannot exercise any great power. By applying a very small amount of strength along this line of minimal resistance, a student can tip over his opponent effortlessly. While this is a fine exercise for developing jujutsu skills, it is not kokyu dosa. In this case, all that is happening is that the students are practicing a sitting form of a jujutsu throw known as *tenchi nage.* Because little strength is needed, kokyu chikara is not exercised and, consequently, never developed.

To practice kokyu dosa properly, you should go directly against your opponent's strength. Go against *all* of his power. Your training partner should hold your wrists as hard as he can, so hard that both your wrists are swollen and bruised on the day following practice. Inhale strongly and cut upward with your open hands. Then exhale and cut downward, tipping over your opponent in any direction you choose. Instead of searching for his weakest point, seek his strongest. When you can go against this strength with little apparent effort, then you are truly using kokyu chikara.

The first time you attempt kokyu dosa (in the proper manner), you may have an urge to label it impossible. The standard cause of difficulty is allowing your mind to be trapped along with your wrists. Your partner seizes your wrists firmly and your mind is trapped at that point—when you look at your wrists your mind cannot move. The key to kokyu dosa is not even to think about your wrists. Look off into the distance and concentrate on your body. As you inhale, think about expanding. Imagine that you are growing so large that your head is touching the ceiling. If you do this correctly, you will find no difficulty in raising your hands against a heavy resistance.

An ancient form of this exercise, called *koden aiki happō nage,* is still used in some schools. In this variation, your opponent will be standing while you remain seated. When you extend your arms out and up, he will seize your wrists firmly. Then you throw him in any of eight directions. The harder he grabs you, the harder he will hit the floor.

Either of these methods makes an excellent warm-up

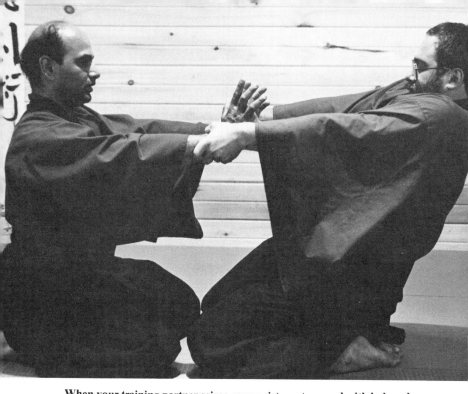

When your training partner seizes your wrists, cut upward with kokyu dosa, as if raising a sword. He will then fall backward.

The exercises of kokyu dosa may also be practiced with one hand.

exercise before class. One of them should be made an integral part of every training period.

NOTES

1. The character for *chikara* is sometimes pronounced *ryoku.*

2. According to legend, it was Prince Teijun (c. ninth century), the sixth son of Emperor Seiwa.

Chapter Five

Kiai: Intense Ki

The result of basic training in any art is a strong, flexible, and relaxed mind and body. If the training has been vigorous, mind and body will be very healthy. The life force will be very high and synchronized. Where the energy of an untrained person will have a sporadic and fragmented quality, the energy of a properly trained man will have cohesiveness and depth.

This is a difficult feeling to put into words, but it is something which everyone has encountered. You will occasionally see a large group of people in a room and one of them will stand out from the crowd. He is not noisy or flamboyant. This individual with strong ki may just be quietly standing along the sidelines; but, for some reason, he is the center of attention. He radiates energy but he does not use it.

As was previously discussed, every living thing has ki. When the level of this ki becomes so high as to seem supernormal, it is referred to as *kiai*.[1] A person with kiai seems to be overflowing with life.

To create kiai requires two things: first, there must be system-efficiency great enough to allow ki to increase; secondly, there must be positive feedback. If there is too much drag within the system or if there is not enough positive input, the energy within any system can never increase.

You decrease the drag within your body by practicing a technique until it can be done with maximum efficiency. You get positive feedback from success. When you initiate an attack and see that all factors of your technique are so perfect that it will succeed, no matter what your opponent does, this gives you a good feeling. After the technique has scored and you have cleanly disengaged, you get another positive feeling. These rushes of emotion are what we call kiai.

It is commonly said (by junior instructors) that kiai is a shout used to confuse an enemy, or that it is similar to the grunt of effort you make when lifting something heavy. Not so! While the sound of kiai may be forced out by the effort of executing a technique and this sound may frighten your enemy, this has nothing to do with the actual meaning of the word. True, kiai is normally associated with a voiced sound, but this is not an absolute requirement. There is such a thing, rare though it may be, as silent kiai.

If you reexamine the causes of kiai, you will note that the moments of greatest intensity occur during the attack and during the withdrawal. This is where the sound will occur.[2] There is no kiai synchronized with the moment of impact of a blow. True kiai is a shout of exaltation—you feel so good that you *must* make a sound. This is much different from the forced shouts of beginning martial arts students. They have seen only the external form of kiai and, not understanding its essence, attempt to copy it.

Because kiai, like the technique that generates it, is done at maximum efficiency, it will have a unique sound. It will have a purity and depth of tone that seems to come from deep within the abdomen. Conversely, the imitation kiai of a beginner, although it may be quite loud, will have a harshness which will appear to come from the throat. True kiai is similar to the trained voice of an opera singer—even when soft, such a tone will have much greater range and penetration than that of a beginner. The actual sound of the kiai will range from a low moan to a sharp bark. In any event, it will rarely sound very human. The first time you hear a real one, the hairs on the back of your neck will stand up.

Though kiai is associated with a yell at the moment of attack, the yell is not an integral part of the attack whereas the presence of kiai is quite necessary to the success of the attack.

Development of kiai is a long and painful process. You start by selecting a single technique and practicing it over and over, not just for days but for years, until you can execute it perfectly. A very rough rule-of-thumb would be ten thousand repetitions for a simple technique.

As you engage in this repetition practice, which is known as *renshū,* you must drive yourself past the point of exhaustion. When you are fresh, it is easy to add slight extraneous motions to the technique. However, when you are exhausted, your body will instinctively seek the easiest path. This will also be the most efficient way. By training to the point of exhaustion and then beyond it, your body will eliminate all unnecessary motion. It is very important that, while doing this, you do not modify the technique. For this reason, a good instructor is critical. Because such a man will know your limits better than you do, he can drive you past these limits safely and, at the same time, ensure that style is not sacrificed for quantity.

When you have physically mastered a technique, you are ready for stage two: partner practice. At this time you practice the application of the technique under controlled conditions. You should start softly and slowly and, as you gain strength, have your partner gradually increase the level of his resistance. After enough of this training, one day you will succeed in executing the technique perfectly, against maximum resistance. In other words, you will execute it in a real situation, or at least one as real as can be simulated in a dojo. When this happens, you will feel a great rush of emotion and the technique will be accompanied by a shout of joy.

Note that your kiai is an emotional reaction to a physical event. Obviously, to increase the intensity of the kiai means that you must increase the intensity of the event. The first thing that comes to mind that you could intensify is the situation itself. A real battle or a major tournament with thousands of people observing will bring about a high level of tension, and the resulting kiai will be much stronger than any arising in a controlled dojo situation.

Also, the quality of the technique is of great importance.

To win only by accident brings relief, not kiai. It is only through winning with a technique of such perfection and beauty that your opponent is powerless to avoid it that you will feel exaltation.

The fascinating thing about kiai is that its limits are far beyond what most people consider to be normal. When you achieve kiai, you feel, in addition to exaltation, a sense of great power. This starts a chain reaction. Because of your feeling of power, you relax a little—you are now so good that you do not have to try so hard anymore. This relaxation results in even greater efficiency. The result is a closed loop with positive feedback.

Although the potential power generated by kiai may at first seem limitless, in reality it is restricted by your physical condition. A senior with well-developed kiai who, for one reason or another, is forced to discontinue physical training could easily put himself in the hospital by generating more energy than his body can handle. Because he has felt his true power, he is not limited by the average person's instinctive urge to hold back.

Another interesting characteristic of kiai is that once felt it does not seem supernormal at all. Suddenly it becomes the normal and proper way to execute any technique; it only appears special to an observer. This can, and generally does, result in considerable mental conflict within the adept. Once kiai has been established in him, he must, by a conscious act of will, hold himself down to the public norm in order to exist within society. He has learned to fly but must keep his wings folded when among the flightless; it is only in the dojo or on the battlefield that he may soar.

There has always been much talk of what a horrible experience war is for the weekend warrior. However, for the professional, war is home. Only on the battlefield may he cast loose the shackles of society and live as men have lived for thousands of years, using all of his powers without restriction. A modern man spends his life protected by the cocoon of civilization and may never see, much less be a victim of, an act of violence. This is a recent development. For most of his history man has lived on the ragged edge, only an instant from sudden and violent death. Those whose business is violence, such as police and professional soldiers, understand this. They know that civilization is only a shell. This is why they are rarely regarded as pillars of society. Rather, they tend to generate a strange uneasiness within the general public. The root of the public unease is a subconscious awareness of the warrior's kiai.

However, from the warrior's point of view he is the normal one. It is the rest of society that is lacking something. Although the warrior may not be able to define it, the thing missing from the public is kiai, the ultimate power of man. Once felt, it is more addictive than a narcotic. This is why soldiers, police, and the disciples of a dojo continue their work. It is only when they are engaged in it that they feel truly alive. To demand that the warrior never again release this power is to condemn him to walk through the remainder of his days in a sort of living death. For, to such a man, kiai is no longer a part of his life; it is all of life.

ZANSHIN

After you have executed a perfect technique, you are left with a good feeling, a sort of aftertaste. This is called *zanshin,* "remaining spirit." During this period, while the aftereffects of the technique are fading, all of the proper things you did during the technique are still present in a heightened state. These include such factors as perfect balance, intense external awareness, and spiritual focus. During this period, which may last for several seconds, you are as close as you can come to operating at peak performance without actually doing anything. It is a moment of great stillness—you do not move and it seems as if the universe is holding its breath. Zanshin is an instant of silent exaltation when you are savoring the memory of perfection.

There was a saying among samurai, "After the battle, tighten your helmet straps," which meant you should not let down your guard just because you had apparently won. Or, as the hunters of big game in Africa say, "It is the dead lion that gets up and eats you." Sayings such as these have con-

fused many beginners into thinking that zanshin is an artifi-
cially maintained state of mind. Nothing could be further
from the truth.

If, and that is a very big if, a technique is done perfectly,
zanshin must be present. Zanshin is just as much a part of
a perfect technique as an echo is of a loud noise. In order to
have zanshin, you must go beyond mere victory and win
gloriously, for zanshin, more than just an echo of perfection, is perfection itself.

Zanshin, the moment of stillness after a technique.

The perfection of zanshin is physically apparent. If you observe an event in which a person has just won a great victory, you will usually see him leap about for joy. However, if he has won purely due to his own skill rather than just through luck, his reaction is different. He realizes he has just done something that is awe-inspiring and he will freeze for a moment to savor the thrill of it. At this moment, all is perfect—every line of his body is a work of art. If you chance to see this happen, it is something you will remember for the rest of your life. Japanese cinematographers are superb in their ability to capture such moments. In a typical Western film a fight scene will be concluded with a sigh of exhaustion. This is not the case in Japanese films, for in these a fight will end with a shot framed for maximum artistic content. It is a moment of glory and all action freezes while it is enjoyed. Although this is an artificial device, it does illustrate the proper emotion.

While it is normal to speak of zanshin as a mental state that follows a perfect technique, it is also possible to achieve zanshin before a technique. Much like a great cat that has spotted potential prey, you freeze into an attitude of complete immobility with every cell of your body intensely alive. With sufficient experience you will come to understand this feeling and be able to achieve it at any time. An excellent example of this ability is seen in the actors of a Japanese Nō play.

It is even possible to retain a state of zanshin semipermanently. Military combat veterans and police are familiar with this. However, this is not necessarily a desirable state in a civilized world. While it may be required for survival in a combat zone, whether that zone is in an urban environment or an Asian jungle, it is not conducive to gentle living for the average person. Being in the presence of a man with zanshin tends to make an average person very, very nervous.

Zanshin, and the ability to achieve it, has a dual value for the warrior. First, because awareness is so heightened, the person in a state of zanshin becomes a very dangerous man. He is capable of reacting with explosive force to even the slightest provocation. Secondly, zanshin offers a measuring stick for progress because it only happens after a perfect technique. Without this, you would never know for sure if you had reached the ultimate level of physical training.

NOTES

1. The *ai* portion of this compound word is a form of the verb *au,* which means "to join" or "to meet." However, when used as the second component of a compound, it means "to happen." Therefore, *kiai* may be literally translated as "life force happening."

2. Traditional ryu use the sounds "ei!" and "ah!" to designate these points. Some also use "toh!" to designate safe disengagement from a failed attack. These sounds are purely symbolic and are not real kiai.

Chapter Six

Aiki: Dominating Spirit

The word *aiki* is written with the same two Japanese characters as is kiai, with the characters in reversed order. While it may be literally translated as "blending spirits," do not make the mistake of adding a sense of equality to this.

Kiai is something that happens within you—you can create a state of kiai even when alone. Aiki, however, is bringing your kiai to bear upon your opponent. When you have extremely strong ki, so strong that it is classed as kiai, it affects your enemy. Because he senses your tremendous spiritual strength, his own will to attack is weakened. Perhaps the best definition of aiki was given by Takeda Sogaku,[1] who said, "Aiki is the art of defeating your opponent with a single glance."

The development of aiki into a usable skill is a gradual process. Although it was created by swordsmen, the art of the sword is not the fastest way to learn it. Much better is a system of jujutsu, especially a ryu which is a derivative of the Daitō-ryu. The reason is that in many other styles of combat, such as karate, you can substitute strength or speed for technical skill and still win. However, in a system such as the *aikijūjutsu* of the Daito-ryu you are encouraged to work slowly and softly against great resistance. Because you are not allowed to use speed or strength, your aiki is forced to develop.

The first stage in developing aiki consists of learning a new technique and then practicing it with a partner until you can do it correctly. Then you select different partners and continue practicing until you are sure you can execute the technique against anyone.

The third stage takes you back to your original partner. Now as you practice he will gradually increase his resistance. He does this slowly, never allowing you to fail. After you can do the technique against his maximum resistance, you repeat

When facing an opponent, you project kiai through your attitude, making him feel powerless to your greater skill.

the process with other partners.

Finally, there will come a time when you know, beyond the shadow of a doubt, that you can use this technique successfully against anyone, no matter how hard they resist it. When you have reached this level, you will naturally start to reduce the amount of effort you put into the technique. You do this because you know you are going to succeed and no longer feel compelled to try so hard.

This is when your aiki will start to develop. Your opponent will sense you are merely toying with him, that you know you are going to win and no longer consider him to be a serious threat. This causes him to feel a certain sense of futility. He will wonder why he should even try, knowing he has no chance of success. His discouragement, in turn, makes it even easier for you to win, so you reduce your efforts still further. The process can continue to the point where you only have to look at an enemy and he gives up.

Again, the aura you radiate, which is the expression of your confidence, is kiai. The effect of this upon the enemy, which destroys his will to fight, is aiki. You feel the kiai; he feels the aiki.

If you think this sounds too esoteric and cannot imagine winning a fight with aiki, consider the fact that parents use this method with their children every day. The method is the same. The only difference is in degree. It is said that the great feudal general Minamoto Yoshiie developed this art to its ultimate state. Yoshiie was the greatest warrior in the history of Japan and was known as Hachiman Taro, "the eldest son of the god of war." Legend has it that all he had to do was order his horse saddled and entire armies would surrender.

The first mention of aiki is found in the ancient scrolls of Japanese sword schools. It is a natural thing and has been around as long as life itself; however, it is only in the dojo that a formalized method for its development may be found. Not in all dojo, however. Only those teaching the older and more traditional ryu have it.[2] In such a dojo they regard techniques of combat merely as vehicles for developing aiki. In more modern schools, the techniques have become so important in themselves, for either self-defense or tournament use, that this goal has been lost. This is not to say that aiki is never seen in a modern school. When it is seen in a modern school, however, it has been developed as an accidental by-product and not as the primary goal of training. Neither is this to say the modern schools are wrong in their approach. Aiki requires decades to develop and this is not to many people's taste. For most students, immediate results are far more valuable than some future intangible.

Aiki is a common factor in all traditional Japanese martial arts and should not be particularly associated with the modern art of aikido. While modern aikido has a historical link with the aiki teaching,[3] this has become so diluted in both theory and practice that it bears little resemblance to the real thing. Aikido is supposed to be a set of physical exercises designed to strengthen the power of aiki. However, what most aikido schools now teach is a very, very soft form of jujutsu based on toned-down techniques from the Daito-ryu. This is further diluted by liberal doses of pseudo-spiritual teachings,[4] which makes the art almost useless for anything other than personal entertainment. The reason for this state of affairs is that too many people remember Uyeshiba as a gentle old man of eighty and not as the tiger he was at fifty. They conveniently forget his statement that "aikido is 99 percent hitting." Uyeshiba most definitely understood aiki but, sadly, his lack of education severely limited his ability to transmit this knowledge to his disciples.

Aiki is the ultimate state of any martial art. It is not an external show—you do not frighten your enemy by either action or appearance. Rather it is a lack of external show. You do nothing because your opponent is not important enough for you to have to do anything. Your very existence is enough to defeat him.

NOTES

1. Takeda Sogaku Minamoto Masayoshi (1857–1943) was the last of the great swordsmen. Very small even by Japanese standards (less than five feet tall), he was known as the

Aizukotengu, the "little demon of the Aizu clan." He was the most famous teacher in northern Japan.

2. In 1941 the Butokukai, the leading martial-arts group of the time, defined aiki as an intrinsic part of *all* classical bujutsu.

3. Modern aikido is the creation of Uyeshiba Morihei (1883–1969). He was a student of Takeda Sogaku and received two of the three Daito-ryu teaching scrolls. The Daito-ryu had traditionally only been taught to senior military officers, but Uyeshiba taught it to the general public. This required many of the rougher techniques to be considerably watered down.

4. Uyeshiba was an ardent follower of the Ōmoto-kyō religion of Deguchi Ōnisaburo. This was very popular among the lower social classes because it preached utopia in this life. The religion is characterized by the achievement of religious ecstasy through long periods of chanting and special breathing exercises. Deguchi believed he was the reincarnation of the Dalai Lama of Tibet and that he was destined to rule Japan.

Chapter Seven

Kokoro:
Mental Attitude

Battles are won or lost because of mental attitude. While weapons and numbers of soldiers are of undeniable importance, it is a mistake to view these things as the most important factors of war. The deciding factor on the field of battle is *kokoro,* "heart," the mental attitude of the warrior. It is this attitude, this kokoro that makes the difference between the soldier and the civilian.

It may seem to be an anachronism to discuss fighting spirit in this age of electronics and missiles, where a soldier rarely sees his enemy. Nothing could be further from the truth. A proper fighting spirit is just as important now as it was a thousand years ago. The only trouble is that it is getting much more difficult to develop.

In feudal Japan less than 10 percent of the populace were members of the samurai caste. Of that group less than ten percent were effective fighting men. Finally, out of this small elite, only one in a hundred could be considered a true master of his craft. This percentage, a small one, seems to be remarkably constant for all ages and all cultures. (There are a few exceptions, such as ancient Sparta, but these are very rare.) So, we are talking about 1 percent of 1 percent of a population. Although patriotic people may not like to admit it, most modern men are unsuitable for combat.

Due to their upbringing, modern men are generally incapable either of generating or enduring violence.

The problem is threefold. First, modern society starts indoctrinating its citizens against the evil of violence almost from the moment of their birth. Then, after eighteen years of this, they put a young man into uniform and expect to turn him into a killer with only a few weeks of training.

Secondly, by means of the popular media, society gives its young a totally false picture of what violence is really like. Modern films, especially those watered down enough for television, show bullet wounds as small, red spots on the shirt of an enemy. This ill prepares a person for the sight of an arm or leg blown off by a modern high-velocity shell.

Finally, the machines of war have outstripped the men who direct them. In the past a battle was limited by the endurance of the troops—when the horses and the sword arms grew tired, the armies would disengage to rest and regroup. Now, however, mechanized units may be required to maintain close combat for days or even weeks. This is quite simply beyond the endurance of the human body. The average soldier in a modern war is a physically efficient combat unit for less than six months. He peaks at about the third month and from that point goes steadily downhill—and this assumes that very little of his time is spent in actual combat. Facing this physical limitation has a profound effect on the spirit of a warrior. Once he realizes that he is not strong enough to use the tools of his profession to their utmost, he starts to doubt all his abilities.

As a strategist, you must bear in mind the fact that you are the product of a modern civilization and that the teachings of this civilization have reached far deeper into your personality than you may realize. You have been conditioned by society's ideals, not by the reality of violence. In order to develop kokoro you must learn to see through this veil of idealism.

Kokoro is not a rigid mental attitude; it is whatever attitude you need to win. The classical method for achieving this attitude is surviving a major battle. However, because survival is largely a matter of luck, this method is not very efficient.

In order to develop kokoro without the waste of war, you must understand both the nature of man and the nature of society. If you can learn to look at both objectively, you may be able to shed some of the social concepts, ideals, and ideas that interfere with combat. Social conditioning runs deep, so expect some mental inertia as you try to free yourself from it.

When you think about war, you must free yourself from the concept of good and evil, moral and immoral. There is no such thing as a good war or a bad war; there is only war and it is always miserable. The time for morality is before or after the battle. During the period of active violence, all such thoughts must be set aside. When beginning a battle you must have only one thought: Winning!

A large man with good technique may be defeated by a small opponent if he lacks this ability to concentrate. The big man wants to win, but not enough to do whatever is necessary. This causes him to pause or hold back some of his power, which is fatal. This spiritual weakness is not shared by the man with kokoro, and that is what makes him dangerous. The simplest definition of a dangerous man is that he is a man who is ready to hit. He can hit anyone, at any time, and in any situation. Clearly understanding that combat is no place for a rational man, he disconnects the rational portion of his mind. The remainder of his being forms an efficient tool for war. He sees nothing but the target and feels nothing but the desire to hit it.

This may sound rather cold-blooded, but so is war. The world would be a much nicer place to live in without the warriors, but they are still necessary. Violent times are only surmounted by violent men; and as long as society refuses to do its own fighting, it must never lose the ability to breed such men.

In addition to trying to fight only good wars, modern man has a predilection for limited wars. He likes these because they give him a false sense of security—if he only fights small battles, he risks only small defeats. In reality, limited war is a contradiction in terms. The proper word for such an event is sport. (*Webster's Dictionary* defines sport as "a specific diversion, usually involving physical exercise and having a set form and body of rules.") A war is not a sporting event and it will never be won by trying to fight it as such.

Consider the typical television fight scene. The good man will knock down the bad man and then step back, allowing the bad man to regain his feet. This is repeated until the bad man can no longer continue. Ridiculous! You must never allow an enemy a chance to hurt you. When you knock him down you should stomp on his head until he stops moving. This is kokoro. The danger is that you may be so well conditioned by society that you pause in this action. That is when the man you knocked down will pull out a gun and kill you.

History abounds with examples of this basic truth. The European phase of World War II was won with unrestricted bombing of the German industrial complex. The Pacific phase of the same war was won with unrestricted submarine warfare against Japan, a thing which was regarded as inhumane and immoral only a few years previously. For the opposite side of the coin, consider Korea and Vietnam. The West lost both conflicts by placing restrictions on the combat troops. In the Middle East you see a fine example of kokoro in the Six-Day War—any war lasting less than a week is obviously the result of enlightened leadership.

The civilian abhors statements such as these. He is prone to say, "Better an honorable defeat than a dishonorable victory." This is pure insanity. If you do not plan on winning you should not fight in the first place. Wars are not won by the best men; they are won by the meanest men. Battle is only a glorious adventure to the historians of the winning side. For those directly involved it is a bloody and painful experience. However, from time to time such a thing cannot be avoided. The only rational solution is to go in fast and hard and get the mess over with as quickly as possible.

How fast is fast enough? For individual combat, you should think in terms of seconds. For warfare between nations, think in terms of days. Any battle that lasts longer than a minute between individuals or a week between armies is being mismanaged.

The secret to this speed is kokoro. Once this is developed, things proceed very fast. At the first sign of danger you go for the throat, leaving all thoughts of rules for after the fight.

Over two thousand years ago in the writings of Sun Tzu (see note five in the introduction), Wu Ch'i said, "A battlefield is a land of standing corpses. Those who wish to live will die." He meant that if you think about self-defense, you are sure to lose because every thought of defense is one less thought of attack. This is why you must drop all thoughts of personal safety and concentrate on destroying your enemy.

As you can see, a proper kokoro is a product of many things. It requires ki, kime, and mushin in abundance. Basically, it consists of eliminating all concepts that do not have a direct and positive bearing on the task at hand. The only thing that exists in your universe is your enemy and your only goal is his destruction.

It is the primary job of the officer corps of any army to instill the proper kokoro in all of the troops. Sadly, this is rarely accomplished. The modern concept of trying to create a citizen-soldier is the greatest hindrance to the creation of this spirit. If you tell a man that he is a part of society, in time of danger he will want the protection of that society. Such is not the Way of the Warrior. It is the warrior's task to protect his society, not to be protected by it.

Combat troops should be isolated from society as much as possible. This will ensure that they live (and die) by the morality of the regiment, not that of the community. To expect a man to live by one set of rules and then die by another is both inhumane and unrealistic. The isolated regiment soon becomes permeated by the regimental philosophy. The members of the regiment are family, and the traditions of the regiment are history. The acquisition of a combat mentality under such conditions becomes almost automatic.

An individual instinctively adapts to the norm. When this norm is violence, the result is kokoro. This is frequently seen among elite military units. They are not billeted among civilians and do not fight for abstract social principles. They fight for the team and that is all they regard as important. This spirit is never seen among nine-to-five troops who, on a daily basis, have their fighting spirit diluted by public morality.

An army with kokoro thinks only about destroying the enemy. It is only when soldiers instinctively move toward the sound of guns that they become a dangerous army. The officer's job is to create this spirit, not to lead. Leadership is only required when dealing with rabble. With true professionals, the officer's task is to restrain them. He holds the troops back until the proper moment and then releases them. Their kokoro does the rest.

For the individual, kokoro is created by the dojo. This is why the dojo is both physically and spiritually isolated from the community. A school that is too open to society will be contaminated by community values. The same is true for a school that uses community habits. The proper dojo is like

Isolated from the outside world, a student strives for perfection in endless repetitions of a kata.

the isolated regiment. It is not open to the general public and it has its own set of rules and values. This is one of the reasons for the use of Japanese customs in a traditional dojo. Such actions as bowing instead of shaking hands and removing shoes upon entry further set the disciples apart.

Business, too, is a form of warfare. A businessman uses papers instead of bullets, but the principles are the same. So is the kokoro. A good businessman must always be prepared to engage in competition, with anyone and at any time. If he is ready to put his fortune on the line, winner take all, he becomes a very dangerous competitor. Few people are prepared to do this, and the presence of such a man makes his more conservative colleagues extremely nervous. The businessman, like his soldier cousin, has only one goal: winning.

A business strategist trains like the soldier in the regiment and the individual in the dojo. He buries himself in his business and makes its rules his rules—business morality becomes his morality and business values become his values. The common practice of business leaders taking an active part in the community should be avoided. Such actions can only weaken kokoro.

If you look back through history at the makers of the greatest fortunes or the generals of the greatest armies, you will find that they were *never* strategic conservatives. The great ones had but a single direction in life—they always moved forward, leaping eagerly into each new conflict. Men of a more conservative bent may have survived but they did so only by the grace of the more aggressive. In all levels of life, the sheep are only safe when the wolves are not hungry.

Kokoro does not invariably result in victory. War is largely a matter of chance. A battle is usually won by the side that makes the next-to-last mistake. All kokoro does is ensure that you waste little time on nonessentials. Because you waste no time, you will make fewer mistakes—and, it is hoped, not the last one.

However, all men die. There is nothing that can be done about this. The only thing that an individual or a nation at war can do is to resolve that, when death is inevitable, it will be both stylish and expensive. This, too, is a part of kokoro.

SHIBUMI

In the science of mathematics, there is a type of formulation that can be called rigorous. This is a formulation that is accurate and not conditional upon anything that is left undefined. Such a formulation may involve advanced and complex manipulations of equations. On the other hand, there is another type of formulation that is called elegant. An elegant formulation is both deep and simple. Probably the most widely known equation of this type is Einstein's $E = MC^2$, which describes the relationship of all the matter and energy in the universe.

In combat there is also this kind of elegance. The Japanese word for this is *shibumi*.[1] This indicates a restrained elegance and style. (A black Rolls Royce is *shibui;* a gold-plated convertible is just gaudy.)

The master strategist, imbued with kokoro, never resorts to flashy or exotic techniques. The strategy he selects will be executed with a perfection of posture and a simplicity of motion that will give it an eternal beauty. His kokoro allows him to focus on winning and to accept the possibility of losing. He does not worry about losing; he just resolves to act with style.

When attacked and forced into single combat, a junior may attempt some form of leaping kick and follow it with a complex combination. Even when he wins, there is nothing glorious about the victory. The master would never consider such a defense. He would likely use a simple sliding motion to the side, evading the attack. This would be combined with a single, accurate strike. Posture, timing, and distance would all be perfect. The embodiment of shibumi, such a man does not fight and win. He just wins.

This aspect of kokoro is reflected in the traditional dojo. Whereas a studio may feature wall-to-wall carpets, music, and a colorful decor, a dojo is quite different. In a dojo the preferred material is natural, well-polished wood, and painted surfaces are usually flat white. Decorations are frowned upon and generally limited to an interesting rock or a flower arrangement.

Shibumi is a state of mind, not an affectation. It is an important element of kokoro because it constrains physical action. Simple, natural motion is always more efficient than complex gyrations. This means a warrior should seek victory by the most direct route possible. It is only when a warrior makes his entire lifestyle shibui that this simple, direct action becomes automatic.

An interesting example of shibumi may be found in the rules of early martial arts contests.[2] In these matches, the referee's cry to denote a point scored was *"ippon!"* This meant "one point." To score an ippon you were required to launch your attack with total commitment, strike accurately, and then cleanly disengage. All of this had to be done with perfect style. All in all, it was a very shibui situation.

However, because ippon was so difficult to achieve, it was rarely seen. The sports organizations soon bowed to audience pressure and created the *wazaari,* a half point. This gave a score for a technique that was less than perfect. This was quickly followed by the quarter point.

The terrible thing about these fractional points is that, by their very existence, they destroy the spirit the martial arts are trying to teach. A competitor, knowing he can win by amassing a series of fractional points, no longer feels compelled to try for the big one. Total commitment is no longer required, so it is rarely seen. Neither do you see kokoro, the warrior spirit.

HARAGEI

One of the most mysterious and intriguing aspects of Japanese culture is the concept of *haragei.* This is one of the many Japanese words that has no exact English counterpart. *Hara* means "abdomen" or "belly"; thus a very, very rough approximation of its meaning is "abdominal art": finding a solution to a problem by an irrational (i.e., nonlogical) method. This is not quite as esoteric as it might seem at first.

In the West, the brain is seen as the source of logic, and the heart as the seat of emotion. The Japanese added the belly to this list, regarding the abdomen as the seat of the soul and the source of instinct. While this may not be true from a physiological standpoint, it has profound ramifications.

Haragei, as a function of kokoro, is an art of many facets, both spiritual and physical. To understand the spiritual meaning of haragei and the reasons for its existence, a quick look at the Japanese language is required.

Japanese is a language for poets. Although in the beginning it appears quite simple and straightforward, the more you study it, the more complex it becomes. The major source of difficulty is the almost endless list of verb conjugations—there is a separate one available for almost any possible social situation. This means that when describing a specific event you must consider both the relative and absolute social status of all parties involved in the conversation, as well as their degree of obligation to each other. Each of these factors will contribute to the choice of exactly which verb form should be used.[3]

Although this use of honorific forms is not of earthshaking importance now, in the past it was a life-and-death matter. For hundreds of years the samurai had a legal right (and a moral obligation) instantly to kill any commoner who failed to show them the proper respect. Such was the source of honorific language, as well as of the Japanese stress on polite behavior. History has momentum, and habits of such intensity and duration are not easily broken. While the choice of an improper verb conjugation no longer carries a death penalty, it will assuredly cause social ostracism.

Because of this heightened social sensitivity, a Japanese is also conditioned from birth against making definitive statements—such a statement will always offend someone, no matter what the statement is. A Japanese hates to say no for this reason. No is a definitive word and could cause offense. A rather beautiful example of this concerns table manners. If served something completely unpalatable, the well-bred Japanese guest would never be so rude as to say, "I do not like this." If pressed, he might say, "I only love this a little bit."

Another example of the same attitude, which can be maddening to Western businessmen, is seen in the Japanese corporate executive. Whereas the Westerner is accustomed to making command decisions on the spot, his Japanese counterpart will require time to gather a consensus before making a final commitment. It is not a case of fearing responsibility; he just does not want to take a chance of offending anyone.

All of this is leading into the problem of personal communication. Listening to two Japanese men talk can be an exercise in frustration for the beginning student of the language. It sometimes seems as if their entire conversation consists of little more than a series of grunts, hisses, and shrugs. The problem is that the Westerner is thinking of language as a way to transmit information. The Japanese, however, regard it more as a way gently to convey an emotion. The entire language is structured to talk about feelings, not things.

Because words create the possibility of making a social error, the Japanese try to use as few as they can. With centuries of practice, they have become very adept at two-way, nonverbal communication, especially where sensing and making allowances for each other's emotions is concerned. The method for this is a combination of sublimating the ego, calming the spirit, and maintaining mushin. Through this method a man becomes hypersensitive to the thoughts and feelings of others. This is most definitely not a form of ESP. By decreasing the background noise of his own thoughts, he increases his sensitivity to the thoughts of others. The adept is not a mind reader. It is just that he is so sensitive to vague hints of voice and attitude that it sometimes seems so.

Haragei is not a logical, or even rational, process. It is what is commonly referred to as a gut reaction.

This is not purely a Japanese phenomenon. For a perfect example of this form of haragei in action, observe a couple who have been living together for fifty years. They are so used to each other they seem almost telepathic. A glance or a shrug has more meaning to two such people than several minutes of conversation would between strangers.

For the swordsman, haragei opens limitless possibilities. First and foremost, you will become so sensitive to the people around you that you will sense danger before an overt move has been made. This, in turn, allows you to start your counter before your opponent begins his attack. At the other end of the spectrum, when attacking as part of a team you can instinctively react with your teammates.

Developing haragei is mostly a matter of slightly modifying your standard training exercises. In the dojo you will normally practice a technique from a specific fighting stance. To develop haragei, take these same techniques and practice them from a natural stance. Just stand naturally and allow your training partner to attack. Try to start your counter at the same time that your partner attacks.

When you can do this, start from a position facing slightly away from your partner. As your ability increases, gradually increase this angle until you are facing away from him. When you move instinctively to counter an attack before it starts and even when you cannot see the attacker, then you are using haragei. This is not nearly as difficult as it sounds. Even a beginner, if he can maintain mushin, can do it.

A final note on this aspect of haragei concerns the often heard, and even more often misquoted, statement of Funakoshi Gichen. He said, "There is no first attack in karate." Many Western students misconstrue this to mean they should let their enemy throw the first punch. This is not what Funakoshi meant at all. Even a cursory examination of the Japanese language would reveal the fallacy in this. Both traditionally and linguistically, the Japanese have always considered an attack to start the instant you think about it.[4]

Funakoshi never meant you should allow an enemy to hit first; he was merely saying you should never hit anyone who has no aggressive intentions.

In addition to the psychological aspects of haragei, there is a physical side which is of equal importance. When you practice haragei, all of your concentration is centered in your lower abdomen. Specifically, the exact point is known as the *itten,* the "one point."[5] This point is about three inches below the navel and corresponds to the center of gravity of the human body. By concentrating on this point, you modify not only the way you think but also the way you stand and move. The process is commonly referred to as centering.

All combat postures are built around an awareness of the itten. Start by pulling your shoulders back and downward. Then slightly tense your abdomen, lower your hips a bit, and empty your mind. Close your armpits—pretend you are holding a marble in each of them—and try to point your navel downward. The total posture should be relaxed but firm. This attitude is often called *fudōtai,* the "immovable body." The corresponding mental attitude is *fudōshin,* the "immovable mind."

This posture must be practiced relentlessly. After decades of standing incorrectly, it will take some time for this new position to become automatic. One standard method for maintaining awareness of it is to tie your belt a bit lower on the hips and a little tighter than is normal. This will help keep at least part of your mind in the correct area at all times.

The initial physical advantages of this position are immediately apparent. Because your concentration is on your center, your motion will become much more fluid and balanced. Instead of moving your body with your feet you will now be moving your feet with your body. There is a classical demonstration of this which most people find very enlightening.

Position your training partner several yards to your front. Have him hold out one arm at chest height across your line of advance and brace himself firmly. Now walk forward as you normally would. As soon as your chest strikes his arm, you will be stopped in your tracks. Even if you approach him with a feeling of pushing hard, it will be very difficult for you to advance through the barrier of his arm.

Now back off and try again. This time adjust your mind and body as previously described for haragei. (It will help in the beginning if you press the palm of your hand against your lower abdomen, momentarily, to increase concentration on that spot.) Walk slowly forward and do not even look at your partner. Relax, breathe softly, and advance your center. If you do this properly, when you meet his arm you will not even be slowed down by his resistance. Comfortably erect, you will push him across the room. This is just as much a mental process as it is a physical one—if you allow your mind to shift from your center to his arm, even for an instant, you will be stopped.

There are many such exercises and demonstrations that you can discover or create with little effort. If you know a kata from the art of karate, you can use that for an interesting personal discovery. Go through it once as you normally do, concentrating on the techniques. Now do it again. The second time through, however, think only about your center. For the average student, this makes a radical difference in both the feel and appearance of the kata. You may suddenly realize why seniors doing kata look so much different from juniors.

Physical power and stability are only by-products of hara-gei; they are not its essence. The ultimate goal is development of a mental power and stability that will allow you to function in combat. This means you must be able instantly to detect the intentions of your enemy and react to them with whatever action the situation merits. The key word here is *instantly*. If your counterattack is based on logical thought, there will always be a slight delay between stimulus and response. The mental strength through which you react instantly is fudoshin, which forms the bedrock of kokoro.

There is an old dojo story about Miyamoto Musashi that is often used to illustrate the nature of fudoshin. It seems that one day Musashi had a visitor to his school. As they were having tea the visitor asked, "Sensei, what is this secret technique of 'a mind like a stone' that I have heard you are teaching in your school?" Musashi replied by calling in one of his students and commanding him to disembowel himself. Without blinking an eye the student drew his knife, bared his abdomen, and prepared to carry out the task. At the last possible instant, Musashi seized his arm and countermanded the order. Again without blinking an eye, the student straightened his clothes and calmly returned to the dojo to continue his practice. Turning to his guest, Musashi said, "That is the spirit of a stone."

This is the hardness of spirit that is required by the warrior. In a long and painful process of spiritual forging, the mind of a man is worked like a sword. It becomes straight, hard, cold, sharp, and well polished.

It may sound as if the ideal fighting man is an unthinking, unfeeling, killing machine. He is. What makes him so special is that he has done this voluntarily. By a deliberate act of will, he turns off the centers of thought and feeling that the common man considers so important. He freely surrenders the values that the civilian holds so dear. By doing this he loses much, but he also gains much. He knows great power and lives with an intensity undreamed of by his sheltered cousins. Living on the ragged edge of life and death, the man with kokoro becomes the stuff of which legends are made.

NOTES

1. *Shibumi* is a noun. The adjective form is *shibui.*

2. The concept of bujutsu as a sport is very modern. The karate contest, so common today, is less than fifty years old.

3. The same is true, to a lesser extent, for the selection of nouns and other parts of speech.

4. In Japanese you cannot say, or think, "I will hit." There is no definite future tense; the present tense of a verb contains elements of the future.

5. Some schools refer to this point as the *tanden, seika tanden,* or simply the *hara.*

Book II
The Power

Chapter Eight
Maai: Distancing

The greatest difference between a junior and a senior strategist is that the senior has mastered the art of using *maai,* the "combative engagement distance," to his advantage. A beginner regards the distance between his opponent and himself as merely something that exists. However, the senior sees this distance as a tool, perhaps the most valuable tool in his arsenal of weapons, and he constantly manipulates it.

The proper use of maai is graphically illustrated when you watch a junior and a senior practicing together. When the senior attacks, the junior will leap out of the way, avoiding the strike by a foot or more. On the other hand, when the junior attacks, the senior will gently sway his body aside, avoiding the attack by only a fraction of an inch. This leaves him in a perfect position for a rapid counter, which, in turn, forces the junior to leap about even more feverishly. The end result is that the senior may appear to be napping while the junior seems to be almost working himself to death without really accomplishing much.

You are not born with a knowledge of distance; it is learned by trial and error. During infancy you learn how long your arms are by experimentation and, by adulthood, you can tell at a glance if an object is within reach. For most people this is sufficient.

However, the Way of Strategy is concerned with weapons other than just the hands. A prime example is the kicking techniques of a karate student. During his initial training he will frequently attack with kicks that fall a foot or more short of the target, because he does not know how long his legs are. Like the average person, he merely knows that his legs reach from his body to the ground—he did not need a more accurate measurement because walking was all he ever used his legs for. But for a student of karate, this must change. He must now learn to use his feet with the same precision and dexterity as the average person uses his hands. He must know exactly how far his legs will reach in any direction. A common exercise used to develop this ability is for the student to use his toes to operate the light switches around his home. This exercise builds strength, flexibility, and accuracy. The student does not kick the switches; he slowly raises his foot, flips the switch with his toe, and then slowly lowers the foot. After a few months of doing this, a student will develop a precise feel for the maai of kicking. A sword student follows a similar regimen by constantly carrying a weapon and using it as an extension of his arm for various tasks.

It is the same for all other martial arts. The practitioner must, by long and arduous training, develop an instinctive awareness of the range of all his weapons. He must also do this for all the weapons he is likely to face.

As you develop your awareness of maai, you learn to judge distance within a fraction of an inch. The degree of precision required is clearly illustrated by a rather nerve-wracking sword exercise known as *dōgiri no kumitachi.*[1]

In this exercise, *shitachi,* the "responding sword," as one of the partners is called, will blouse the front of his jacket and assume a middle position. *Uchitachi,* the "attacking sword," will attack strongly with a horizontal slash at waist level. In response to this, shitachi raises his sword and leans slightly to the rear. He evades the attack by just enough to allow his partner's sword to graze the loose front of his jacket. Then he immediately leans back in with a counter-cut. If properly executed, his counter should land before the attacker's sword stops moving.

At first the attacks are always the same. As training progresses, however, both the distance and speed of the attacks are varied. Heavy wooden swords are used for this, and a miscalculation can cost you some fractured ribs. Although you may occasionally see some seniors using shinken, "real swords," this is a bit too dangerous for most people. Let alone the fact that a slight error will result in disembowelment, even a correct exercise results in a ruined training uniform. Using either a bokken, "wooden sword," or a shinken, this is a superb exercise. There is nothing like being a fraction of an inch from death or severe injury to sharpen your concentration. There are numerous exercises based on the philosophy of dogiri no kumitachi—if you do not have exercises similar in your school, it is easy enough to create some.

In addition to learning the basic close-miss distance of any weapon, you must learn the standard three maai of combat.

The proper striking distance for any technique is known as *uchima,* "striking distance." This is the distance at which you normally fight. This space requires that you take one step to deliver the technique. The step allows you to drive in with maximum power and have your body weight behind the strike. The action of closing the gap is called *uchikomi,* the "striking step." Being too far away to attack with a single step is *tōma,* "far interval." Being close enough to strike without taking a step is *chikama,* "close interval." Fighting at chikama is faster than at uchima; but, because you cannot get your weight behind the strike, it is weaker.

In warfare, all weapons have their maximum range. While the maximum range of a sword, a gun, or a missile can be easily determined, the range of an army or an idea requires much deeper study. No matter what weapon you are using, or what weapon is being used against you, you must study it carefully and understand its exact maximum effective range.

A point often overlooked is the fact that, in addition to a maximum range, many weapons have a minimum range. If this is the case, you can be just as safe (and much more

effective) operating inside the minimum range as you would
be outside the maximum range. An excellent example of this
in modern warfare is the anti-aircraft missile. Planes frequently attack at treetop height to avoid these. At such a
short range the missiles have neither time to launch nor room
to maneuver before the attacking jets are there and gone.

NOBASHI NO HEIHO

Nobashi is the strategy of stretching out your enemy. This
is done by forcing him to attack from a distance slightly
beyond uchima.

This is a fairly easy strategy to implement because it is
natural to move away from danger. A beginner will commonly assume a position well beyond uchima due to his fear
of being hit. Even a senior may use an open interval when
he wishes to take a break from combat. They both feel safe
because it is very easy to counter any attack delivered across
such a gap—the attacker must take a small step to get to
uchima and this gives the defender plenty of warning.

Nobashi uses this natural tendency to fight at a distance
to stretch out your opponent's attack. You carefully maneuver to place your enemy slightly beyond his uchima. Because
he is only an inch or two beyond what he considers a perfect
distance, he may be lured into attacking without taking an
extra step to close the gap. Consequently, his technique will
be slightly overextended. The technique will then be both
weaker and slower, making your counter much easier.

There are many ways to push your opponent back. The
simplest method is to adopt a *zenkutsu,* "forward leaning,"
posture. This will make you seem a bit closer than you actually are. Another way would be to adopt a very aggressive
attitude. This spiritual intensity will make you seem physically closer. Against a beginner, you might try drawing his
attention to your sword or hands. If he can be tricked into
setting his maai from these, he can be positioned wherever
you want him.

Whatever method you use—you may have to use a combination of tricks—you do not wish to push your opponent

back too far. Just an inch is enough. If he sees that he is obviously well beyond the proper striking distance he cannot be lured into an attack.

In a throwing type of art, such as judo or aikido, you can apply the nobashi strategy by approaching your opponent with your weight well forward. Then, as he reaches out to grab you, settle into a balanced stance. The shift in your balance should be very small, about one-half inch is enough. This small shift will force him to lean slightly forward to grab you. If your shift is too large he will take a small step to regain his balance. However, if your move was just right, he will be so slightly off balance that he will not even notice it. Now that he is stretched out a little, it is very easy to throw him.

To practice this variation of nobashi, have your training partner repeatedly seize the lapels of your training jacket. After he has firmly planted himself, try to move about. If you have executed the strategy properly you will find this very easy. He may think he is holding you firmly, but, because he is fractionally off balance, you can walk about at will, dragging him along with you. After you have mastered this with a basic lapel grab, *katadori,* you can proceed to more varied attacks.

For a striking art, such as karate or boxing, the training is similar. Now, however, instead of trying to move while being held, you will block a strike. Try to make the power of your block as consistent as possible as your partner repeatedly attacks with the same technique. Your strategy is to move about slightly in an effort to force him to overextend his attack by about one inch. If you are too far away, he will not strike until he adjusts the maai. However, if you are at a more or less proper distance, he will stretch his attack a little. When he does this, you will see the result in the effect of your block. Normally it would only deflect his arm; but if his punch is extended, the force of your block will affect his posture. Watch the line of your partner's shoulders very closely as you practice. When the impact of your block changes this line, you have executed nobashi properly.

In warfare between armies, the proper maai is determined

by many factors. Primary among these are the ready reserves of fuel and ammunition. Although a slow, steady thrust can be sustained by standard supply lines, a quick surge is another matter. If intelligence is of such quality as to allow knowledge of your enemy's supply capabilities, this can offer an excellent opportunity for a successful counterattack. By timing your counter to the point at which the enemy's advance has been stretched to its maximum limit but its supply corps has not yet been able to adapt to the new front, nobashi no heiho can be applied with devastating results.

Business use of nobashi is slightly more complex. If you think of your competitor's advertising as a weapon, then its range is determined by his advertising budget. To stretch him out would mean you force him to go over his budget on a certain campaign. If you time your counter properly, he will not have enough funds to oppose it.

On a smaller scale, you can use this strategy in a debate.

If you leap in with a counterproposal each time your opponent presents his viewpoint, he will remain strongly antagonistic. To use nobashi in this situation, just relax and listen. Sooner or later he will say everything he can in support of his argument and grow tired of the sound of his own voice. Then you immediately step in with a single, well-thought-out statement. Such a statement will have a much greater effect than if it had been delivered during a pause in your opponent's argument.

In all applications of nobashi, it is best not to get greedy—do not try to stretch your opponent out too much. You must use this heiho with a delicate touch in order to keep it from becoming too obvious.

TOKOSHI NO HEIHO

Tōkoshi means "to cross a great distance." This strategy may be used to good effect when you are fighting at an open interval, *toma,* and are forced to take several steps in order to close to a proper attacking range.

When you are fencing at an interval which requires two steps to close with an enemy, you will normally take a small step and then a large one. By closing the gap in this manner and throwing yourself into the second step, you can generate maximum power in your cut. If you reverse the process and take the large step first or make both steps equal in length, the power of the stroke will be reduced. Taking the small step first gives you a physical advantage. However, there are times when this physical advantage is outweighed by the psychological advantage of tokoshi.

Tokoshi no heiho states that when you are faced with a large distance, you cross it immediately. To be the first to close the maai places you in a positive attitude; to hold back creates a negative, defensive spirit.

There are times when the movements of a battle may carry you away from your opponent. This space allows you time to rest and regroup your forces; and no matter how fast your enemy attacks, you will have ample time to mount a solid defense. This is a very common attitude. It is also a very negative way of thinking and should be avoided. It is better to be the first to close the gap, thereby forcing your enemy onto the defensive.

Beginners find tokoshi no heiho very difficult. The source of their problem is that they forget a fundamental truth: there is no safety in war. Even in the rear lines you may be injured by an enemy raid. The only true safety in a time of strife is after you completely destroy your opponent, crushing him so thoroughly that he no longer has the capability of hurting you. To do this you must be prepared to go in harm's way.

If you flee from an enemy you may be struck from behind because you are unable to block an attack from that direction. If you wait, you allow your enemy to attack at his own pace. If you advance you may also be hit, but at least you will have some control of the timing and direction of the attack.

Among swordsmen there is the maxim: "When afraid, clench your belly and step forward!" Although most students have heard this, few bother to give it much thought. Even fewer try it. That is unfortunate, because it does work quite well. There is something about tightening the abdominal muscles that controls fear. When this is combined with deep abdominal breathing, as is used for kokyu chikara, it has excellent results.

It is very important to use tokoshi when you are faced with a large opponent, someone you have little chance of defeating. If at the first sign of danger you always step forward, you will often find that this action alone is enough to stop a fight before it starts. By not holding back you generate a very positive image, both in the eyes of your enemy and in your view of yourself. This will weaken your opponent's spirit and strengthen yours. His initial reaction will probably be to take a small step back to readjust the maai. You should be ready to take immediate advantage of this.

In a contest it is normal to take a few seconds to feel your opponent out before launching your first attack. After the command to start the round, you move around to see how he reacts to various feints. To use tokoshi in a contest, you should take one large step forward as soon as the round begins. Do this instantly, without even a second of delay. Your opponent, who was thinking about you, will now start to think about the maai. Keep the pressure on and you can easily control him.

Most governments do not understand that strategy between nations is the same as strategy between individuals. The result is that many wars are started, not because one nation was too aggressive but because another country was not aggressive enough. (One wonders how long the war would have lasted and how many lives would have been saved if the United States had entered World War II in 1939 instead of two years later.) A country should learn to use maai with the same skill as the individual swordsman. By suddenly taking a large step toward an enemy, a nation can forestall an attack. This step does not have to be a military one. There is also maai in politics and economics.

Tokoshi no heiho requires no special skills other than bravery, so there is little you can practice to make it better. This is one of the few strategies that a beginner can do just as well as a master. The only difficult part is remembering to use it in time of need. To practice for this, always be alert for possible applications, constantly look for tasks in which you can do the hard part first. If you do this often enough to make it automatic, then you will instinctively do the same thing in a time of danger.

SHIKKOTAI NO HEIHO

This was a favorite technique of Miyamoto Musashi and his Nitenichi-ryu. To use *shikkotai* means that you stick as close to your opponent as a coat of lacquer. Because most techniques have a minimum effective range, by sticking close to your enemy you deny him room to operate.

This strategy is often seen in an engagement where the effective lengths of the weapons are dissimilar, such as a spear against a sword. If you fear the range of the spear and opt to fight from an open distance you are actually enhancing your opponent's position. However, by moving in very close you deny him the advantage of his longer weapon.

Even when you think you are operating at a close interval, such may not be the case. There is a strong tendency among juniors to crowd in only with their hands and feet. The timid will hold their bodies back slightly, at a seemingly safer distance. Guard against this. Always crowd in first with your body and then with your hands and feet.

Once you have closed with your enemy, concentrate on cutting him. This must be all that you think about. He will probably flinch from the body contact and try to step away. If you are ready you can cut him instantly. He will be thinking, "Withdraw and cut," while you are thinking only, "CUT!" This gives you a great tactical advantage.

To practice shikkotai, a set of kendo armor[2] may be used to great advantage. This allows you actually to hit without injuring your training partner. Constantly strive to get in as close as you can while keeping your sword ready. Then, as your partner steps away, strike firmly. You may do the same thing in a karate match. The key to making this strategy work is your posture. If you are not perfectly balanced you will be unable to take advantage of your opponent's opening motion.

In a battle, when faced by an enemy having both infantry and artillery, closely engage their infantry. When you do this they are unable to use their artillery without hitting their own men—you have negated part of their army without having to engage it.

As a businessman, open a store next door to your largest competitor. Then anything he does to increase his business will also help you—his advertisements become your advertisements. If you were on the other side of town, he might regard you as merely friendly competition. But now you are right next door and he will get very nervous. This may cause such a state of tension in his staff that he loses the ability to compete. Worrying more about you than his own company, he becomes easy to manipulate.

In a karate or boxing match, evade your opponent's attack and slide in close. As you do this, hold one fist ready. As he steps away, hit him in mid-stride. He may have been able to block your punches when operating from a stable stance but he will find it very hard to do this while backing up.

There are obvious times when you will not want to use shikkotai. One such occasion would be when your opponent is using a short sword and you have a long one. In this case you will constantly have to guard against him closing in on you. This means you must learn to use a long weapon at short range. There are many ways to do this. Although these are giho, not heiho, and thus are not the proper subject of this book, they are so rarely taught that a few are included to give you an idea of how to get started.

With a sword, step away with your right foot and cross your wrists. Do the same with a spear or staff. With a pistol, clamp your wrist firmly against your hip and turn your palm slightly upward. To shorten the range of a kick, bring your kicking foot to your buttock instead of to the knee of your supporting leg. To punch at short range, rotate your fist to the outside instead of inward. To turn in a crowd, use the footwork of the karate *tekki* kata. There are hundreds of other possibilities. With the above indications as a guide, you should be able to figure out most of them yourself.

The enemy is not necessarily a physical thing. It can be

a philosophy, an industry, or a market. Whatever its nature, the strategy of shikkotai requires you to get in as close as possible.

NEBARI NO HEIHO

Nebari means that when your opponent sweeps your sword aside, you stick your blades together as if they were glued. This strategy may have a Chinese source, for it has a close philosophical resemblance to strategies in the art of t'ai chi ch'uan. It is also used extensively in the *aikijujutsu* of the Yamate-ryu.

When your opponent sweeps your sword aside to clear the centerline and cut you, lightly hold your blade to his and refuse to disengage. This will place him on the defensive—instead of thinking about cutting you he will be thinking about freeing his sword in order to cut. As he attempts to disengage, you can cut him easily.

This strategy is frequently confused with shikkotai no heiho. The difference is that in shikkotai you are sticking your body to your opponent's body. Here the focus is on the weapons.

The best exercise for practicing this strategy is *nagashi undō.*[3] By devoting some time to this, you will rapidly learn to stick your sword to your opponent's blade through all manner of maneuvers. You should augment this with some blindfolded practice. This will teach you to feel through your blade and not have to look to see where your opponent's sword is.

Because a stroke from nebari is frequently launched from an awkward position, it will usually be weak. You should develop the habit of always following it with a second, stronger cut. As your opponent attempts to disengage, you cut and cut again, with a rhythm of "one-TWO!"

Another application of nebari is seen in the *tachi no kata, mawashi.* In this classical exercise, when your opponent attempts to circle his sword under yours, you follow it around. Then, with a flick of your wrists, throw his blade off center and cut. (If you are very strong you can flip your opponent's sword from his grasp with this technique.)

A boxer or a karateka uses nebari by sticking to his opponent's punching arm. Instead of blocking a punch and then crisply returning to your original position, as you normally would, soften your arm at contact. As your opponent withdraws his fist, follow it while maintaining light contact. This will shift his attention to his arm, and when he makes an attempt to break away, you can hit him.

On a battlefield the principle is the same. When the opposing army sends out a raiding party, do not clash with it and then disengage. If you do, it will be free to move about and can cause considerable damage. By maintaining contact, however, you can control its movement. Then, when the army makes a tactical mistake, attack with force.

Like most strategies, nebari no heiho operates on two levels: the mental and the physical. Physically, this strategy ties up your attacker and restricts his motion. Mentally, it is even more powerful. By drawing his attention away from your body and to his weapon, you can attack him with little opposition.

Sometimes an enemy may even place himself in nebari. An example of this would be when your opponent seizes your sword arm to stop you from cutting. This is a very stupid and dangerous act, for you can then use the rest of your body to destroy him. (When trying to immobilize an opponent, you never use the grip of your hands. You should use an open hand and bent wrist to hook his arm—this is called *tensho*. As you do this, you keep your attention focused on his body and do not think about the arm you are trying to control.)

The counter for nebari is *hanashi no heihō*, "letting go."[4] If your weapon or technique is immobilized, then you give up, let go, and try something else. This is often forgotten in the heat of combat—there is a dangerous tendency to try to force a technique through to completion. The secret is to never allow your attention to waver from your true objective: the destruction of your enemy. If you are always striving toward this goal, you will not even notice letting go. Also, you will be able to do this instantly. In combat, where even the blink of an eye can be fatal, this speed may be the difference between victory and defeat.

FUKURAMI NO HEIHO

Fukurami means to expand your enemy. This strategy is based on the fact that normal power, tai chikara, is delivered with a compression of the body. This heiho should not be used against a master of kokyu chikara.

Open by luring your opponent into close range. If you wish to be more aggressive you can move in on him. His reaction will be to crouch slightly—this is an instinctive act when close to danger. You accentuate this action by attacking strongly at an upper level. Chase him around, always attacking high, until his posture is obviously compressed. Then, when he attempts to disengage and open the maai, allow him to do so easily.

As he steps away he will automatically start to correct his posture. And, as he straightens and expands his body, he will inhale. This is what you are waiting for. As he breathes in and straightens, attack strongly at a low level. Because he can only cut strongly while exhaling, you have little to fear. Also, most people relax their abdominal muscles when they inhale. This means a low strike to the body will be devastating.

You can practice this strategy as you did shikkotai, with kendo armor. It will help if you have your partner tense his lips so that you can hear his breathing. You should practice until you can force him to inhale deeply at the time of your choice. You will also have to devote considerable time to the study of combination attacks—the transition from upper to lower level cuts is not easy.

In a judo match, when your opponent has attempted an unsuccessful throw, there may be a moment of stillness. He is straining to force the throw through to completion, but you have braced against it, so all motion stops for a second. When this happens, place your hands against his body and attune yourself to his breathing. As he strains to throw you his body will compress and he will exhale. When he gives up on this technique and shifts position to try something new, he will straighten and inhale. If you are prepared for this, you will find him very easy to throw.

In a karate match, things will happen quite a bit faster. You should watch the line of your opponent's back and shoulders. If you see his back is bent or his shoulders are not level, it means that his body is compressed. Realignment of either back or shoulders will normally be accompanied by an inhalation. This is the moment when you should attack. Because of the speed of a karate match, you may find this very difficult. You should maintain mushin and not allow yourself to think about his breathing. If you allow your mind to become involved, you will never be fast enough to strike him while he is inhaling.

On a battlefield, when an attacking force is pinned down by heavy fire, the soldiers will automatically seek cover. In such a situation, increasing your fire will have little effect. However, if you slacken your fire, the enemy troops who were pinned down in a bad area will seek better cover. Then, as they move, you can increase your fire with devastating effect. This alternation between heavy and light fire will be much more deadly than a sustained barrage.

To counter fukurami, use kokyu chikara. This allows you to strike firmly while inhaling, expanding your body as much as possible for maximum strength, and retreating.

This action may be augmented by the use of *sanchin*. Sanchin is a breathing method taught in some traditional schools. This method lets you keep your abdomen hard even while inhaling.

To practice sanchin, press the fingers of both hands firmly into your abdomen and tense your abdominal muscles to resist this pressure. Inhale by pushing your abdominal muscles forward against the pressure of your stiffened fingers; exhale by compressing your abdomen. Take care that you do not relax your muscles for even an instant during this process. Once you have succeeded in this, have your training partner rain a steady series of blows on your abdomen as you breathe. With a little practice you should be able to endure his maximum effort while maintaining a steady breath cycle. Sanchin is actually a process for strengthening the entire body, not just the abdomen. An adept can even survive a full-power strike to the throat without injury.

A combination of kokyu chikara and sanchin will not allow you to escape an attack delivered with fukurami no heiho. Even though you cut while moving away, you will normally still receive your opponent's strike. However, sanchin gives you a better chance of coming away from an exchange of blows as the winner.

There is an old saying in bujutsu that states: "When a void is found, a technique will fill it." Fukurami is but one application of this dictum. When you use this strategy you should imagine that your enemy's inhalation is creating a vacuum and that this vacuum is pulling your technique forward. Do not think of forcing yourself forward to attack; pretend that your opponent is pulling you forward by creating a vacuum.

SHUKOTAI NO HEIHO

The strategy of *shukotai* teaches that you should fight with shortened arms, holding your weapon a bit closer to your body than normal.

When fencing you should guard against extending your arms too much. This is a common mistake among beginners. Because they are a little timid, they overextend their arms in an effort to keep their opponents as far away as possible.

By keeping your arms bent a little more than normal, you close the maai slightly. Then, if your opponent wastes a count by stepping back to adjust the distance, you can cut him instantly. All you are doing is closing the gap by an inch or two in order to reduce your reaction time by a fraction of a second. A fraction of a second is not a very large advantage, but in combat you take everything you can get.

The application of shukotai does not have to be continuous. For example, when fencing, a momentary application of the strategy can be used to disrupt your opponent's timing. When you sense your enemy is ready to attack, bend your arms and lean forward sharply—your sword stays where it is and your body moves forward toward it. When you do this you shorten the maai, forcing your opponent to modify his attack. As he pauses, you stretch out and hit him quickly. This idea may be used for a wide variety of combat arts.

Yoko gamae is the posture used frequently with shukotai.

In army tactics, it is a common practice to place the point troops at a considerable distance ahead of the main body. This gives the bulk of the army an additional moment of warning, greatly increasing their reaction time. Among well-trained troops, the distance to the point men should be reduced. Because they do not require time to get ready for combat, this shortened distance will allow the main body of troops to get into action much faster.

The training for such an army should be identical to that for an individual. They must be drilled on exactly what to do at the moment of contact with an enemy force. Each member of the unit must know where to go and what his field of fire should be in any situation. Then, when contact is made, the entire force will leap into action and deliver a decisive blow before the enemy is prepared.

In a karate match, you fight with shortened arms by stopping all your techniques about 10 percent below full extension. Fight for a while without letting your kicks or punches extend to their maximum range. Your opponent will gradually start to adjust his maai to this range. Then, once you have lured him in, allow your techniques to go to full extension. Suddenly, all those punches and kicks he had been successfully dodging will start hitting him. (If your opponent was an accomplished one, he probably was not even blocking your shortened attacks; he was only swaying his body back to avoid them by an inch.)

Reaction time depends on two factors: distance and speed. As you experiment with this heiho, keep this in mind. If you fight for a while with slow reactions and then suddenly go to full speed, it is the same as being physically closer. This requires extraordinary self-control but it works magnificently.

An army takes advantage of this time element by converting a standard infantry unit to air-mobile or mechanized infantry. A unit could even be trained to march further and faster than normal. By whatever method, the unit becomes capable of closing with an enemy force in less time than is expected.

A business firm does the same thing by setting up an emergency resupply method for its branch stores. Then, when there is an unusually heavy demand for a certain item, they can restock the branches very fast. This allows the company to gain a step on its competition.

Shukotai no heiho can even be used to good effect in something as simple as a debate. As your opponent espouses his viewpoint, try to determine where his argument is leading and prepare your rebuttal in advance. At the instant he stops talking, leap in with your own argument—do not delay for even a fraction of a second. What you wish to do is catch him before he has had a chance to mentally shift gears from attack to defense.

It is normal for your opponent to expect a certain measurable time between his stimulus and your response. Shukotai is merely a method to make this time a little shorter than he expects. Frequently, this will be all that is necessary to ensure your victory.

NOTES

1. A *kumitachi* is an informal kata. The moves are pre-arranged as in a formal kata, but there is less stress on form.

2. Kendo armor is used in the sport of kendo. It consists of a face mask, chest protector, hip pads, and padded gloves. The sword, called a *shinai,* is made of split bamboo. This combination allows full-power strikes.

3. Nagashi undo is described in Chapter Eleven.

4. Hanashi no heiho is explained in Chapter Fourteen.

Chapter Nine

Hyoshi: Timing

There is a rhythm to the universe. There is a rhythm to life and a rhythm to death. Each living thing beats to its own rhythm. If you understand this you can always achieve victory.

Rhythm is determined by many things. A large man will fight to a slower beat than a small man. The same is true for a larger weapon or a larger army. Strength and physical condition are also important factors. An individual who has trained hard can operate at a faster count than someone who has not trained so rigorously. Rhythm is also determined by spirit. This last point merits careful study, for a senior opponent may try to conceal his true spirit.

In any type of engagement you strive to learn the natural rhythm of your enemy. Then you use *hyōshi,* "timing," to turn this against him.

Strategies involving timing are often used by .guerrilla forces. Their small units are ideally suited to operate at a very fast beat. Relying on high mobility, they use a series of fast attacks and withdrawals. When a large army, slowed by heavy infantry and artillery, tries to fight such a commando unit, it is hopelessly outclassed. The guerrillas never remain in one place long enough for the large army to bring its heavy firepower to bear.

There are only two options in such a case. If it is not required to control a large area, the army can opt for maximum defense. It can set up defensively and wait for the commando to come to it. This only works if the valuable real estate is not spread out. The second option is for the army to discard its heavy equipment and break into small units. Then it can fight the commando unit with guerrilla tactics. Because the large army has a solid support force, even if this is not carried into the field, the army should be able to operate at a faster pace than the enemy commando unit and keep this up for a longer time.

In any case, the battle between the army and the commando unit is only a matter of rhythm. The large army must either speed up the battle or slow it down if it hopes to win. When opposing forces have different structures, the attacker must never be allowed to operate at his preferred speed. This last statement is possibly the most important single sentence in this book! Study it deeply.

Businesses also have rhythms. The corporate board that trains itself to make fast and accurate decisions is much more dangerous than one that takes its time and only makes a final decision when forced to. Armies, during a time of peace, play war games to keep their command structure in fighting trim. Companies should follow their example. If a team of executives does not have a problem to solve, it should create one just to keep in practice.

The executive structure of a company heavily weighted down with departments and divisions of authority will operate more slowly than that of a company composed of only the absolute essentials. This also applies to an army or an individual. When you study the history of war, it becomes evident that battles are won through speed and mobility. Victory is achieved by the first army to bring its forces together at one point. Perhaps the greatest example of this was the Golden Horde of Genghis Khan. In this army, everybody rode and everybody fought.

Careful consideration is necessary here. Although the large sword cuts deeply, the short sword cuts fast. This is true for warships, armies, and companies. You must always study the arena and select the weapon that is most appropriate. The samurai wore two swords. The long sword, *katana,* was the primary battlefield weapon. The short sword, *wakizashi,* was used for close combat in restricted areas. This was a good system and you should copy it.

A navy fleet of heavy ships is accompanied by a group of fast destroyers. An army does the same thing by having a force of light-infantry raiders available. As an individual, you should be sure that your knowledge of large, powerful techniques is balanced by an ability to use small, fast ones. This combination of speed and power is necessary if you are to master timing, for you must be able to fight at any speed, not just your favorite one.

The study of hyoshi is one of the most advanced and fascinating areas of strategy and it is a never-ending process. You must develop a great deal of empathy for your opponent. Forgetting yourself, try to get inside your enemy, to sense his very heartbeat. And, as you do this, never forget that in order to defeat your opponent's rhythm, you must first match it.

HAN'ON NO HEIHO

A *han'on* is a half-step. To use this strategy you discern the rhythm of your enemy and then hit him on the half-count. Because he is fully engaged in transforming the end of his last attack into the beginning of his next one, you will win easily.

To practice this heiho, a long training hall is very beneficial. Start at one end and have your partner attack with a continuous series of cuts. As you retreat, count his cuts: "one ... two ... three." When you have established his rhythm, counter-cut with a rhythm of "one ... two-THREE!" At first you should actually count aloud. The sudden sound of your own voice shouting "THREE!" will trigger your body into action. If you do this perfectly, it will seem as if you are almost casual as you step in and cut—you will feel absolutely no need to hurry. Conversely, your partner will feel totally helpless. He will not be able to coun-

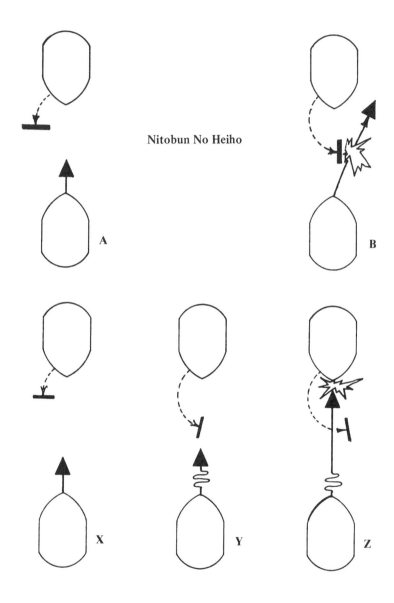

Nitobun No Heiho

The attack (A) is initiated and your opponent immediately starts his block which (B) deflects your attack. You initiate an attack (X) and your opponent starts to block. After he is committed (Y) you pause for a fraction of a second and then continue your attack (Z), passing behind his block.

ter your cut no matter how fast he moves.

This training method can be used in a variety of arts. No matter what the attack, just synchronize with the series, count the beats, and then speed up your count. A beginner will require some time to match the tempo—he has to count several attacks in order to catch the beat. However, the number of strokes required is reduced with practice. A perfect master of this strategy will know the rhythm of an attack before his opponent moves.[1]

Rhythm is subject to entropy. This means that a fast, highly organized attack cannot be maintained forever. Be alert for this. If you observe the rhythm of your enemy changing, you can hit him on the half-count. However, in this instance you are adhering to the old tempo and he is the one whose changing rhythm creates the opening. This is very useful against an opponent who attacks with a very fast combination of techniques. Because of his speed you have little hope of matching the rhythm and no hope at all of exceeding it. So, watch and wait. As soon as his initial barrage falters, step in and strike.

Han'on may be used against any attack where your enemy's power is pulsating. (You cannot hit on the half-count unless there is a count to start with.) For example, assume someone grabs you by the arm and starts dragging you across the room. He is walking normally: left-right-left-right. Because you are off balance you cannot resist him. To use han'on, skip a step. Move your feet: left-right-left/left-right. As soon as you do this you will find that instead of being led, you are now the leader.

The obvious counter for han'on is not to fight with a fixed rhythm. However, because your body has a fixed mass, it is natural to tend to move at a fixed speed. You must constantly guard against this habit.

KATSURI NO HEIHO

Katsuri means that you win by changing speed. You force your enemy to fight at a rhythm that is unnatural for him. If you can do this, victory is assured.

Because there is a rhythm to everything—a rhythm to an attack and a rhythm to a defense—it is very easy to become trapped by a certain tempo of fighting. Watch for this and, when you sense your opponent is getting comfortable at a certain speed, suddenly change it. Han'on no heiho is one form of this.

In many cases, suddenly slowing down will work just as well as speeding up. If you attack with a series of fast strikes, your opponent will react accordingly. Then, when you suddenly decelerate, he may overreact and not be able to slow down enough to counter your attack.

A particular series of sword forms from the Yamate-ryu is a beautiful example of the change-of-speed strategy. In each of these kata, the attacker closes in with a series of four steps. Each of these steps is exactly twice as long and twice as fast as the preceding one—the first step is very slow and small; by the fourth one, the attacker is throwing himself forward. This constant acceleration is much harder to deal with than an advance at steady speed.

A similar strategy is seen in the *kōryū no ken* of the Tenshin-ryu. In this sword kata, the attack is delivered with a rhythm of one . . . one . . . one, two . . . one, two, three!" Advancing with a broken rhythm like this is very disorienting for an enemy.

In the business world you apply this strategy by constantly varying the pressure you put on your competition. With a constant pressure, no matter how great it is, a competitor may learn to live with it. In fact, it may even be beneficial to him—a company that has it too easy has no incentive to improve. However, a constantly varying pressure is very hard for a competitor to adjust to. It is as if he were trying to lift a barbell while you were randomly adding or removing weights from either end. Because you are the only one who knows what is going to happen next, your competitor cannot establish a firm budget for advertising, production, or any other phase of his operation. This is devastating.

Katsuri is an important feature of guerrilla warfare. A raiding party strikes and withdraws over and over again and always in a random pattern. To enhance the effect, the size of the force should be changed with each attack. Altering the style of the attacks is also recommended. The defending army becomes so involved in trying to adjust to a constantly changing conflict that it soon ceases to function as an effective fighting unit.

An army forced into a set battle, such as in World War I, offers a good opening for an application of katsuri. If you assume parity between the opposing forces, you can also assume the enemy support forces will be able to adjust to any level of pressure—they will be able to get the required food and ammunition to the front no matter how hard you attack. To confound this process, use katsuri no heiho.

Starting with a small raid at squad strength, escalate each new attack. This forces the enemy supply corps constantly to adjust to increasing demands. Even the line commanders cannot concentrate on their jobs—they are always worrying whether they will receive the increased amount of supplies required for use against tomorrow's larger assault.

When you sense an inability in your opponent to cope with the situation, immediately accelerate to the divisional-level attack. In some respects, it can be even worse for your enemy if he manages to adapt to your attacks. If this happens, after attacking at regimental strength do not advance to the divisional level. Instead, drop back to the squad level. This leaves the defending army with his front lines clogged with tons of unused matériel and his supply corps operating at full speed. Your enemy now has only two options: he can use these supplies by launching an attack, which forces him to desert a strong defensive position, or he may send the supplies back to the rear. He cannot just leave the supplies in the trenches for later use; there is no room for them. (An army uses an unbelievable amount of matériel in combat. After several hours of sending supplies forward for a battle that never happens, there is not room to turn around in the front lines.)

In individual combat, take care you do not become so involved with changing speed that your cuts become weak. This is very, very likely to happen. A simple method for getting around this problem is to concentrate on your breathing. Set the rhythm of your sword to the rhythm of your breath, then concentrate on breathing strongly at various speeds and forget your sword. The secret for breathing strongly at different speeds without losing power lies in the sound of your breath. A normal cycle of inhale-exhale has a sound of "ah-ha." By changing this to a sound of "ah-he," or any other combination of tones, the rhythm can be radically altered. A little experimentation will quickly reveal several advantageous patterns.

You should also practice breaking one half of a breath cycle into two or more parts. For example, instead of exhaling with a sound of "ha," try breathing out with a sound of "ee-ya." It is still one continuous exhalation, but it is stressed at two points. (Remember to use your abdomen for proper breath control—it is near to impossible if you breathe with your chest.) This pattern of breathing allows you to execute two techniques on a single count. Again, a bit of experimentation will reveal many variations of this, and the advantages are obvious.

You can think of katsuri no heiho as an expanded version of han'on. Han'on is used as a defensive counter; katsuri may be used for either attack or defense. Like han'on, katsuri will disrupt your opponent's strategy.

HITOTSU NO TACHI NO HEIHO

Hitotsu no tachi means the "sword of one," and most swordsmen consider it the king of strategies. This heiho was created by Ito Ittōsai, the founder of the Ittō-ryu.[2] Although the story of the creation of hitotsu no tachi is widely known, it bears repeating here.

It seems that one night Ittosai was meditating in a temple. Sensing some unknown danger, he spun around while drawing his sword and cut downward. There was a man behind him with a drawn sword in the midst of an attack; the unknown assailant was killed instantly. Ittosai was enlightened by this event and formed his new school based upon it.

The basic strategy consists of a single stroke of the sword which serves as both attack and defense, hence the name "sword of one." Hitotsu no tachi requires great speed and steady nerve. At the instant your opponent starts a cut toward your head, step straight in and cut down strongly. As your sword passes his, it will act as a narrow wedge and force his blade aside. Your blade continues straight down, cutting his head, while his stroke is deflected harmlessly to the side.

This action must never be done with a feeling of trying to sweep your enemy's sword to the side; you should be trying to cut his sword in two lengthwise. As you can see, the physical action is quite simple. However, it requires extreme mental discipline—you will rarely see a junior use this strategy successfully because of this.

As you execute your counter-cut, your mind must be focused on killing your enemy. If you have even the slightest thought of trying to deflect his sword, your cut will be greatly weakened. Your sword must slice downward in a perfectly straight line, cutting through his attack and continuing to the target. If you allow yourself to look at, or even think about, his sword, you will invariably hit at it instead of him, and your cut will be carried off the proper line of attack. Even if you successfully deflect his attack, which is very doubtful because you are changing targets in midstroke, your cut will land off target. Also, because much of the energy of the stroke was used to deflect the enemy attack, your sword will not cut deeply.

Hitotsu no tachi is an all-or-nothing type of strategy. To use it successfully, you must not have the slightest doubt that it will work. If you do not believe in it, you will instinctively adopt a defensive attitude. This will make your cut either too weak or too slow to accomplish its task.

Obviously, your cut must be stronger and faster than your opponent's. It is for this reason that the Itto-ryu and its myriad branches place great stress on repetitive cutting exercises. (In some schools, 90 percent of all training consists of the basic cut, kiri oroshi.) To prepare for this strategy, you should do endless repetitions of kiri oroshi with a heavy wooden sword to develop speed and power. Your mushin must also be highly developed—without this you cannot react with the required speed.

When engaged in partner practice, a set of kendo gloves is very useful. This technique is known as a knuckle buster. If your stroke is a fraction of a second too slow, your partner will strike your hands; if you are a bit too fast, you will hit his fists. Only when the timing is perfect will the two swords make clean contact.[3]

During the early stages of training, your partner should cut slowly and softly. He should also hold his sword in a very relaxed manner and allow it to bounce to the side easily— because the swords are hitting at a reduced velocity, there will not be enough energy generated to deflect his blade if he resists. At high speed, this relaxation is not required. Even though the angle of impact is very small, there will be ample force generated to knock his sword well to the side.

Although it is very easy to do this technique under controlled conditions at reduced speed, actual application is much harder. Be prepared for several years of hard work if you desire to achieve any real proficiency in it.

In the art of karate, there is a technique known as *nagashizuki,* the "flowing punch," that is an applied form of this heiho. As your opponent launches a punch toward your head, mirror his action—if he strikes with his left fist, you will punch with your right. As you thrust, lower your hips slightly and allow your right fist to rotate to a thumb-down position. Because your fist is rotated ninety degrees further than normal—in a classical karate punch you only rotate your fist to a palm-down position—your right arm will be curved upward and your shoulder will be elevated. The slight dip of your hips will allow your fist to pass beneath your opponent's punching arm. As it does this, the curvature of your arm will deflect his punch upward and to the outside. Ideally, his fist will miss your head by about an inch while yours will cleanly strike his face.

As was the case with swords, if you attempt to block your opponent's attack, the strategy will not work. You must concentrate only on his face. If your spirit wavers and you allow yourself to think about the oncoming fist, you will instinctively try to block it. If this happens, there will not be enough energy remaining in your punch to do any serious damage, even if it does land near the target.

An army can use hitotsu no tachi by launching its counter-attack directly through an attacking force. This is contrary to the usual practice of first stemming the attack and then

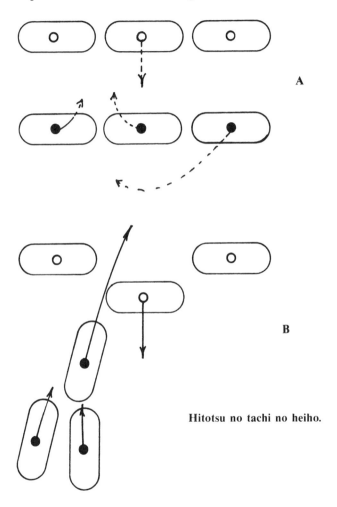

Hitotsu no tachi no heiho.

countering to the weakest area. To use hitotsu no tachi, launch a full-scale attack at the advancing element of the enemy force. The other units of the opposing army will be well dug in, occupying strong defensive positions, so attacking the attackers is not as dangerous as it might seem.

Assuming the initial format of the battlefield consists of opposing regimental fronts, the sequence is as follows: when one battalion of the enemy force advances, you immediately shift to column formation. Your leading battalion attacks the leading corner of the enemy force and advances toward the rear of his formation. Your second and third battalions follow closely, engaging both the advancing enemy battalion and the stationary enemy forces. As your troops advance, they must stay in a tight enough formation to be within range of both enemy battalions. This gives you an advantage of three-to-two in firepower. Conversely, if your regiment becomes too stretched out, the enemy battalion will have a two-to-one firepower over your lead battalion.

In order for this strategy to work, you must strike fast and hard. For example, if you are using infantry, it should attack on the run. If the troops slow to a walk, it will be disastrous. If you can attack with your full regiment, savagely, it will be like throwing a brick through a plate-glass window—the enemy formation will be shattered.

Once you have penetrated the enemy line you will be operating in a zone of great confusion—the rear echelon of an attacking force is never as stable or well protected as that of a defensive army. If you have a mobile force, you can race about for some time before encountering any great resistance.

In an engagement such as this, regard the troops of your opponent as his sword. The head, which is your true target, is his command and control structure behind the front lines. You should always concentrate on this target and not become distracted by local firefights.

Hitotsu no tachi no heiho is a favorite strategy of seniors. They have the strength and skills to make it work consistently. It is a sterling example of strategy at its best. You use one technique, with perfect timing and total commitment, to destroy both your enemy and his attack. Your technique is simple, elegant, and devastating.

NOTES

1. When you hit on the half-count before your opponent's initial move, it is called *sensente,* "regaining the initiative."

2. Ito Kagehisa devised the theory that all actions of sword are based on one technique, which he called *kiri oroshi,* "cutting downward." He changed his name to Ittosai and founded the Itto-ryu heiho. Ito Kagehisa (1560–1653) is considered the greatest of all swordsmen.

3. Kendo gloves are only designed to protect the knuckles against a shinai. The Itto-ryu has a special set of very heavy gloves for use with a bokken, but they are both expensive and difficult to obtain.

Chapter Ten

Sudori: Passing

Everything that moves has momentum. Because individuals, armies, and even ideas have momentum, a strategist can use this to his advantage and create a situation of *sudori*.

If your opponent has a well-balanced defense, you may attack over and over again with little chance for success. However, if you first lure him into motion, he may be unable to change directions fast enough to counter your attack. It is this fact, that it is very hard for a person in motion to quickly change directions, that is the essence of this heiho.

SUDORI NO HEIHO

When faced by an enemy who is in a solid defensive position, cause him to move. Then, while his momentum holds him on a straight line, counterattack on a diagonal.

An excellent example of this strategy is seen in the group of jujutsu throws known as *sudori nage*. One form of these throws is used against an opponent who is rushing forward to attack you. Against such an attack, wait until the last possible instant and then step forward and drop to the ground. Because your opponent is unable to stop in time, he will trip over you and crash to the ground, head first. Obviously, your move must be precise. If you move an instant too soon, your opponent will be able to stop in time, which places you in a helpless position at his feet. Conversely, if you delay too long, he will crash into you. It is only when you time your move perfectly that the throw will work.

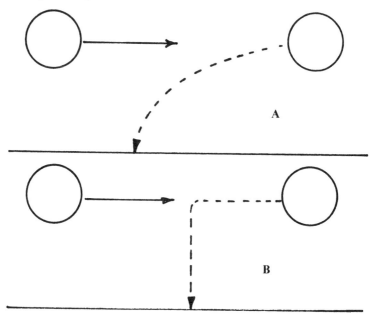

In an improper sudori nage, (A) the gradual drop allows the attacker enough time to stop, but in a proper sudori (B), the rapid change in direction prevents the attacker from slowing down in time to avoid falling.

When you step forward and drop to the ground, you must never start your move gradually—this is called telegraphing a technique. You remain motionless and then move briskly. The most common mistake in this particular technique is for a student to try to lower himself to the ground. This is much too slow. You should step forward, lift both feet off the ground, and drop like a rock. Although there are several variations of this throw, the classical finishing position is one of *zarei,* a kneeling bow, at right angles to your opponent's line of advance. As you drop you rotate, landing on your shins and forearms, as if you were bowing from a position of seiza.

An example of a well-executed momentum throw.

Armies have a great deal of momentum. Once an enemy army has committed itself to a certain line of attack, it is very hard for it to change direction. This is an ideal time for you to use a flanking move. If you attempt this while the enemy is still dug in, the move may be repulsed. However, if it is executed while he is involved in a major attack, it will be some time before he is able to divert enough troops to properly defend himself.

In single combat, adopt a diagonal stance, such as *sochin dachi*. In this stance, your feet are placed at an angle of forty-five degrees to the line of attack. As your opponent charges forward, merely bring one of your feet to the other one. This action will shift you off the line of his attack, either diagonally forward or to the rear. Which direction you select depends on what technique you plan on using. For example, in a karate match if your opponent attacks with a kick, close to your front foot. The momentum of his attack will carry him past your side and you can easily counter with a strike to his head. Make no attempt to block his attack, just bring your feet together and strike in one motion. Your strike should land before he has a chance to recover from his kick.

Perhaps nowhere is this strategy more used than in a modern air battle—a pilot being attacked by missiles makes great use of momentum. If he evades too soon, the missile has room to turn and remain tracking; if he dodges too late, he will be hit. However, if he times his evasion perfectly, the speed of the missile will prevent it from making a radical course change and he can escape. As in all forms of sudori no heiho, this demands steady nerve and a good eye for distance.

In a debate, you can use momentum by allowing your opponent apparently to win by pursuing a particular line of reasoning. Then, once he is securely trapped by his own logic, you switch tactics and destroy him with a completely new argument. For this to work, you must allow him to feel enough success to build up strong momentum. If you rebut his initial arguments, he will stay too defensive.

For a final example, consider the case of two opposing riflemen. If you assume your enemy is of equal skill, you have only a 50-percent chance of winning. To use sudori to create a passing situation, rapidly retreat beyond your opponent's maximum effective range. In order to maintain contact, he will be forced to pursue. However, by this time you will have reestablished a firing stance. This will give you at least one clean shot while he is on the move. In order to return your fire, he will either have to stop and assume a stable stance, at the cost of time, or fire on the move, at a cost of accuracy.

Sudori no heiho is a combat application of Newton's first law of motion.[1] Because the momentum of anything depends upon its mass and velocity, make sure you consider both of these factors when setting up a passing situation. If your opponent is small, he must be forced to move much faster than a bigger man. The same is true for an army or an idea.

SUIGETSU NO HEIHO

Suigetsu means "the moon in water." To use this strategy, you present your enemy with a target and then, when he attacks, you evade and counter with a single motion.

This may sound identical with the previously discussed sudori no heiho. It is, in fact, a form of sudori. The difference is that sudori no heiho is concerned with the end of a technique. Suigetsu, on the other hand, is concerned with the beginning. It is a method for luring your opponent into motion and then using his momentum against him.

Typically, in kenjutsu, you thrust your sword toward your opponent's face. Then, when he attempts to sweep your blade aside, circle your sword under his and cut his wrist. This is a popular strategy among beginners because it is so easy to do. However, do not make the mistake of regarding suigetsu as only a beginner's technique. It has great value for strategists of all levels.

Training for this heiho focuses on the study of motion. Given a particular motion of an enemy, you practice an evasion that takes advantage of it. Just evading the attack is not enough. You must evade in such a manner as to place yourself in an advantageous position. Once you have developed such an evasion, you then combine it with a cutting technique and practice this combination until it can be done as a single motion. This is of critical importance. Your evasion and counter-cut must always be done on a count of "ONE!" and never as "one-TWO!" If you evade the attack and then cut, even if your technique scores, it is not suigetsu.

For a very simple application of suigetsu, stand facing your partner, while holding your sword low and to your right side. Remain motionless as he approaches. Then, as he cuts downward toward your head, slide forward and to your left. As you pass, cut upward across his body. You become like the reflection of the moon in water. You can be seen and reached for, but never grasped.

Suigetsu requires an advanced state of mushin if it is to work well. As your opponent launches his attack, you must hold this state and remain completely uninvolved with his action. When your spirit is like a pool of calm water, your evasion and counter will be a reflection of his attack. You will not respond to his move; you respond with it. This mental aspect of suigetsu is readily apparent when you observe fencers of different grades using this heiho. The swordsman who applies suigetsu only on a physical level, while frequently successful, will always appear rushed. On the other hand, a fencer who maintains a tranquil spirit will appear to be moving in slow motion—his opponent will always seem to be a count behind, no matter how hard he tries to catch up.

When using suigetsu, you should not settle for just showing your opponent a target; you must make the lure irresistible. One way of doing this is to show him a threat.

If you just present a target, a senior may recognize this as an attempt at suigetsu and take an appropriate action. He might use *nagashi giri,* a flowing cut which follows as you attempt to evade. He might also attack with a style you have never seen before, thus spoiling your planned evasion. However, if you present him with a threat, he may be lured into eliminating the threat first and then attacking. This involves him in two separate actions. Because your evasion and counter are done on one beat, you will hit him on the half-count,

Gedan kamae, a low-guard position, is frequently used to create a suigetsu situation.

before he enters phase two of his strategy.

This element of suigetsu, presenting a threat instead of merely a target, is very important for armies. If you present only a target, the enemy advance will be orderly. This makes a counterattack very difficult. It is much better to feint a sharp and damaging raid, followed by a slow withdrawal, staying at the edge of enemy range. This may cause the enemy troops, in the excitement of the chase, to pursue a little faster and further than they should. In this disorganized state, they are ripe for a counterattack. George Armstrong Custer is perhaps the most famous victim of this strategy.

In a karate match, extend your leading hand toward your opponent's face. When he attempts to brush it aside, snap your hand away with a rolling motion and strike his face. You must evade his block by the absolute minimum distance possible; if your circular evasion is too wide, your strike will be delayed enough for him to bring his arm back and block it. Practice this action in slow motion at first. Thrust your hand forward and then roll it around your opponent's blocking arm, maintaining contact all the way. If this is properly executed, you should be able to hit his face before his blocking arm stops its original motion.

In judo, set yourself up as an obvious victim for a hip throw. As your opponent steps in to throw, step to his side in the direction of his rotation and drop to one knee. The power of his turn will slam him to the floor. You should not have to use your hands or apply any extra energy to throw him—he does it all himself. (This is a hard fall, so practice with care at first.)

A businessman can use suigetsu to expand his company. First, market a good product. Then wait for another corporation to retool in order to manufacture a similar product. As soon as it has done this, but before it starts making a profit from its investment, execute a takeover bid. This has a very good chance for success because your company, with a good product on the market, is financially strong. The other company, however, has invested much of its operating capital into new machinery. The advantage to acquiring a company like this is that you become the owner of a new plant that is already prepared to manufacture your product.

Suigetsu no heiho is a superb strategy and may be used in any form of conflict. Because of its stress on motion, it is also an excellent training method for other techniques. Study it carefully, for its variations are wide and its theory is very, very deep.

IRIMI NO HEIHO

Irimi, the "entering body," is an ancient fencing strategy that makes excellent use of momentum. When your opponent attacks, you move in such a manner as to place yourself at his rear corner, making it very easy for you to cut him and almost impossible for him to counter.

To practice the basic form of this strategy, stand facing your opponent while holding your sword low and to your right side. Your left foot should be well forward. When he attacks, leap forward and slightly to your right with a strong, counterclockwise hip rotation. You will pass very close to his left side with a leaping turn and cut his back as you land. You should finish this move positioned at his left rear corner, with your right foot forward and facing his left shoulder.

A variation of this move is used when your enemy rushes in very fast. In such a case, if you leap forward you will wind up too far to his rear to cut him strongly. So, instead of leaping forward off your left foot, pivot to the rear on your right foot. You should still wind up in the same relative position.

The important point is to finish at your opponent's rear corner, diagonally facing his back. You should practice with a variety of attacks until you learn to adapt your leaping turn to any amount of enemy motion. Check your final position by leaning forward without moving your feet. You should be able to touch his shoulder with your hand. If you cannot touch him without taking a step, you are too far away; if you can touch his shoulder without leaning forward, you are too close.

Irimi is *not* a dodge to the side. You must pass as close to

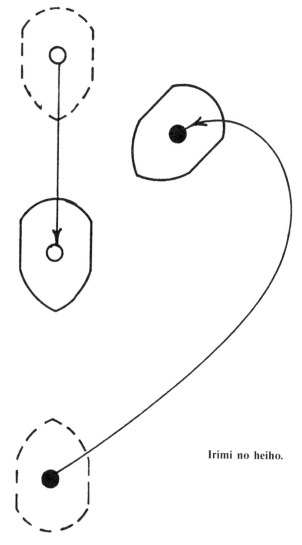

Irimi no heiho.

your opponent as possible, close enough to brush against him in passing. If your leap is too far to the side, he may be able to twist enough in mid-step to cut you. However, if you pass very close to his side, the passing angle becomes too acute for him to follow you.

Although which side you move to may well depend upon your relative positions at the start, you should make an effort to get to your opponent's dead side. This is the area to the

The proper finishing position for irimi.

rear of his forward leg. For example, if he steps forward with his right foot, try to get to his right rear corner. You do this because it is very difficult for him to turn in that direction. On the other hand, if you moved to his left rear corner, he could quickly pivot to face you.

The problem of reaching his dead corner when you are caught with the wrong foot forward is solved by a variation of the strategy which is known as *gyaku irimi*. Proceed as in the basic form but, instead of leaping to your right front corner, leap slightly left with a stronger hip rotation. You are jumping toward your attacker's right rear corner instead of to his left rear. Instead of facing him as you pass, your back will

be toward him. If your distance is perfect, his right shoulder
will brush across your back as you pass. You finish as in the
basic form, cutting as you land.

Gyaku irimi is much more difficult than the basic irimi.
Also, because you are turning your back to an enemy, it is
not for the faint of heart. (If you begin this strategy with
your sword sheathed and draw it as you turn, it is known as
yamabiki no ken. The name comes from the fact that you
do not hear your opponent's kiai when he attacks. You are
behind him so fast that you only hear the echo.)

One of the most impressive demonstrations of irimi no
heiho is using it to escape from a circle of enemies. When you
are surrounded, wait for the attack and then use irimi to leap
through the attacker's line. If you time your rotation properly, you can pass through a very, very narrow gap. As you
turn, push against the shoulder of the man you are passing.
This will cause him to stumble into the center of the circle,
becoming the new target of the blows which were intended
for you. If this technique is done with vigor and spirit, it
seems almost magical. You are surrounded by several men,
they attack strongly, and suddenly you are standing outside
the circle watching their blows land on one of their own
number. For many years this was a secret technique of the
Takeda family. It was only taught to senior military officers.

Philosophically, this strategy depends upon a constant
awareness of *sankaku tobi,* the "triangular leap." Normally,
when fighting, a person is aware only of himself and his
opponent. *Sankaku* means you think of the battle as a
triangle: you are at one point, your enemy is at the second,
and the third point is a void. When you leap into the irimi,
you do not do this with a feeling of escaping. Rather, you
have a feeling of being drawn forward into the only other
proper place on the battlefield. You are not moving *from*
a place of danger but *to* a place of advantage. By thinking
this way you can maintain a positive spirit of attack instead
of a negative spirit of evading.

In the past, armies have rarely used the principle of irimi
because it is very hard to turn a large group of men. However, modern communications equipment has changed this.

These devices allow the shape and organization of a unit to be limited only by the imagination of its commander. This means the army does not have to have a front. It can now be shaped like a disk with the commander at the center, and any direction can be the front. Such an army can leap forward and then sharply pivot for an irimi. (Naval fleets have used such formations for centuries.)

The obvious advantage of the disk-shaped formation is that it makes a fast pivot possible. By advancing at an angle and pivoting, a regiment can imitate the action of an individual. This kind of regimental pivot is much faster than one in which the unit has to turn its axis.

Mention should be made of the technique known as *irimi nage,* the "entering throw." This throw is a specialty of the Daito-ryu and its many offshoots, one such being modern aikido. The technique consists of an entering motion to your attacker's dead side, followed by a pivot in the opposite direction to throw him. You spin into your attacker's side and guide the energy of his attack into a circle. Then, when he starts to recoil, you spin in the other direction and throw him onto his back.

The original strategy for this throw was borrowed from the Itto-ryu. It was based upon a repeated crossing of the line of attack, both to evade cuts and to cut the enemy on the half-count. However, because this technique is rarely practiced with swords anymore, the throw is rarely done correctly.

Most students move altogether too much when using irimi nage. Properly, irimi nage should be done with a minimum of motion and a maximum of timing. Also, many students attempt this throw with too much distance between themselves and their opponents. The art of entering requires that you pass as closely as possible, forcing your enemy into a sharp turn. In irimi nage, your bodies should be pressed firmly together.

It would be very beneficial for most aikido students to practice this technique with swords, in its old form. When your opponent tries to cut you, slide to the left and cut his sword down. Then, as he pivots toward you and raises his sword to cut again, slide to the right and cut his wrist. This action is based on the old Itto-ryu techniques of *myō-ken,* the "mysterious sword," and *zetsumyō-ken,* the "exquisite sword." As in most techniques from that ryu, although the action is simple, the theory is deep.

Whether dealing with an individual or with an army, never lose sight of the first rule of combat: Attack! Irimi no heiho is a very beautiful and very effective strategy. However, due to its nature, it is very easy for it to degenerate into a series of evasive leaps. Guard against this. Never think about avoiding the attack; concentrate only on cutting your opponent's back. The result of this concentration will be a strategy which is both beautiful in appearance and deadly in application.

HITO E MI NO HEIHO

Hito e mi means that you weld yourself and your opponent into "one body." In some schools, this action is referred to as blending.

When you are attacked, it is instinctive to try to evade the danger. By countermanding this instinct and blending with the attack, you can achieve a tactical advantage in certain situations. There are two methods of blending with an attack: you may adopt a mirror image or an identical image. A mirror image is yo no tachi, the "positive sword," and an identical image is in no tachi, the "negative sword." These two styles of combat are also referred to as *gōhō,* the "hard method," and *jūhō,* the "soft method."[2]

The difference between the positive and negative methods is the relative direction of force. If the attack and defense move in the same direction, it is the soft style; if they move in opposite directions, it is the hard style. A soft-style defense is usually more technically complex than the hard style. Therefore, soft methods are usually thought of as being more sophisticated. On the other hand, although hard-style techniques are usually simple, they are also fast and decisive.

For an example of hito e mi applied in the style of yo no tachi, assume your opponent is attacking with a downward

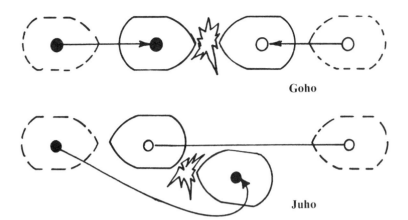

Goho

Juho

cut. Slide straight forward and twist slightly to the left—do not try to dodge his sword, just twist left. As you do this, lower the point of your sword and brace your right wrist against your hip. Your opponent's blade should miss you by a fraction of an inch as he impales himself on your sword.

You can use a similar action when unarmed by placing your right hand on your hip. Then your opponent will strike your elbow with his solar plexus. In either case, the feeling is that of two individuals being welded together by their techniques. This is goho—the line of the attacking force is directly opposite to the line of your defense.

When beginners try this technique, they will invariably flinch from the attack. Instead of stepping straight forward, they will move to the side. To correct this, place a strip of tape on the floor and use it as the line of attack. Start with the inside edge of your right foot touching the tape, do the technique, and then look at your foot. The inside edge should still be touching the tape. All you are doing is stepping forward while rotating the left side of your body over to the same side of the line as your right side. Your opponent's sword should pass *very* close to you. Ideally, it will shave the hairs off the back of your left hand.

If, instead of clashing with your opponent's energy, you blend with it, it is called in no tachi. For example, in the preceding exercise, continue your twisting action until you are facing the same direction as your attacker. Now you may

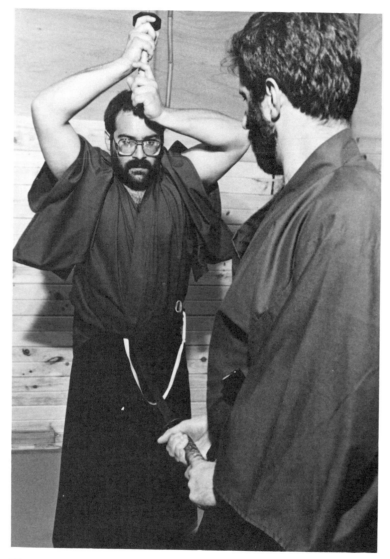

Hito e mi: if the uchitachi (facing) continues his attack, he will skewer himself on his opponent's sword.

easily grasp his right hand with yours. You should be in identical positions, with your back touching his chest. If you do this rapidly and then cut down, you can throw him over your hip. If he resists and tries to pull away, turn with his pull. He will have to rotate his right hand, forcing himself into a wrist lock. In either of these variations, use a minimum of force. If your timing is correct it will take less than a pound of pressure to throw him or establish the wrist lock.

You could also use an irimi motion and move to his right side. Matching his position and standing very close, hook his right wrist with your right hand and place your left hand on the back of his neck. If you continue his original motion, you will throw him forward. If he resists and pulls back, you can pivot left and throw him to the rear with irimi nage.

There is a profound spiritual element in this strategy. No matter what variation of the heiho you use, you must never think, "I am doing this to him." Your attitude must always be, "we are doing this together." There is an excellent little demonstration of the efficacy of this way of thinking that you should try.

Have your training partner assume a forward stance, *zenkutsu dachi,* with his right foot well forward. He should lower his hips and brace himself strongly. Now grab him and try to move him around. You will find this very difficult, if not impossible. Once you have convinced yourself of the futility of this action, step around to his right side and assume a stance similar to his. However, do not spread your legs as far apart as his or tense your muscles; just stand in a casual and relaxed manner. Drape your left arm softly across his shoulders and take his right wrist lightly with your right hand. Now, imagine that you are both made of hot wax and are melting together. Take a deep breath, exhale slowly, relax, and lead him away.

As long as you are thinking, "we are one," this exercise will be very easy. However, as soon as you start to think of yourselves as being two individuals, all motion will slam to a stop. The trick is to use no more force to move both you and your partner than you would use to move yourself—you should hold him as lightly as a feather. This exercise clearly illustrates the fundamental principle of juho: the harder you try, the worse the results will be.

If you have been trained in how to hit, you may wish to try another exercise which will demonstrate the hard aspect of blending. For this you will need either a *makiwara*[3] or a large punching bag. (Do not attempt this unless you have had formal instruction in how to hit with your fist or you will break every bone in your hand.)

Take a good stance facing the target and hit it as hard as you can. Note the effect of your punch, paying particular attention to the sound of impact. Now try it again. This time, as you hit, look intensely at the target and think, "we . . . are . . . ONE!" At the moment of contact imagine that you and the target are being welded by the technique. You should find the results quite a bit more impressive than your first attempt. This is a very difficult exercise and only seniors will have much luck with it. Very few beginners are capable of hitting anything without holding back a little.

A final exercise for blending uses *katatedori,* a wrist grab, as the attack. Stand naturally with your right foot slightly forward and extend your right arm. Your partner will adopt an identical stance and grip your wrist with his right hand. You now imagine that your bodies become one, letting your individuality gradually dissolve. If you do this properly, any move you make will force your partner to do the same. However, if you are not blended, you may move around freely, but your partner will remain stationary.

The art of jujutsu makes extensive use of this principle. Also, many people think the word *ai* from *aikido* denotes this blending action.[4] This is not quite correct. *Ai* does mean that two things are meeting, but the phrase *hito e mi* captures the true feeling much better. *Hito e mi* may be literally translated as "unifying action." Some aikido schools compound the problem by placing undue importance on the fact that *ai,* "to meet," is a homonym of *ai,* "love." This results in a loss of the true meaning of *blending.* In reality, blending is just a method for dominating another person.

Applications of hito e mi range from the mundane to the ethereal. Something as simple as pushing a bicycle up a steep hill becomes easy when you stop fighting it. Just stand naturally beside it, place your hands lightly on the seat and handlebars, relax, and walk up the hill. Instructors, or at least the great instructors, make frequent use of this strategy when teaching. Instead of listening to their own words, as an instructor, they learn to listen from the viewpoint of the student. This is called empathy.

As an executive in the business world you may do much the same thing. Instead of telling a crew what to do and insisting they do it because you are the boss, blend with them. No longer directing, you are now guiding. The advantage of this soft-style leadership is its efficiency—the workers no longer instinctively react against authority. The disadvantage is its slowness. When time is of the essence, you should rely on the classical methods of creating conditioned reflexes: stern discipline and hard training.

In any application of hito e mi no heiho, your primary considerations are the lines of force of the conflict. You must adopt an objective attitude. Do not think about what your enemy is doing; think only about his motion through space. Then adjust your technique to this line of force, moving with it or against it. In either case, weld yourself to your opponent and move with him as one person.

HAPPO BIRAKI NO HEIHO

To be in an attitude of *happō biraki* means that you are "open on eight sides." Standing in a natural position, you are apparently open to attack from any direction.

In reality, you are poised and ready for the attack. This is a very advanced strategy, and it requires a healthy dose of zanshin in order to be viable. To survive from such a position means that your haragei must be at such a high level that you can sense an attack from any direction and instantly react to it.

A swordsman assumes a posture of happo biraki by standing in a natural stance, with his sword dangling from his hand. The blade is not in any particular attitude and no great effort is made to conceal the sword. If you stand with your left foot slightly forward, your sword will hang behind your right leg, but do not try to force it into that position.

You will find the initial move from happo biraki somewhat difficult, and quite often it is technically complex. Generally some form of *tsubame gaeshi*[5] will be used. This is a fast, whip-like, side-to-side slash, and to generate any speed with this technique will take some practice. The secret is using a rolling, relaxed snap, as if you were cracking a whip. Your sword should finish in a vertical position, in front of your left shoulder.

Happo biraki is an applied form of zanshin. Your enemy will first think, "he is wide open to an attack." However, a second look may make him think, "he knows he is open to attack and is waiting for it." This moment of indecision, a form of mental inertia, is called a *suki*. A suki is a gap in your opponent's concentration. This is the instant in which you can attack and be assured of a victory. You must not hesitate—a delay of even a fraction of a second will allow your opponent to recover and block your attack. Also, any hesitation on your part is another suki, which makes you vulnerable.

There is a particularly fine training method for this strategy. The students are lined up facing a wall, and the instructor stands several yards behind them. He has a large rubber ball, which is attached to one end of a long cord. He ties the other end of the cord to his wrist. Selecting a target at random, without any warning he will hurl the ball at one of the students. The student's job is to sense the missile, turn, and block it before he is hit. Then the instructor reels in the ball and repeats the drill.

The amazing thing about this exercise is not that the students can do it at all, but that they can do it so easily. It is not unusual for even beginners to become quite adept after only a few hours of training. The secret, of course, is total relaxation. The warning you feel signaling the time to turn and block will be so subtle that even the slightest amount of physical or mental tension will mask it. This is not ESP. Even if the instructor throws with perfect silence, the ball will make a sound as it passes through the air. It will also compress the air in front of it. If you relax you can hear and feel these signals.

An organization, whether military or corporate, may use happo biraki by appointing an overseer. His job title should be taken literally. He has nothing to do with the day-to-day operations of the organization; his only task is to sense that something is about to happen and warn the others. Although this may seem a bit mystical, it is very practical. Quite frequently those with the authority to trigger an organization into motion are so loaded down with operational responsibilities that they cannot detect minor danger signals. If the person in happo biraki is not conscientious, this is a waste. However, if he does his job only once, it can save the group. Many large organizations waste more money on less important gambles.

The most obvious example of this strategy is the military sentry, not the ceremonial guards you see, but the real sentries that you do not see. A soldier only walks a post to look pretty. An actual sentry will be motionless—he doesn't draw any attention; he just senses what is going on around him.

This strategy, like all the others in this chapter, makes use of momentum. You either lure your opponent into the attack—if you do that, this strategy becomes a form of suigetsu no heiho—or you freeze him in a moment of indecision. In either case, his inertia will allow you time to cut.

ENGETSU NO HEIHO

Engetsu is the "full moon" technique. Although the physical applications of this strategy are too theatrical to be of use against any but the most junior of opponents, its spiritual principles merit study. Therefore, this strategy is more often used as a training method than an actual combat technique.

Execution of this technique usually involves the swordsman's adopting a large and imposing attitude while slowly moving his sword in a circular pattern. Then, with no warning, he will suddenly attack from a random position along the circle.

This strategy is not well thought of because of its large initial motion. Although a beginner may be both confused and fascinated when he sees this, a senior is apt to attack the instant the sword is moved off the centerline. However, as a training method to learn how to attack strongly from any angle, engetsu can be quite valuable.

The great seventeenth-century strategist Miyamoto Musashi said, "Make your fighting stance your everyday stance and your everyday stance your fighting stance." This is the essence of engetsu.

The mistake made by beginners who attempt this strategy is that, while they move their swords in a large circle, they actually attack from one of the standard positions. The beginner is limited by his training to the use of a few classical stances, but the person who has mastered engetsu is freed from these restrictions. Instead of learning only to cut from the standard eight positions, known as *happō gamae,* he can cut freely from any direction.

The mastery of engetsu requires long training. You must master 360 cuts instead of only eight. Although you can think of any of these 360 cuts as only a variation of whichever of the eight basic cuts is nearest it on the circle, each must still be practiced rigorously.

Philosophically, this is very important. A beginner will automatically shift to a standard fighting stance when threatened, then launch his attack. This is what you are learning to avoid. Instead of using the normal sequence of "see-prepare-attack," you should operate on a single count. You see and simultaneously attack, from any attitude. This gives you a major time advantage.

The opening phase of engetsu is called *asahi,* the "rising sun." This move is seen in many kata. As you slowly raise your sword, carefully rotate it. At some point, the blade will catch the rays of the sun and reflect them into the eyes of your opponent. Then, when he blinks, attack strongly.

Asahi illustrates the essence of engetsu no heiho. You must be able to attack in the blink of an eye from any position. If you pause to shift to a standard position, this moment will be lost.

Spiritually, you must come to regard yourself as a very, very dangerous person. Whether sitting, standing, or lying, you must be able to attack in any direction. Up, down, left, right, front, or back must all be the same to you. This ability, when using a sword, is called *iaijutsu.*

Naval warships frequently rehearse for engetsu. Normally,

The technique of asahi, from the **Taikyoku No Ken kata**, in which the swordsman flexes his wrist in order to cause light to be reflected from his swordblade into his opponent's eyes.

a warship will fire its guns from an attitude known as "battle stations." However, this takes time, up to several minutes for a large ship. To fill in this gap, a warship practices shooting from the hip: launching a missile or torpedo from its cruising attitude. Although this shot will not be well aimed, it will be very fast. If the ship can launch an attack within ten seconds of discovering an enemy, the resultant confusion may be enough to allow it to assume a proper battle stance.

An infantry unit uses engetsu by having each of its members preprogrammed to respond to an attack. The unit is taught that enemy fire from any direction should be automatically returned in a certain pattern. Each man has his role in the pattern. Although the men may not actually hit anything, flying bullets have a tendency to drive the attackers to cover. This will allow the unit commander enough time to devise a more appropriate counter.

Although it is not readily apparent, engetsu is another momentum technique. It is actually an expanded version of happo biraki. Like happo biraki, it is not concerned so much with your enemy's momentum as it is with your own inertia. By learning to attack from any position, you seize the initiative and the momentum of attack from your opponent.

NOTES

1. An object in motion will stay in motion, in a straight line, unless acted upon by some outside force.

2. Some ryu show a marked preference for one or the other of these methods. No ryu, however, uses one of the two styles exclusively.

3. *Makiwara:* a striking post. It is made by sinking a tapered post into the ground with the small end up. The end is wrapped with coarse rope and used as the target.

4. *Ai* is the combining form of the verb *au.*

5. *Tsubame gaeshi:* the "swallow-tail counter." It takes its name from the side-to-side flick of a swallow's tail in flight. This technique was made famous by Sasaki Kojiro in his duel against Miyamoto Musashi in 1612.

Chapter Eleven

Chushin: Centering

The single factor which is common to all forms of conflict is control of center. From hand-to-hand combat to a chess match, this is of primary importance.

When you control the center, your techniques will have only a short distance to travel in order to reach the vital areas of your opponent. Conversely, his techniques must circle around this central area in order to reach you. For long-term gains you should always try to dominate the center at the beginning of the engagement. The initial costs will be far outweighed by later benefits. The only sure way to win without doing this is to make the fight very short.

Before you can dominate the center you must identify it. The *chūshin* can be a physical place, such as the point midway between two individuals. It can also be an area, like the central squares on a chessboard. It can even be an idea. For example, if a business owns the patent on some basic machine, then all of its competitors must use a longer and more involved means to achieve identical goals.

There is a variety of methods used to instill this concept. Most of these training devices require much time and effort. However, there is one training method which works both fast and well. This is the *nagashi undō* of the Tenshin-ryu. This "flowing exercise" will, within a matter of minutes, teach a

157

Naginata chudan gamae, control of the center.

raw beginner how to control center.

Nagashi undo is a two-man exercise using bokken. You face your training partner in any attitude you desire and, using any technique, try to cut him without being touched yourself. The restrictions are that you must cut as softly and slowly as possible, using the entire length of your bokken. Using speed to score a point or strength to resist an attack are strictly forbidden. These restrictions force both partners to rely entirely on body motion for attack and defense.

Holding your sword very softly with only your fingertips,

you freely engage in a series of cuts and parries. The goal is to draw your sword slowly and softly, from hilt to tip, across your opponent's body. You accomplish this by maneuvering him into such a position that there is nothing he can do to stop you.

After only a few minutes of practicing this exercise, each man will realize that he will be cut the instant he loses control of center. Conversely, the only way he can score a clean cut is to gain control of this area. Because the cuts of this exercise are slow and soft, students may practice it with minimal supervision. The instructor's only task is to ensure that their competitive instincts do not come to the fore—the students might forget the purpose of the exercise and start using speed or strength instead of strategy to score a point.

Among seniors a bout of nagashi undo may stretch on for a very long time without a point being scored. In such a situation, about all you can do is continue patiently, hoping that your partner will make a mistake before you do. This type of conflict is usually lost by the first person who becomes bored or frustrated, as is the case in most fights between seniors.

CHUSHIN DORI NO HEIHO

This strategy, "taking the center," has almost limitless variations. While an army may dominate the center of a battlefield by force of arms, in other arenas the action is more often psychological than physical.

Junior students of strategy will habitually place the chushin at a point exactly halfway between themselves and their opponents. If faced with a beginner who does this, you can take control of the center by radiating more spiritual energy. By suddenly using kiai you will overlap the center with your spiritual presence. As he instinctively moves back, pursue him relentlessly—the beginner will find it almost impossible to stop retreating.

Every individual has what is called his personal space. This is a zone of about three feet in radius around you. (The exact size is primarily a function of your self-confidence.) If a stranger enters this zone you will begin to feel uncomfortable.

Assume the personal spaces of both you and your opponent are exactly three feet in radius and that you are standing six feet apart. By the simple act of moving forward one inch you have overlapped the chushin with your personal space. If your spirit is stronger than your opponent's, you now have dominated the center. Instead of concentrating on the control of center, your opponent will now shift his goal to getting you out of his personal space. He will probably do this by taking a small step back. If you are prepared for this action you can hit him easily.

Chushin dori is an excellent method for winning a debate. If your opponent is presenting a solid and logical argument, move closer to him. Gradually his attention will shift from his logical argument to the emotional problem of an invasion of his personal space. Once he has made the transition from logic to emotion, he is a victim for even a second-rate argument.

In business, to control the center you first examine the market to determine what the customers want. Then you examine yourself to see what you can provide. You establish the center halfway between these points. The customer has to make certain concessions in order to get your product; you have to make other concessions to get the customer's money. Then you apply chushin dori no heiho.

In a normal transaction a customer will know exactly what a product is worth and what his own financial capabilities are. To use chushin dori you convince him that either, or both, of his conceptions are wrong. There are many ways to do this. Whatever the method, you are controlling the center, the fine line between "buy" and "don't buy." If you do this with delicacy, the customer will go away poorer but happy. If you are too heavy-handed he will just go away.

There are many cases in which a center has to be established where none has previously existed. A good example of this is seen in the art of leadership. A good executive, within moments of his arrival, will firmly establish the point midway between leader and follower, respect and familiarity.

He will then totally dominate this point. Once he has done this, leadership becomes very easy. He starts hard, without a trace of compassion. This is because it is easier to close the maai than to open it. If he begins with a familiar attitude, any change will be viewed as a retreat. (A good leader is always hated the first day and loved on his last day. An executive who tries to start as a friend is not trusted the first day and not respected on his last day.)

A good leader must also be able to vary the chushin as the situation demands—the center at an office party is different from that at a board meeting. But, no matter what the situation, a good leader will never lose sight of the center or allow its control to slip from his grasp.

Domination of center requires not a little courage, because you must expose your center in order to control your opponent's. Lack of this ability is seen in many karate matches.

When observing these matches, you will often note people who prefer to fight from an oblique stance, turning their chests slightly away from their opponents. Because most vital areas of the human body are on the centerline, they feel safer this way—it makes their opponents' efforts to hit anything important more difficult.

Although they may win in such a stance, the victory will never be decisive. It is much better to use the classical karate stance, derived from kenjutsu, and face your opponent squarely. This places all your body's weapons, not just those on the leading side of your body, in position for attack or defense. This position also has a great psychological advantage. Turning away from danger is negative; facing it is positive. You will never control the center with a negative spirit.

The classical karate stance is rarely taught anymore. Modern karate uses more high kicks and the stances have been modified to take this into account. In the classical stance, which looks a little like an old boxing stance, your leading arm is held forward with the back of the fist facing your opponent. The important point is that both your fist and elbow are exactly on the centerline. (The standard mistake is allowing your elbow to move to the outside.) By holding your forearm on the centerline, you have dominated it.

By placing your hand on your opponent's hip and locking your elbow, you can prevent him from throwing you.

Any technique from your opponent must now go around your forearm to reach your body.

Chushin dori offers an excellent counter for a judo hip throw. When your opponent spins in to throw you, do not try to resist him. In order to throw you over his hip, he has to move his itten into your center. You should concentrate only on this point. As he spins in toward your center, extend your arm and place your palm on this imaginary point. His hip will slam into your palm and because he cannot get his itten to the center, all motion will stop. You will discover that you can counter his maximum effort with just a touch.

As pointed out in the discussion of haragei in Chapter Seven, concentration on the itten generates physical stability. There is an interesting little exercise that illustrates the psychological effect of chushin dori on this kind of stability.

Have your partner stand in a natural stance and concentrate on his itten. Now push against his chest with your fingertips. He ignores your push; the harder you press against him, the harder he concentrates on his center. You should find him hard to move. He will feel relaxed but stiff. (If he just tightens his muscles he will be very easy to tip over.) Now touch him lightly on the abdomen and run your finger up his chest to his shoulder. If you then immediately give him a push, he cannot resist it. This is because his mind has followed your finger up to his shoulder instead of remaining locked on his itten. You may use this principle in any throwing art.

This process of shifting your opponent's center is even more impressive when you do it from the rear. Have your partner stand as before, but this time he faces away from you. Do not draw your finger up his back to shift his center, just concentrate on where you want his itten to be. If you imagine that his center of balance is in his head, you can push him with just your fingertips.

Chushin dori has many variations. Remember, there are actually three centers for you to work with: your personal center, your partner's center, and the center of the combat zone between the two of you. Chushin dori no heiho is the art of manipulating these points to your advantage.

HARAI NO HEIHO

When your centerline is threatened, you can use *harai* to sweep your opponent's sword aside. This clears the centerline for your own attack.

To sweep your opponent's sword, the tip of your blade should move in a small circle. If the tips of your swords are crossed, with your blade to the right of his, you move the tip of your blade in a clockwise circle. You can stay to the right, knocking his sword up and to the left, or you can circle under his sword, knocking it up and to the right. (If you start with your blade to the left of your opponent's sword, reverse this action.)

The actual sweeping action is done with a flick of your wrists and nothing more. If you use excessive force, the tip of your sword will be carried off the centerline and no advantage will be gained. Practice until you can slap your opponent's sword several inches to the side, with an absolute minimum of motion on your part. In no case should the tip of your blade ever cease to point at your opponent's body.

Excessive use of force is the first major mistake of beginners. As long as the tip of your enemy's sword clears your body as you step forward, that is enough. Ideally, it should slice through your sleeve but not touch your arm. If you have knocked it any farther to the side, you have wasted time and energy.

When you have completed the first small circle with the tip of your sword, which slaps your opponent's sword aside and clears the centerline, continue the circle and cut him. You never use two linear motions for this; your cut is always an expansion of the harai. The tip of your sword should follow the line of a helix. If the second circle is small and you take a short step, you will cut his wrist. If you expand the circle and take a bigger step, you can cut his head. This is stronger than cutting his wrist, but it is also quite a bit slower. If you opt for the wrist as your target, immediately follow this with a second cut to his head or body. Strike his wrist with a feeling of hitting a rubber ball and then bounce straight into the second cut. With one breath, cut "ta-TAH!"

The instant after harai, with uchitachi driving in strongly.

You must start your attack step with the harai, not after it. This means that if you are standing in the normal middle-level position with your right foot forward, you begin the step as the tip of your sword starts moving. As your sword slaps your opponent's blade aside, your right foot must already be driving in powerfully to close the maai. Your cut is delivered as your right foot comes down. Your right foot is the first thing to move and the strategy has been completed before it comes to rest.

To practice this action, use a solid target. Execute the harai against an imaginary sword and strike the target firmly as you hurl yourself forward four feet. (Mark a start and finish line on the floor to ensure that you are covering this much distance.) The sound of your bokken hitting the target should be synchronized with the sound of your right foot hitting the floor.

Herein lies the second great mistake of beginners. Because the junior is not altogether certain the strategy will work—that confidence only comes from long experience—he hesitates. He does not commit himself to the attack step until he is sure his opponent's sword has been swept far enough to the side to permit a safe entry. This, of course, is much too late. By the time he actually launches his attack, his opponent has had enough time to recover from the harai. The usual result is that, as he steps forward, the beginner skewers himself on his opponent's blade, which has now returned to the centerline. The failure of this delayed attack forces the beginner to use an even more powerful harai the next time he practices it. This returns him to his first mistake.

Using too much power in a harai is an attempt to correct the effect, not the cause, of a mistake. If the timing of your footwork is proper, you can easily pass the tip of your opponent's sword safely, even after a very small sweep. The error of delaying the main attack is often made even by seniors, who should know better. By waiting for a fraction of a second to make sure the opening move has worked, the main attack is always doomed to failure. In all cases, harai requires outrageous boldness.

A good example of military use of harai is seen on the artillery barrage. The barrage is walked in ahead of the infantry—the gunners increase the range of their cannon with each round fired, so that the shells fall just ahead of the advancing infantry. This allows the foot soldiers to make contact with the enemy before the barrage ends.

You can apply this strategy during parliamentary procedures by calling for a vote on your own program immediately after destroying your opponent's argument. There will be an instinctive reaction among the members of the group to believe that, because you have proved your opponent's position to be wrong, your position must be the right one. If you move fast, they will not have time to consider that both of you may be wrong.

In a karate match, you can use harai as if you were fencing. Drive forward with your left foot and strike with your right hand. As you do this, use your left hand to sweep aside any obstructions.

In this type of strategy, as in many others, success is highly dependent upon how deeply you believe in yourself—self-doubt causes hesitation, which destroys the effectiveness of the technique. There is an ancient dojo story, which is often used to illustrate the amount of confidence required for this heiho.

It seems that once, many centuries ago, there was a new master in town, and a group of students were discussing him. Because the new swordsman was such an unknown quantity, everyone was waiting to see him in action before they challenged him to a match. (In those days a fencing match frequently resulted in death or a crippling injury.)

Upon hearing the students' talk, the dojo headmaster snorted and said, "Come on. Show him to me and I will test him." The students quickly replied, "Oh no, sensei! Don't you be the first. Let someone else challenge him so you can see how good his techniques are." The sensei responded, "I don't care how good his techniques are because I *know* how good mine are!"

(He won, defeating a halberd with only a folding paper fan.)

It is this degree of self-confidence that you need if you are to use harai no heiho properly. You have to leap in with your main attack, *knowing* that your sweep will work. Harai is classified as one of the family of techniques known as *kissaki waza,* "tip techniques," because it normally begins at a range where the tips of the two swords are touching. At this range there is no time for the slightest hesitation.

HIJIKI NO HEIHO

Hijiki is another kissaki waza. It is designed for use against a very strong fencer who is trying to dominate the center.

(Against a weak swordsman, this technique will not work.)

With the tip of your blade, apply a steadily increasing pressure against the side of your opponent's sword. Act as if you are trying to force his blade off the centerline so you can slide in with a thrust. In an effort to maintain control of center, he will instinctively resist this pressure.

When a sufficient amount of pressure has been built up, suddenly drop the tip of your sword about an inch. This sudden release of pressure will cause the tip of your opponent's sword to spring to the side, opening the center for your attack.

As in harai, your follow-up cut must be delivered in the blink of an eye. This means that you must launch your attack as you start to lower the tip of your sword. If you wait to see how far his blade springs to the side, he will have time enough to recover before you can cut him.

To use this strategy with an army, apply pressure against one segment of the enemy line. Then, when enemy strength concentrates there, suddenly disengage and fall back. The enemy force will surge forward in pursuit, creating a rift between that unit and the remainder of its line. You launch your true attack at that rift. As in the case with individual swordsmen, this only works against a strong and aggressive enemy.

When your opponent is trying to press you against a wall, resist firmly. Then suddenly relax and slide to the side. His own strength will slam him into the wall and your positions will be reversed—now you are holding him against the wall.

If an opponent grabs you by both lapels or sleeves and tries to pull you forward, resist him. Then step quickly to your front diagonal and lower your hips. His sudden backward surge, combined with your lowering action, will slam him onto his back.

When engaging another swordsman, if you cross swords, a position known as *tsuba zeriai,* press forward as hard as you can. When the pressure has built up, suddenly step to the side and cut your opponent as he stumbles past.

There are numerous other variations on this strategy. They

are all based on the principle of generating a lot of potential energy in your opponent and then suddenly releasing your resistance to it—something moves, generally too much. The secret to making this strategy work well is in the increasing pressure. If you apply a steady pressure your opponent may learn to adapt to it and have time to think about what is happening. Increasing the pressure denies him the luxury of such an analysis.

MOMIJI NO HEIHO

A *momiji* is a red maple leaf. To cut with a feeling of momiji means that softly, like a falling autumn leaf, you strike down your opponent's sword to clear the center. This sounds simple and it is simple. All you have to remember is not to try too hard. That is *not* simple. Momiji no heiho is best accomplished by pretending your sword is a large feather—stroke gently with it.

A quick exercise will demonstrate how this works. Have your training partner hold out his arm parallel to the floor and tense his muscles. Now try to push his arm down. Even if you try to slam it down with a blow of your forearm, it is very hard to move. However, if you touch his arm as lightly as a feather, it is easy to force it down. Do not look at his arm or think about it. Just very, very softly stroke it downward with your fingertips. Breathe gently and use no more force than you would use with a newborn infant.

The essence of this teaching is: if you give your opponent nothing to resist, then he cannot resist you. If you have any difficulty with the exercise, remember this and reduce your effort.

When fencing, you will normally use this strategy in response to an attack. Evade your opponent's cut and then, lightly, cut his sword. This will force his blade further along its trajectory than he intended it to go, clearing the center for your counterattack.

In business or with an army, there are many uses for momiji. When you use a very gentle pressure against an enemy, you may find that you can move him around much easier than with brute force. If your touch is gentle enough, he may not even realize he is being manipulated until it is too late.

For example, in a debate you use this strategy by not disagreeing too much with your opponent—the greater your disagreement, the more he will resist. Argue with an attitude of, "Yes, you are right, but . . . ," and he will have nothing to resist. You keep doing this until he agrees with you.

In judo, the initial stage of a throw is called *kuzushi*. This is an action used to break your opponent's balance. It is usually done with a push, pull, or twist. Most beginners get much too physical, using more force than is really necessary for this. This causes their opponents instinctively to resist, making the throw itself very difficult to accomplish. It is much better to use a very small force for kuzushi. Then you can break your opponent's balance without him realizing it.

(If you want to be tricky, you can use an obvious kuzushi as a feint. Jerk your opponent forward as if you wanted to throw him to the front. When he flinches back against that action, throw him to the rear. This would be hijiki no heiho.)

Momiji should be applied with a feeling of shattering a brick with a feather—even though your body remains very soft, your spirit is very heavy. This requires great mental discipline. You instinctively try harder when you encounter resistance; momiji requires that you reduce your efforts.

SURIAGE NO HEIHO

Suriage is a strategy designed for use when you have crossed swords with your enemy and the position is frozen—neither of you can disengage without risking being cut.

When your swords are crossed, step in quickly while relaxing your arms. As you do this, lower your hips. Do not bend forward—lower your hips by bending your legs and keep your back perfectly erect. Now, somewhat slowly, rise while thrusting upward with your sword. Note that the bulk of the lifting action comes from your legs and not your arms. The lifting action is applied to the hilt of your opponent's sword, not to its blade.

Because his sword is being forced upward, opening his center to attack, your opponent is forced to step back to regain control—he cannot cut you without doing this because you are too close. As he steps back you should be in a fully extended upper-level position. As his sword disengages and starts down, follow it and cut his head.

Suriage is often seen in the sport of kendo, but few students of that art understand its theory well enough to do it well. The most common error is trying to use the strategy at too great a distance. That seriously reduces its power. Also, even if you manage to lift your opponent's sword at this open interval, you are too far away to cut him. Suriage should always be done so close that the hilt of your sword brushes against your opponent's chest as you thrust upward.

In the art of jujutsu, there is a technique named *tenchi nage,* the "heaven and earth throw." This is an empty-handed application of suriage. To practice this throw, have your partner grasp both your wrists firmly. Point your left hand downward and, with your right hand, do a suriage. You should be so close to him that the edge of your right hand slides across his chest as you thrust upward.

The opposing actions of your hands, one pointing up and the other pointing down, will bend his back and twist his shoulders. He can then easily be thrown. In older styles the throw is done with a strike; modern schools use a push. Actually, both methods are wrong. If you execute the suriage perfectly, your opponent's posture should be so distorted that the only thing holding him up is his grip on your wrists—if he lets go, he should fall. The actual throw should be mostly a process of shaking him loose.

Many students confuse suriage with kokyu chikara. Although tenchi nage does have a superficial resemblance to kokyu dosa, the philosophies and theories behind the two techniques are entirely different. Kokyu chikara is an application of breath-power against an enemy's physical strength. Instead of using the strength of your arms against your opponent's strength, you give up. Stepping in closely, you change the angle of attack and use your legs instead of your arms. You may use kokyu chikara to augment this, but you do that with any technique having vertical motion.

Due to its limited number of applications, suriage is on the borderline between giho and heiho. The essential teaching of this strategy, the item which makes it so important, is that everyone has a zone of strength. This is a spherical area around the abdomen—within this zone your opponent can generate great power. Suriage teaches that if you get between this sphere of power and your opponent's body you can operate with little opposition.

Chapter Twelve

Minari: Appearing

There are a variety of ways in which a strategist can use appearance to achieve a tactical advantage. These range from appearing stronger than he really is, which may cause his opponent to pause, to appearing weak, which can lure his opponent into attacking with less than maximum power.

Most examples listed in this chapter are concerned with enhancing your appearance. First and foremost, your appearance has a tremendous influence on your spirit, which can cause a chain reaction of events. You appear strong, so you begin to think strongly. This, in turn, makes you act strong. The result is that, by appearing to be more than you really are, you frequently accomplish more than you normally could.

The second major advantage of enhancing your appearance is its effect on your opponent. A positive image can cause your enemy to delay, or even cancel, his plans for attack—the best victories are always the ones you win without having to fight.

Finally, a positive image is the sine qua non of a true strategist. It is a sign of personal discipline, and discipline is something seniors have in abundance.

Although your emphasis should be on the positive appearance, there may be times when you might wish to take a

A strong appearance reflects a strong mind, and will tend to dismay the opponent.

negative route. For example, if you want to lure your opponent into an attack so you can use suigetsu no heiho, you should appear weaker than you really are. You can adopt a negative appearance by reversing many of the strategies in this chapter.

MINARI NO HEIHO

When studying *minari* you should not consider your true face, the real you; instead, consider what your opponent sees when he looks at you. What you regard as a proper appearance is not as important as what he thinks a proper appearance is.

There are many factors to appearance. Clothing, grooming, and weapons are the most obvious ones. However, even more important is your posture. A strong posture is universally accepted as the sign of a strong body and spirit. For example, it is known that muggers frequently select their victims by the manner of their walk. Where one person is obvious prey, another can walk in relative safety, simply because he does not walk like a victim. By acting as if he will never be attacked, he probably never will be. This is an excellent day-to-day application of minari no heiho.

The classical exercise for improving posture is walking while balancing a book on your head. This has been practiced by generations of young ladies and it works as well as any other exercise. Try to develop an erect, military posture. Always keep your shoulders back and down, your chin tucked in, your chest out, and your back ramrod straight. You can augment the basic exercise by clamping a marble in each armpit. (In kenjutsu, this slight tension is called "closing the armpits." It is used in most fighting stances.)

In addition to its psychological advantages—proper posture makes you feel stronger and your opponent feel weaker—good posture has a direct, physical advantage in combat. With a straight back you can turn faster than when you slouch. A curved spine is like a bent shaft in a motor.

About clothing, grooming, and weapons, little needs to be said. Good grooming and proper clothes are a sign of a successful man; clean, well-cared-for weapons are the sign of a professional warrior.

Businesses are the greatest practitioners of minari. Business people know from experience that a prosperous appearance may be just as important as actual profits. More than one company has survived, not because it was successful, but because it looked successful. In any business, if you take the attitude that your company is the best in the field and act the part, the public will generally assume this to be the truth without bothering to check the fact.

In business, it is always better to overdress. Then, if you walk into a formal meeting, you will be ready. On the other hand, if you step into an informal situation, you may ask, "Would you mind if I remove this damn coat and tie?" This establishes you as just one of the boys, a working man who is required to wear a suit by his boss. In other words, you can easily fit into any situation. However, if you start your day dressed casually and are forced into a formal situation, there is not much you can do about it.

In the business world, proper appearance means a suit. This is just as much a uniform for the businessman as a military uniform is for a soldier. Without this uniform, even though you act and talk like a professional, there will always seem to be something missing. You may be superb at your job, but the public will have subconscious reservations about your true ability. This places you in a negative position. However, when you dress as the public expects a professional to dress, people tend to accept your authority much more readily. This positive psychological position can be used to compensate for any actual weaknesses you may have.

Although there are some exceptions to this rule of formal dress (such as the entertainment world), these are few and far between. Nobody takes actors seriously except other actors. The same is true for any other subculture that wears costumes instead of clothes.

In any conflict, you must first determine what the standards for the arena are. Observe the competition and determine their style of dress, posture, and attitude. Then you exceed this, establishing a new standard which is slightly above them. This places you in a position of command. It is very hard for someone to compete with you when, subconsciously, he does not feel that he is your equal.

(Many martial arts instructors fail to heed this dictum. An instructor may spend decades mastering his craft and then wonder why he does not receive the same respect as other professionals. For the answer to that question, all he has to do is look into a mirror. Although he may have thirty years' experience and be a professional in every sense of the word, that is not how he is seen by the public. A sensei who truly understands the Way of Strategy will dress and act formally at all times. He takes the same rules that govern his actions in the dojo and applies them to his daily life.)

A positive, powerful appearance is of benefit in many situations. A negative appearance is like a cancer. The man who dresses and acts casually will soon develop a casual posture. Even worse, he will start to think casually. This is suicidal for a strategist. The perfect strategist never relaxes— he is formal in all situations. He even sleeps at attention. (This is not meant to be hyperbole—check your bedding when you awake in the morning. The covers should not be wrinkled.)

To counter the effects of minari, you must learn to look past the *omote* and see the *oku,* looking through the surface to see what is hidden.

The samurai used to say, "Do not be influenced by the color of your opponent's armor." In feudal Japan, a senior officer wore much more colorful armor than did a foot soldier. When a swordsman was faced with an opponent who wore this fancy armor, he might make the mistake of assuming his enemy's fighting skill matched his outfit. The resultant pause could be fatal.

When you study an opponent, you must see his true abilities rather than his apparent strengths. In the military or in business, this information is supplied by various intelligence services. In single combat, you must be your own intelligence service, but the rules are the same.

At first glance, an opponent who is much larger than you may seem very dangerous. Look again. Observe his posture and his walk. These will give valuable clues about his balance. If his balance is bad he cannot exert significant power, no matter how strong he is. (An entertaining exercise is to sit in your car and observe the people walking past on the sidewalk. It is amazing how many of them appear to be constantly falling. They tip their bodies with each step and then catch themselves at the last moment.)

Observe your opponent's attire next. Neatness is a sure sign of mental discipline. The style will indicate whether he is a leader or follower. Leaders dress conservatively; followers dress more rakishly. Followers think their clothes are avant-garde. Actually, they are just copying a smaller group of people. They do this to feel special, which is the first sign of a weak spirit.

Finally, look at your enemy's muscle tone. This is an indication of his speed, strength, and endurance. If his muscle tone is significantly better than average, it is also an indication of good discipline.

When all of these items are combined, they may give you a picture which is quite different from your original impression. When a cat is sick, the first sign is its failure to properly groom itself. It is the same with a person. Dangerous men have personal appearances which are just as polished as their techniques. Conversely, the man who never thinks about how he looks has a flaw in his spirit. As a strategist, you must look for such openings and use them to your advantage.

OBIYAKASHI NO HEIHO

Obiyakashi means to threaten your enemy. This is a specialized form of minari and/or maai.

Normally, to threaten an opponent is both time consuming and dangerous; and it is rarely worthwhile. This strategy can only be used against a beginner and then only in certain limited situations. You must never attempt to threaten a senior. Time spent threatening is time subtracted from hitting. If you are busy threatening a senior with what you are going to do, he will be busy actually doing it to you.

However, against a beginner a threat may be useful. The question at this point is usually, "Why bother with a strategy that is only viable against an inferior swordsman?" The answer is best stated by an old Japanese adage: "Even monkeys fall out of trees." This means you may make a mistake, no matter how good you are. Therefore, even a beginner should never be taken lightly. (Most students learn this the hard way in a dojo. Injuries to senior students are usually caused by beginners. A master will hurt you if he wants to; a beginner may kill you because he does not know how to control his technique.) Always use every strategy available to ensure victory. You never give a stronger swordsman an even chance if you can help it. Neither should you give a weaker opponent any advantage.

Although you use both appearance and position to threaten, they are really the same thing. If you use appearance to seem bigger, it will also make you seem closer to your enemy than you really are.

The standard method of threatening with position is to change the maai, entering the personal space of your enemy. Your enemy undoubtedly has a solid objective and strategy in mind. When you step forward into his personal space, you destroy all this. Now, instead of concentrating solely on attacking, he is forced to think about a possible defense. The time of transition, while he is mentally shifting gears, is when you should launch your attack. During that instant his mind is floating and he does not have a firm plan of action.

This strategy is most easily practiced in a karate or kendo format. Holding a rather open maai, allow your opponent to attack over and over again. Then, once he is in a very aggressive frame of mind, take a large step forward and adopt a powerful stance. You only hold this position for a fraction of a second and then attack. As you step forward you should note a minor hesitation in your opponent as he shifts from attack to defense. That is the moment in which you should attack.

Obiyakashi can also be used between nations. (A country has a personal space, just like an individual. It is just bigger.) If you advance on the borders of an enemy country, it will begin to shift to a war footing. This is when you attack. You advance, pause until it starts mobilization, and then advance again. Although appearances may be to the contrary, a country is weakest during the transition period. A nation at peace is well organized. So is a nation at war. A peacetime army may be small, but it has a solid and familiar command structure. However, during the transition from peace to war organization, the sudden influx of new troops changes everything. The military commanders are floating and incapable of rapid and unified action. With no one sure of who is in charge of any given operation, they are ripe for defeat.

If a business has had a monopoly in a certain area for some time, you can easily use obiyakashi against it. Simply move your company into the same area. The management of that company may feel very solid and comfortable, but as soon as you move next door, this harmony is destroyed. For a short time they will be floating, having no clear idea of their response—they have not yet made the transition from servicing their own customers to competing with you. During this phase, they can do neither effectively. However, you have your goals firmly established. This gives you a considerable advantage.

(Note: The "same area" in business can refer either to a physical location or a product. Moving your hardware store next to the only other hardware store in a town is the same as manufacturing a product which was previously only produced by one company.)

You must have a firm goal when you use obiyakashi. If you are moving toward a sharply defined objective, your opponent, in his moment of confusion, will be able to offer only minimal resistance. You must threaten, pause, and attack. If you have not established your target in advance, you will never be able to do this fast enough.

Even so, walk with care. You should never threaten a man you are not going to fight, and if war is your intention, it is best to get on with it.

UTSURAKASHI NO HEIHO

Emotions are contagious—by feigning a certain feeling, your opponent may be lured into feeling the same thing. As a strategist, you use this to your advantage.

For example, you might adopt an appearance of extreme

tension. Sink into a deep and powerful stance and gradually tighten your muscles. Continue tensing your muscles until your entire body is trembling with suppressed energy. After a few moments of this, when your opponent starts showing signs of equal tension, suddenly relax and glide in for an easy strike. If you do this quickly, your enemy will be so tense that he cannot evade your attack. This is a case of threatening your opponent with potential energy.

Another method of using *utsurakashi* is to appear very casual, as if nothing of importance is about to happen. Then, when your opponent relaxes, attack savagely.

When taking part in a contest, meet your next opponent outside the arena with a smile and a handshake, giving the appearance that you regard this as only a game. Then, when you actually face him for the match, act as if you are planning to kill him and eat the body. His momentary confusion in trying to shift from sport to total war will render him incapable of attack for a few seconds.

In a corporate board meeting, you can use a similar method by shifting your attitude after the meeting has been called to order. This sudden change may shock the other members enough to freeze them into an intellectual immobility.

Utsurakashi no heiho may be used at all levels, from the interpersonal to the international. It is commonly seen in international diplomacy, where the face that one country shows another may have little relationship to its true feelings. In business also, more than one company has been lured into a feeling of false security by a statement of, "we are not competitors; there is a big enough market for both of us." In either case, the results are usually fatal.

The mind has an inertia. By using utsurakashi to transfer a feeling, you force your opponent's mind into a certain channel. Then, while it is locked into this pattern of thought, you quickly change your attitude and attack.

RYOTE NO HEIHO

Ryōte means "both hands." In a limited sense, this means

you are ambidextrous and can fight equally well with either hand. This is a valuable ability, but this is not the true meaning of the strategy.

As pointed out earlier, there are two fundamental styles of conflict: juho and goho. Juho means you do not offer your enemy any direct resistance—your style of fighting stresses mobility and varied techniques. When your enemy pushes, you pull. When he strikes, you evade. Goho is the opposite of juho. Using goho, you directly oppose your enemy with strength and kime.

In its fullest sense, ryote means that you should be able to use both these methods with equal facility. Normally, you would pick one style to start an engagement and finish with the other.

For example, in a karate match you can start by adopting a deep stance and using only major techniques. By giving your opponent the impression that you are going to rely on brute power, you can influence his strategy. He knows a light attack will have little effect on you, so he, too, will concentrate on major techniques.

Once he has settled into this pattern, suddenly shift your style. Moving to a higher stance, attack with a series of techniques which stress speed and mobility. In doing this you are presenting an entirely different face—it is as if he is fighting a new opponent. If your opponent adapts to this new style, you can always shift back to your original format.

By shifting your fighting style in this manner, you can stay on the offensive. Your opponent, however, is always on the defensive, trying to figure out what you are doing before he commits himself to the attack.

A superb example of this heiho was the use of cavalry as mounted infantry. A cavalry unit, although very mobile, cannot deliver accurate fire from horseback. Knowing this, an enemy army could plan accordingly—it could risk certain attack formations against a cavalry troop that it would never consider using against dug-in infantry. However, by giving the command "dismount and fight on foot!" a cavalry commander had the best of both worlds. The enemy force was then faced with an opponent who, within a matter of seconds, had completely changed its appearance and style of combat. This was, in many cases, much more effective than having a permanently mobile cavalry unit or a consistently dug-in infantry detachment.

Ryote no heiho is based on the axiom that it is impossible to be both strong and mobile at the same time. When you tighten your muscles you cannot move about freely; when you are moving you cannot exert great strength. This is true for an individual or an army. By learning to fight in both styles, you give your enemy two men to oppose.

KOCHIKU NO HEIHO

A *kōchiku* is a tall bamboo. By making your body like a tall bamboo, you can weaken your opponent's spirit.

When engaged in combat, there is a great tendency for a beginner to crouch. He does this in an effort to protect the vital areas of his body. Aside from the fact that this greatly reduces his mobility, it is a sign of a defensive spirit. You should avoid this at all times.

When you face another swordsman, stand as tall as possible. Stretch your body upward, as if you were suspended from heaven by a string attached to the top of your head. Stretch your spirit upward also, approaching combat with a large and imposing appearance. Make your body like a bamboo standing tall and straight above the forest.[1]

When your opponent, crouching to protect his vital points, compares his height with yours he will shrivel even further. Seeing you standing tall and straight while he is crouching, his spirit will weaken and he will feel inferior. You should accentuate this disparity by always moving to higher ground and attacking at an upper level to keep your opponent's head down. This destroys his spirit.

There are always those who prattle on about unifying the mind and body. How ridiculous! Your mind and body are always unified. When they are not, it is called being dead. There is no need for esoteric exercises to unify your mind and body; they are as unified as they are going to get from the moment of your birth. Because they are unified, if you engage in exercises to strengthen your body, you will simultaneously strengthen your spirit. Also, because body and spirit are one, if you allow one to cower from an enemy so will the other.

Just as foolish as those who talk about special exercises to unify mind and body are the people who state that external appearance is not important, that the only thing that

Kochiku, another aspect of minari, means to stand tall, giving your opponent more reason to fear you.

really counts is what a person is like on the inside. This philosophy is only espoused by the weak and inefficient. Anyone who has personally dealt with power knows that a man is a complete unit—one part of his being affects all the others. A person who has poor physical posture will also have poor mental posture. Casual clothing is a sign of a casual mind, and sloppy speech patterns indicate sloppy thinking.

Kochiku no heiho is an outgrowth of the Japanese successes as behaviorists. They learned the value of this system of training during centuries of warfare and it is the fundamental philosophy of all traditional dojo. An instructor realizes he cannot directly manipulate your spirit. However, he knows from experience that he can mold it by molding your body. It was during the process of straightening a student's body in order to straighten his spirit that kochiku was discovered.

It is not that a senior strategist devotes much time to thinking about his appearance—that would be an affectation. It is simply that his external appearance is always correct due to years of disciplined training. With each year of training, he becomes more and more like his sword: straight, hard, and polished. He pays no more attention to his appearance than does a mirror to the image it reflects. The surface of the mirror reflects what is before it; the surface of the man reflects what is beneath it.

A graphic illustration of this can be seen in any dojo. When you watch a mixed class, you can see a great difference between the appearance of the juniors and seniors. Beginners will always seem in the process of losing their uniforms— perhaps a belt will come untied or a jacket will be in disarray. The seniors, however, will always be neat, no matter how violently they are practicing.[2]

Because the seniors look neater, they also seem taller than the juniors. Their physical precision seems to add a couple of inches to their height. They stand straight and tall, appearing to look down at the beginners. They do not do this pretentiously; it is much closer to the way an adult regards a child. Kochiku is unique among strategies because it is automatic, a part of your daily life. After a few years of training you will find that it requires a conscious act of will to slouch.

The effects of this are so immediate and so obvious that it is amazing more people do not use the heiho. Take the time to engage in this experiment: First, change into a good, three-piece suit, then pause to consider your feelings. Next, switch to a casual outfit and do the same. You will discover that both your physical posture and mental attitude are quite different. If you study the way people react to both of these appearances, you will note an equally great difference.

Kochiku takes advantage of the fact that most people assume that an expensive frame contains an expensive painting. You adopt an affluent attitude, maintain a perfect posture, and stand on high ground to appear taller than your opponent. This gives you a spiritual advantage because, from infancy, people are conditioned to accept a taller person as an authority figure.

You can use this strategy to great effect in competition. When you step up to the line and face your opponent, stand as tall as you can and adopt an imposing attitude—stretch your body upward and act as if you are looking down at him. To your opponent you will appear taller. He will assume that this means you are also stronger and better than he is. Even if he is a much better fighter than you, this strategy will provide you with a few seconds of spiritual superiority. If you hurry, you may win the match before your opponent discovers how weak you really are.

An army may use this strategy by giving an appearance of superiority over its enemy. Note that the advantage need only seem to exist. Of course, it would be much better to have a real kochiku, but if that is impossible, creating a belief in superiority is better than nothing. In many cases, reality is only a state of mind—what you are is less important than what your enemy thinks you are. If the enemy army sees your forces holding an apparent advantage, it will approach the engagement with an overly cautious spirit. This gives you a real advantage.

A corporation gives the impression of great height by having an imposing front office. Note the preference by large companies for penthouse offices in tall buildings. An expensive penthouse does not accomplish more work than a cheaper basement facility, but it has a tremendous effect on the people who visit it. The basement office serves the customer; the penthouse suite controls him.

This is an example of a Westerner using a traditional Japanese strategy without realizing it. The executive may understand the advantages of an impressive facade, but it may take him an hour to explain them. The Japanese strategist, on the other hand, merely looks at the skyscraper, nods, and says, "kochiku no heiho," expressing the entire concept in one phrase.

Because when you stand tall and straight it is easy for you to turn, you should use kochiku with circular attacks. You enhance the effectiveness of these attacks by forcing your opponent to crouch. His poor posture makes it very difficult for him to turn enough to counter your move.

By adopting a bold front with an army or a business firm, you force your enemy into a defensive attitude. This attitude, too, is a form of crouching, and his ability to turn is greatly restricted. Again, attack with a circular motion. With an army, this would mean a flanking attack. In business, you would not try direct, head-to-head competition; change your advertising strategy to attack your competitor from a new direction. For example, if your competitor is stressing quality, adopt a campaign that says: "The superiority of our product is so obvious, it does not merit discussion. However, you may not be aware of the superior service our company offers."

Kochiku is the strategy of making your opponent feel that you are much better than he is, with a resultant weakening of his spirit. There are many methods, both psychological and physical, and they all justify intense study.

NOTES

1. There is an *okuden* here, a hidden teaching, so study it well.
2. This is also true for military-recruit training centers.

Chapter Thirteen

Sente: Initiating

Sente is the "leading hand." This refers to the man who hits first. This is a very important strategy, because, as an axiom of combat, the man who lands the first solid blow will usually win the fight.

Westerners have been raised with some rather insane slogans and theories. Notable among these are: good guys always win; fight fair; and, give him another chance. None of these have any basis in reality.

A good man does not win because he is good; it is only the strong of mind and/or body who win consistently. Fighting fair means following someone else's rules. This is proper in a sporting contest but in a war it is madness. In a real fight you always want your enemy to fight according to a set of rules. Then you fight without rules. As for giving an enemy another chance, that does not even rate discussion.

Rules of war are created by people who do not fight. War is an ugly business and there is nothing you can do to change this fact. Therefore, when conflict is necessary, you should get it over with as fast as possible. The best way to do this is to hit first and destroy your enemy with one blow.

ICHI NO HYOSHI NO HEIHO

Ichi no hyōshi, the "rhythm of one," is done with a feeling

189

of *ikiuchi,* "striking in a single breath." This means you step straight in and cut down your enemy with one stroke of the sword. There is no thought of get ready, get set, GO! You just *GO!* This strategy is a distinctive feature of all Japanese martial arts.

Ichi no hyoshi is an alien concept to the Western mind. From childhood, you have been raised with the concept of preparation: you prepare for a test at school, you take your mark for a footrace, and you get ready for combat. All these preparations are the mark of a loser.

As mentioned earlier, in combat there is a thing known as a suki, a momentary gap in your opponent's concentration. Typically, a suki only lasts a fraction of a second. You must seize this opportunity instantly, detecting the suki and attacking while your opponent's mind is floating. In the East they say, "when a void is found, fill it with a technique." The Western equivalent is, "strike while the iron is hot." Both statements are based on the same concept: sente.

The average person's reaction time is about one-tenth of a second. Depending upon the situation, this can seem to be either a blink of an eye or an eternity. The rhythm of one is a strategy for taking advantage of this instant of time. It teaches you to spot an opportunity and attack while your enemy is trapped by his reaction time. This is done by creating conditioned reflexes.

When a master typist is at work, he does not look at the keyboard. At the master level, a visual stimulus will cause the correct finger to move without a conscious act of will. The reason he types so fast is not because his fingers are moving fast, but because he wastes no time thinking. Ichi no hyoshi is a combat application of this principle. When you detect a suki, if you have created the proper conditioned reflexes, you will cut instantly—it is as if you had touched a hot stove and your hand had jerked of its own volition.

There are many ways to demonstrate this concept when you introduce a new student to the Way of the Sword. One of the easiest is to watch the tip of his sword when he cuts.

Start by positioning the student in an upper attitude. Then instruct him on command to cut downward as fast as he can. As you shout "now!", carefully observe the tip of his sword. Usually it will move backward a fraction of an inch before starting forward with the cut. This is an indication that, instead of thinking only about cutting, he is thinking, "get ready—*cut!*"

If the backward motion is large, position a bar horizontally behind his sword. Then every time he moves his blade back it will strike the bar, giving him instant negative feedback. For fine tuning, constantly urge the student to relax and maintain mushin. Also tell him to imagine that his sword is being pulled forward into the target. Comment on the quality of every cut. By a process of trial and error, the student will eventually develop the proper motion.

A more advanced training method is to have the student sit in a position of seiza. Stand behind him and, with no warning, toss a ball of paper forward over his shoulder. Throw the ball so that it strikes the floor at a point about five feet in front of him. When he sees the paper ball, the student draws his sword and cuts at it with a horizontal stroke. (Beginners should use bokken instead of shinken. If they get in too much of a rush with a real sword, they may cut through their scabbards and amputate a few of their fingers.)

A beginner will find this exercise impossible—the ball will strike the floor before he even starts moving. However, once he learns the correct mental attitude, it becomes quite easy. In fact, he will soon reach the point of having to slow down in order to hit the target; at full speed his blade will move too fast and pass under the ball. As in the standing exercise, the key is relaxation and mushin.

This is not nearly as hard as it first seems. When the student fails, constantly remind him to relax and empty his mind. Usually a beginner will fail ten or twenty times in a row. Then, by accident, he will have the proper mental attitude and start succeeding every time.

It is very important for you to note that there is nothing physical about this strategy; it is purely mental. You are not making your sword move faster. In fact, you will often be slowing it down. However, by eliminating all preparatory thoughts, you begin to gain a tremendous time advantage.

This is the secret behind Miyamoto Musashi's statement that "the sword that cuts fast cuts nothing." Ichi no hyoshi no heiho is a strategy for cutting slower than your opponent but getting there first.

To apply this strategy in the field, you must develop a comprehensive set of techniques. These techniques are then practiced until they become conditioned reflexes. This type of training is called *renshū,* and it is done with an attitude of forging the mind and body into a weapon. The key is constant repetition, training to and then beyond the point of exhaustion. This is no fun, so a high degree of self-discipline or a strict instructor is needed for success.

A fine example of renshu is the emergency drills for the crewmen of warships. Sailors are trained to handle a wide variety of emergencies until they can do their assigned tasks automatically—every contingency is planned for and re-hearsed until the crew operates like a finely tuned machine. When the crew is well trained, a sailor can be aroused from a deep sleep and be at his proper post and well into his assigned task before he is completely awake. The process of acquiring this ability is never enjoyable, but it wins battles.

An army patrol uses a similar strategy by training each of its members to respond automatically to any situation. When the point man makes contact with the enemy, each member of the patrol races forward to his assigned spot and lays down a predesignated pattern of fire. Contrast this with the reactions of an untrained unit. Untrained men will drop to cover and await further orders. Although that may seem safer, in reality all it does is give the enemy force time to get orga-nized.

In the business world, use of ichi no hyoshi is devastating. Because business conflicts move at such a slow pace com-pared with hand-to-hand combat, if you react in a fraction of a second instead of days, your competitor does not stand a chance. This means that, like the swordsman, you must create a set of conditioned reflexes for your business. For example, your advertising department should have appro-priate campaigns ready for any situation. In addition to being prepared for positive actions by your competitors, they should be ready for their own company's mistakes—the effect of an error is greatly reduced if your positive advertising is aired the same day as the negative news reports.

Top-grade competitors in sport karate tournaments are masters of this heiho. In this type of match, the blows are stopped a fraction of an inch short of the target, which makes speed of primary importance. To win you must spot an opening and launch your attack in the blink of an eye— the tiniest delay between stimulus and response will eliminate any chance of winning.

Ichi no hyoshi no heiho is a very simple strategy and anyone can master it. All it takes is a few years of brutally hard work. Limit the number of your techniques and repeat them over and over until they become as automatic as breathing. Then forget about getting ready. Just stand quietly, waiting. When an opening presents itself, your technique will happen automatically. If it is properly done, you will not even have time to realize what is happening.

MUNENMUSO NO HEIHO

Munenmusō means that you are free of all thoughts and plans—you disconnect your mind and allow your body to operate on its own. This is a very difficult concept to master.

A beginner always wishes to know how it is possible to cut with no thought of cutting and no target in mind. According to his reasoning, any physical action demands some form of mental direction. Munenmuso shows that this reasoning is faulty—you do not have to direct your physical actions with your mind.

In the beginning of your training, you are a man with a sword. Then, after several years of training, you become a swordsman. The physical and mental differences between these two states are easy to see and understand. However, there is a third level. In the third stage, you are no longer a swordsman, you are a sword. You no longer direct your cuts, because there is no you left. Your ego has been transformed into a weapon. Everything that is you has been welded to your sword; you *are* your sword. At this level you are truly

Poised and ready, with no thoughts and no desires.

following the Way of the Sword, and words are no longer a suitable method of communication.[1]

One small (very small) example of munenmuso is occasionally experienced while driving a car. You may suddenly realize you are several miles farther down the road than you were the last time you noticed—it is as if you have lost a few minutes of time. Who was driving the car during this interval? *It* was. You were not conscious of driving or paying any attention to your surroundings, you just did it. This only happens to experienced drivers and only on familiar roads; new drivers are far too nervous to let go like this.

It is the same in war. Only after long years of experience, when you have seen and done everything, will munenmuso occur.

In the dojo you will discover an excellent method for developing this strategy: the kata. What makes this method so valuable is that you are never good enough at the kata to satisfy your instructor. Even after decades of practicing the same set of moves, he will always manage to find a flaw in your performance. After a few years these flaws become infinitesimal, a matter of a fraction of an inch or a degree of an angle. You are still hounded to correct them, for your goal is not to be good, or even great. Your goal is absolute, 100 percent, total perfection. Obviously, you will never achieve this. However, in this case, the trip is more important than the destination.

The beauty of kata as a training device for munenmuso is that it forces you to think about the kata instead of yourself. This is called going into the form. (There are several stages of studying a kata. They are marked by going into, or coming out of, the form. Each stage has a different purpose.) After enough time you cease to be aware of yourself and only see an image in the mirror. It is as if you have become this image. There is no you left; there is only technique. Like an Alice in Wonderland, you enter the world of no thoughts and no plans.

Seniors love this type of thing. Because they have eliminated the need for thought, they have much more time available for technique. This, in turn, means they can move much slower and still win.

It is not unusual to see some grand old swordsman gliding slowly around a class, striking at will. He may be so ancient as to seem near death. His sword is constantly trembling with the palsy of age, yet somehow his cuts always score. And somehow, even though he moves slowly, he can never be touched. The old man acts as though he is out for a casual stroll, while the beginners race around frantically trying to score a point. No matter how hard the juniors work, their best efforts will rate only a senile giggle from the old master.

Invariably, the juniors will reason there is some secret

Shitachi leaps into the air in a dramatic move from Ten No Kata. Caught in a kneeling position when his opponent attacks with two rapid cuts, he leaps high into the air, blocks twice and switches his foot position, to land in an advantageous position. The camera has captured him in the midst of executing a perfect maru-dome block.

trick involved. How else could a weak old man constantly defeat strong young men? To their questions the elder will only reply "kata," and giggle again.

There is a trick to munenmuso, but it is not a secret. The trick is practice, practice, and more practice. You combine this with time, a lot of time, and the result is a sword that wears a man.

SEKKA NO HEIHO

A *sekka* is a spark from a flint. This is a specialized form of sente—your technique is like a spark generated by your enemy's attack.

To use this strategy with a sword, cut with a twitch of your hips. Do not raise the tip of your sword even a little; just go straight in. Imagine a line from the tip of your sword to the target. Your blade travels along this line as you leap forward, driving strongly with your hips, legs, and shoulders.

A classical example of this strategy is seen in the formal sword kata known as *ki musubi no tachi.* In this form, you begin by facing your opponent with the tips of your swords touching. As he raises his blade to cut, slide straight in and cut his wrist. The traditional method of teaching this is to advise the student to imagine there is a string connecting his opponent's sword to his own belt—as soon as the sword moves, he must move his center forward as if he is being pulled. If you do this with the correct spirit, you should cut your opponent's wrist as his hands are on the way up, not after he has actually started the cutting action.

It is all too easy for this to degenerate into a mere touch, as is often seen in modern kendo. Properly, you should be able to cut quite deeply with this technique. This requires a thorough understanding of the Way of the Long Sword. In particular, you must understand the theory of cutting and the role that the *sori,* the curvature of the blade, plays in this action. A person who cuts only with his arms will never be able to cut very deeply with sekka.[2]

While the strategy of ichi no hyoshi may be used at any time, sekka is usually used as the response to an attack. Standing calmly, you await your opponent's opening move. Then, without an instant of delay, you leap forward and strike. It is as if he is the steel, you are the flint, and your technique is the spark.

An essential element of this strategy is that it must always be augmented by power from your center. This is true for an individual or an army. In individual combat, if you cut only with your hands, your blade can be easily slapped aside. This leaves you open for a counter-cut such as *kotegiri,* a quick slash to the wrist. Thus, if you cut only with your hands, you may lose your hands. It is the same with troops. If the group that first contacts the enemy is not supported by the main body, it will be lost.

A military force wishing to use this strategy must learn to attack in a straight line from any position. It wastes no time with consolidation or organization; the troops just charge directly toward the enemy. A key requirement for success is the proper training of junior officers. Each and every one must live by the naval dictum: "A captain can do little wrong if he lays his ship alongside that of an enemy." Officers and men must be trained to react instantly and aggressively to any enemy move. (Note: Troops trained in this manner will require keepers.)

The valuable thing about this heiho is that it catches your opponent in the middle of his attack. He is physically committed and will not be able to counter your attack.

You can occasionally use this in a debate. If you have determined where your opponent's argument is leading, counter it before he states it. In other words, if he is saying, "A is less than B, B is less than C, C is less than D, therefore D is greater than A," you can easily counter with sekka. As soon as he says "B is less than C," jump in with a statement which proves how small D really is in the absolute sense. Because he has not even mentioned D, this should destroy his whole chain of thought. The fact that D really is bigger than A is of little importance. His confusion will allow you ample time to capture the leading role in the debate.

All variations of sekka no heiho are based on the simple axiom that a straight line is the shortest distance between two points. For more advanced studies, you should give careful consideration to the fact that this is only true on a plane surface. On a sphere, the shortest distance will be a great circle; on other surfaces, more complex lines are required. For example, consider what your line of attack should be when you are separated from your opponent by several yards and both of you are standing on the side of a small hill. If you experiment with this on broken terrain, carefully measuring various routes, the results may be surprising.

NOTES

1. See Chapter Two.

2. The arms play a secondary role when cutting with a Japanese sword; most of the work is done with the hips. You drive forward, allowing the blade to hit the target at a forty-five degree angle to its long axis. The sori makes it bite into the target.

Chapter Fourteen

Kawari: Changing

Things have inertia. So do ideas. If you understand this inertia, you can change your strategy and attack before your opponent can change directions.

It is easy to use your enemy's physical inertia against him. To do this, you should increase the range and power of his attack. If you force him to come in fast, over a considerable distance, he will generate great momentum. You can force him into this type of attack by adopting a very agressive attitude. He will then, instinctively, fight from an open maai. Also, because he realizes that a weak attack will not work against you, he will attack very strongly.

To create mental inertia, allow your opponent to succeed with a certain strategy. The longer that his strategy works, the more resistant he will be to changing it. A change in your strategy when your opponent is locked into a pattern of success is much more effective than if you had tried it after he had failed in several attacks.

SANKAIKAWARI NO HEIHO

Sometimes, when fencing, you may attack several times and be unable to penetrate a strong defense. *Sankaikawari,* the "mountain-sea change," should then be used.

There are large changes in strategy and there are small changes. In this heiho, your change should be very, very large. The difference between your old strategy and your new one should be as great as the difference between a mountain and the sea.

For example, you can shift from the offense to the defense. Your enemy's defenses are too strong for you to penetrate, so give up. Suddenly shift to a defensive attitude and retreat a few steps. This may lure him into attacking. Then, while he is busy chasing you instead of concentrating on his defenses, attack again. Now your attacks will be against a greatly weakened defense.

Another way of applying sankaikawari would be to make a radical change in the target and style of your attack. After making a series of large cuts toward your opponent's head, suddenly drop to the ground and attack with short thrusts at his body.

The previous two examples illustrate the difference between mental and physical inertia. In the first case, your enemy's forward motion was used to reduce his defensive capabilities. In the second situation he had been successful in his upper-level defense. Once settled into that rhythm, it is hard mentally for him to shift to a lower defensive position.

Whatever the change you elect to make, it must be done with speed; a gradual shift would allow your opponent to adapt. You should change strategies as quickly as you flip a light switch, going from light to dark in an instant.

Superb examples of this strategy are seen in football games. An offensive team will make a series of long passes to spread out the defense. Then they will switch to a running attack, with great success. Reversing the pattern works equally well. By starting with a series of running plays, the offense tightens up the defensive team. Then they shift to the long pass. The value of a big change is clearly seen in these two examples. A shift between short runs and long passes will work well. However, a combination of screen passes and sweeping runs will not be as effective—there is not enough difference between these two types of plays to take advantage of the opposition's inertia.

To get ready to use this strategy, divide all the techniques you know into sets according to similarity. Then practice fighting with each of these sets until it is comfortable. For example, a karate student could assemble a set of kicking techniques and practice them from an erect posture. Then he could have a set of powerful punches that he uses from a very low, solid stance. A third set could consist of fast, snappy techniques, delivered from a mobile stance.

Typically in a karate match, your opponent will devote the first moments to studying your style. Then, after he has seen how you react to a few feints, he will commit himself to the attack. However, by fighting with a variety of styles, you can keep him confused. Start by fighting in one style—do not use a technique from one of your other sets, no matter how tempting it may be. Then, when you sense your opponent has figured out your style—he will start to get aggressive—make a radical change. It should now seem like he is fighting a completely new person. Even your personality should be different.

The result of making a big change is that he must curb his aggression and start all over, moving about carefully and feinting to see how this new style of yours is going to react. If you keep this up, he will always be on the defensive while you are always attacking. If a certain style is effective, continue to use it. But, as soon as your opponent starts to defend well against these attacks, shift to something new.

This strategy works best when an art has a wide variety of techniques to choose from. Obviously, it is a natural for karate. However, even in an art as limited as boxing, it can be used effectively. For example, you can practice a left-lead style which is characterized by long-range jabs and mobility. To complement this set of techniques, develop a right-lead style which relies on powerful hooking attacks to the body. Start the match in one style and then suddenly shift to the other. During the moments of confusion when your opponent is trying to adapt to your change, you should score well.

Sankaikawari is also very effective in advertising. As a manufacturer, you may be stressing the economy of your product and competing head-to-head with another company that offers the same thing. If you suddenly shift to stressing performance, you will have no competition until the other company generates a new advertising campaign. If your competitor should also change his ads to stress performance, you can shift again. Now you push the quality of your product. During each of your changes the competing company will be trapped by inertia—it will need time to analyze your new ads and then respond to them.

The best counter for sankaikawari is another sankaikawari—you respond to a big change in strategy with an equally big change in your own strategy. You normally try to avoid this type of situation, because by using a certain strategy your opponent has demonstrated his familiarity with it. It is usually best to select a strategy that your enemy does not know. However, in this case, fight fire with fire. When your opponent uses sankaikawari, do not attempt to adapt to his new style. Take a third path. To use the previous business situation as an example, when your competitor shifts from stressing economy to stressing performance, you should change to quality or style.

With an army, use this heiho by changing your style of combat. Integrate your armor with your infantry and proceed methodically from one enemy strong point to the next, fighting set battles as they occur. After a time, the enemy will start to concentrate along your line of advance and his resistance will grow increasingly strong. When this happens, free your armor and let it operate as a separate unit, striking deep into enemy territory and bypassing strong points. While the enemy commanders are struggling to adapt to your change of strategy, attack with your infantry.

The key to using sankaikawari no heiho effectively is making your change of strategy as large as possible—the greater the change, the greater your enemy's confusion. Your shift must also be fast and without warning. If you take immediate advantage of this, you should only have to do it once. If you are having to use several changes during a battle, the problem is normally that you are changing too slowly, allowing your opponent time to adapt to the new strategy.

RYUCHO NO HEIHO

Ryūchō, to "flow or bounce," is a variation on sankai-kawari. The rules which apply to the mountain-sea change strategy also apply to this one.

In combat, there are two basic methods of connecting various techniques to form combinations: one technique can flow into the next, or you can bounce from one to another. Combinations from the art of karate offer excellent examples of this idea.

If you execute a *mawashigeri,* a horizontal, circular kick, and it misses the target, your kime will snap the foot to a stop. (At the completion of any technique, you tense all your muscles for a fraction of a second to ensure maximum power transmission.) The secret to ryucho lies in how much kime you apply.

If you tense your muscles very strongly at the end of your kick, your foot will bounce back to its starting position. In this case, it is natural to follow the recoil of your foot with your body. Then it is equally easy to follow the mawashigeri with a jab from your opposite hand—you kick with your right foot and, as this foot recoils, punch with your left fist. This is the bounce method of creating a combination. The recoil of the first technique provides the initial movement of the second one.

Bounce Method

Flow Method

Your opponent evades your kick and closes the distance...

...only to be met by your punch.

Or continue turning and shift feet.

Then score with a back kick.

To create a flowing combination, which is called a *nagashi waza,* do not use as much kime. In the preceding example, if you reduce the amount of focus at the end of the kick, your foot will be slowed down but not stopped. As it continues on its original trajectory, allow your body to rotate with it. Then, as you turn, you can easily follow your first kick with *mawashi ushirogeri,* a spinning back kick. Note how the first technique flows naturally into the second one.

This procedure can be used to create sets of techniques in most arts. Once you have rehearsed these, apply them as in sankaikawari.

Starting with flowing techniques, you set up your opponent. After he has seen a few of these combinations, he will understand your style and be able to predict where your next technique is coming from. When you sense he is preparing to counter, shift to the bounce style. You should score with your second technique because it is launched from an unexpected direction. Again using the preceding examples, your opponent was expecting your mawashigeri coming from his left to be followed by a mawashi ushirogeri, also coming from his left. However, you recoil strongly from the first kick and attack with a left jab. As he dodges to his right to avoid the anticipated kick, he should step into your punch.

When commanding an army, use ryucho when you are faced with a series of objectives. Start by taking them one at a time, halting to regroup after each battle. Then suddenly take two in one thrust, not pausing for an instant after the first battle. Just allow the momentum of your troops to carry them on to the next target. Because the defending troops at that post were expecting a short delay, you will destroy their timing.

Ryucho no heiho has many variations, so you should study it carefully. This requires a detailed technical analysis of your art. Examine the techniques one at a time, focusing on the natural recoil. By varying this recoil, new combinations should be easy to discover.

MAGIRI NO HEIHO

When you stir up your opponent's spirit with a series of

small changes, it is called *magiri.* By changing your strategy frequently and randomly, you confuse your enemy and gain the advantage. These changes can involve technique, target, or timing.

For example, in a karate match, attack with a low-level foot sweep and then a high-level strike. Follow this with a middle-level thrust. This is a very common application of magiri. By attacking a wide range of targets with an equally wide variety of techniques, you spread out your opponent's defenses enough to allow penetration.

Assuming an equal level of training, as is normally the case in a tournament, your opponent should be able to block just as fast as you can attack. To negate this ability, apply magiri to your timing. Instead of attacking with a rhythm of 1 ... 2 ... 3 ... 4 ... 5 ... 6, break your offense into a random pattern such as 1, 2, 3 ... 4 ... 5, 6. By mixing up your techniques, targets, and timing, your opponent will not know what to expect or when to expect it.

You should also consider that the lack of a pattern is, in itself, a pattern. This means that if you never repeat a target and then attack high-low, your opponent will be ready for a middle-level technique. Random does not mean that you can never repeat something; a series of three identical techniques aimed at one target can be part of a random pattern.

Also, do not become trapped into doing only the most logical thing. Occasionally pick a secondary target or use a technique which does not logically derive from the preceding one. This will keep your opponent totally confused.

This illogical behavior is very important when both you and your opponent are senior. He will expect a beginner to do something stupid and will be prepared for anything when he fights one. However, he will not expect another senior to make a big mistake. In such a case, a bad technique may catch him by surprise. There is an amusing dojo story that illustrates how this can work.

One day the headmaster of a dojo was training with one of his senior students. They had been fencing for several minutes when the instructor made a pivot, pinched a nerve in his knee, and dropped to the floor like a stone as his leg collapsed. The student, with seemingly one big step, instantly retreated twenty feet and adopted a tense defensive posture.

The instructor looked up and asked, "I am all right, but what are you doing way over there?"

The student nervously replied, "Sir, I never saw you make a move like that before. I did not understand what you were doing and did not want any part of it."

The point of this story is that, by doing something so completely unexpected, the instructor destroyed his student's offensive strategy. In this case, because of the instructor's accidental fall, the student was unable to follow up on his advantage. However, the message is clear: a bad mistake can create a better opening than a good technique. (Note: Due to its magnitude, this example is closer to a sankai than it is to a magiri.)

The objective of magiri no heiho is to stir up your opponent and diffuse his defensive capabilities. Then, when he is spread out, you have a good chance of scoring with a single well-focused attack. This is slightly different than sankai-kawari. In that strategy you make one large change and take immediate advantage of it. Magiri, on the other hand, is done continuously. Its goal is not a momentary confusion but an overall weakening.

It is important to use magiri in an aggressive manner, because it takes some time to take effect. This delay can allow you to start thinking about your own survival. Then, once you fall into a negative attitude, your techniques become very weak. To counteract this tendency, always attack. Pursue your opponent with a barrage of techniques, never allowing him to rest. This will generate maximum confusion.

Magiri is a fundamental concept of guerrilla warfare. By refusing to become involved in a set battle, yet constantly raiding your enemy from a wide variety of angles, you gradually weaken him. In this manner a relatively small force can defeat a large army.

When engaging in guerrilla warfare, some paramilitary groups make the mistake of falling into a pattern. Although they attack different targets at random intervals, if they fail to use different techniques they may be destroyed.

But most groups avoid this pitfall by varying both the style and strength of their attacks. For example, when using a commando unit, you should vary the strength of a raiding party from individual to battalion level. If you always attack at squad strength, the enemy commander has only to disperse his troops at platoon level to defend himself. However, if you use variable strengths, he never knows what to expect. This forces him to concentrate his forces while trying to control a large area, which is impossible.

A viable counter-technique for this guerrilla use of magiri was not available until fairly modern times. Now, however, modern communications and transportation equipment allow an effective response. A properly equipped army can totally eliminate guerrilla opposition.

The defending army is broken down into units of squad strength, and each unit is supplied with a helicopter and an integrated computer-radio. The individual units are then distributed in a grid pattern. The computer-radio is programmed to transmit unit location and enemy strength at the touch of a button. The general receives this information and, again with the touch of a button, transmits an attack order of any desired level. Upon receiving this order, the computers decode it and display course-to-target information to the appropriate units. The computer will also spread out the attack commands to various units to prevent one area from becoming stripped of defenses—this takes into account the possibility that the enemy move may be a feint.

When adopting a grid-dispersal system of troop deployment, each unit must be fully mobile. The system will not work if only a portion of the troops is designated as a strike team while the rest are dug in. Partial distribution would result in certain areas being thinly covered, allowing a substantial enemy formation to form. By having his army totally dispersed, a general can prevent this from happening. He can also, with a single command, focus any desired amount of force, from one squad to his entire army, on any point.

Such a system of combat allows the modern army to use its greatest asset, modern technology, to maximum effect against a small and mobile enemy. All that is required in addition to standard equipment is a pocket-sized computer integrated with each unit commander's radio. The maximum distance between each unit in the grid is a function of response time: the time it takes for a helicopter to get airborne from a cold start plus its air-travel time to potential targets.

Conflict between individuals is the same as conflict between armies. To defend yourself against an opponent who is using magiri, you too can use a grid-dispersal system of defense. This means you adopt a perfectly balanced defensive posture. Do not be lured into focusing your attention on any specific area. The secret to this lies in not looking at your opponent; always look through him and off into the distance. This lets you counter his attacks objectively, maintaining your tranquil spirit. It is only when you allow yourself to consider what your enemy is doing and become personally involved with it that you can become confused.

To use magiri in business, you should consider the axiom that a company can only be competitive in two of three possible areas: cost, quality, or service. Pick any two of these, but you cannot handle all three at the same time. Applying magiri means you should select only one area instead of two. In that way, your company will become far better in the area you focus on than your competitor, who is trying to do two things at once. This, in turn, will force your competitor to focus more of his attention on your chosen area. You, however, are constantly changing. For a week you advertise lower prices, then for a month you stress better service. This is followed by a return to your original ads or a shift to stressing quality. The result is that your opponent is forced to try to compete in all three areas, which is impossible.

Magiri no heiho is a strategy of constant variation. You fight fast and slow, hard and soft, simple and complex. Your targets and techniques change from second to second. Even your personality changes. Sometimes you are very aggressive and sometimes, for no apparent reason, you shift to the defense. You become a random series of logical and illogical events, always moving and never predictable.

Your opponent is forced to try to deal with this. He is allowed neither the time to rest nor a chance to use a coherent strategy. It will drive him crazy.

Although magiri no heiho is an ancient strategy, its most famous exponent was Miyamoto Musashi. He used countless variations of this heiho to win many of his sixty duels. He was especially adept at using changes in timing to confuse and frustrate his enemies.

HANASHI NO HEIHO

Hanashi, "letting go," means that when one strategy does not work you let go of it and try something new.

Although becoming entrapped by some particular method might seem a pitfall only a junior would fall into, such is not the case. Past successes can make a strategy so attractive that even a senior can become ensnared by it. Examples of this are almost infinite in number and variety.

During World War II, battleship admirals were slow to adapt to modern air warfare, with disastrous results. It seems to be taking an equally long time to convince many modern admirals, men who were raised on a diet of successful aircraft-carrier operations, of the value of small patrol craft armed with antiship missiles. A general can be just as susceptible to strategic prejudices as an admiral. Many such men are learning the hard way that the helicopter armed with antitank rockets is making armor tactics from the past obsolete.

Hanashi is based on the principle of juho, nonresistance. Most people do not fully understand this. They think of its most well-known application, jujutsu, as merely a Japanese form of wrestling. Although they may know that jujutsu is based on nonresistance, they do not consider that this requires mental as well as physical flexibility.

One method of increasing your mental flexibility is described in Chapter Three. You should pursue this, and any other training methods that seem appropriate, with great vigor. Remember, your goal is not to think about different things, but to think about things differently. For an example of the degree of mental flexibility required, consider the difference in value structures and lifestyles of a New York executive and a Southern farmer. You must learn to think like either of these men with equal ease. It is only when you can make a mental transition of this magnitude that you will be able to use hanashi.

Although it is most frequently applied to physical strategies, hanashi actually means that you must be able to let go of an idea. You must learn to think and act in any required pattern, not just in your favorite way. Miyamoto Musashi stated this best when he said, "A swordsman should not have a favorite sword." A gambler must know when to fold his cards, and a businessman must know when to close a company. It does not matter that it was a good poker hand or especially enjoyable company; when it is time for hanashi, a person must let go and not look back.

It is frequently seen that the ability to utilize this strategy decreases with age. Old armies and old navies have a great tendency to stick with outmoded techniques simply because they have always worked in the past. A glaring example of this is the little-known fact that many European nations were still using horse cavalry when the Germans attacked with tanks and aircraft in World War II. Even the United States, a relatively young country, was no exception to this. Moving from the field of battle to the field of business, the first companies to offer time-payment plans and mail-order sales were thought insane by their more conservative colleagues.

Because of the tendency for mental inertia to increase with age and success, hanashi is one strategy in which a beginner may have an advantage over the senior. The beginner has so few victories that he has not yet built up prejudices, either for or against, the various techniques of war.

Hanashi no heiho is one of the most difficult of all strategies to teach, because the average person's attachments and prejudices go so deep. Although many people believe that they are quite flexible, they rarely are. There will always be hard spots within their spirits, areas of ideals where there is no give at all. If you do not think this is true for you, try to pet a tarantula with the same affection that you pet a cat. Although your rational mind may tell you there is more to fear from the cat than the spider, old phobias are deeply rooted. While this may seem to be a radical example, it is not. For example, the strategy of *aiuchi,* discussed in Chapter Eighteen, requires that you acquire the same attitude about dying as you have about living.

A good physical example of hanashi can be seen in the technique known as *jodan hazushi.*[1] To practice this, stand in a middle-level attitude and let your training partner grasp your wrist firmly. If you try to pull free you will find it very difficult. To use hanashi in this situation, let go of the idea of escape. You should even let go of the idea that you are being held. If you can completely ignore your partner, simply raising your sword to the upper-level attitude, his hand will pop free from your wrist.

This exercise is a good example of how closely your mental and physical attitudes are related. On your first attempt to free yourself, because your body was trapped, so was your mind. Try it again. You will note that, as soon as your partner seizes your wrist, your attention is drawn to that spot. Because you were thinking about your wrist, even though you wanted to escape, you could only try with a portion of your spirit. However, when you shift your thoughts from your wrist to raising your sword, you can free yourself with little effort.

Jodan hazushi is an example of a situation where your instinctive reaction is not the best method. Your natural reaction to being grabbed is to try to escape. However, in this case you let go of your natural instinct and do something different.

When fencing, you may have attacked several times only to have your cuts easily avoided by a skillful opponent. So, give up. Cease your attacks and just stand there. Now, when your opponent raises his sword to strike, you can cut him with ease because he will be thinking about attacking instead of evasion.

When trying to throw your opponent in a judo match, if he resists strongly, give up. Then quickly turn and throw him the other way. He was pulling away from your original throw, so you throw him in the direction he is trying to go.

Whatever your goal may be, remember that there is usually

more than one path to the top of the mountain. If one route is blocked, forget it and try another. As long as you never lose sight of your final objective, you will win.

A method which has proven its effectiveness should not be given up simply because it is old. Neither should it be retained for that reason. Hanashi no heiho does not mean that you should try something new simply because it is new; it means you should not stick to something old just because it is familiar. It is this fine line, the division between effective and familiar, which requires careful attention.

In business, a rigid adherence to old, familiar ways will only cost you money. In combat it can cost you your life.

HENKA NO HEIHO

Henka are variations on a basic technique. Although there are some techniques that can only be done in one way, they are the exceptions rather than the rule; most techniques will have hundreds of possible variations.

For strategic purposes, you should concentrate most of your attention on studying the different possible conclusions of basic techniques. These henka are usually taught during the intermediate stage of training, after you have developed a strong foundation of fundamentals.

To apply henka no heiho during a fight, you avoid repeating the ending of any technique—each time you use a technique, finish in a different manner. This prevents your opponent from developing a proper counter for it. For a simple example, consider the *maegeri,* front kick, of karate. If it is your habit to return your kicking foot to its original position after the technique, change it. One time, after the maegeri, allow your weight to shift and bring your foot down well forward. The next time you use this technique, do not put your foot down at all. Just kick again from where it is.

With a sword it is standard practice to return the blade back along the line of the cut. Vary this by occasionally following through and cutting from the opposite direction. Another option is to stop on the centerline and immediately thrust.

Henka is not a major strategy—it seldom results in immediate victory. However, because your opponent must wait for the end of your attack to see where you will be, you will frequently be able to launch a second attack before he counters. In addition to this advantage, your enemy is forced to design a new counterattack for each of your techniques as it occurs. One defensive strategy will no longer work because you are using so many variations.

NOTES

1. This is one of the Daito-ryu *aiki inyōhō* waza.

Chapter Fifteen

Kage: Concealing

Kage is a very popular word in the language of strategy. It is used as a component of the names of many techniques. Literally it is translated as "shadow," but figuratively it has many meanings. These can range from the act of concealing your strategy from an enemy to suppressing his techniques. This group of strategies contains some of the deepest and most esoteric theories in combat, so study them with care and be prepared to spend several years before you achieve a full understanding.

Great victories are mostly achieved through great intelligence work. You try to conceal your intentions from your opponent and he tries to hide his plans from you. The first person to penetrate this shield, to see through the shadows of deception, is usually the winner. The actual intelligence gathering may be done by a government agency, a unit of a general staff, or an individual's five senses, but the process is basically the same. In all cases it should be augmented by a healthy dose of intuition.

Concealing your strategy is a delicate art, one that takes a lot of effort to master. Among beginners there is a tendency to telegraph a technique—they reveal their intentions by some slight motion. The fastest way to cure a beginner of this dreadful habit is to strike him with a stick. Every time

What happens next? The cut following this posture from the iaido kata, Tsubame No Ken, is blindingly fast, brutally powerful, and toward the rear. An excellent example of kage.

he makes a telltale move, hit him. He will soon learn to explode into motion without giving his plans away with some extraneous action.

To see through the shadows means that you sense what your opponent is about to do, even when he is trying to conceal his plans. One of the many ways to do this is to use your ears to listen to his breath—he will probably attack after a

Waki gamae is a posture frequently used with various applications of kage.

deep inhalation. This tells you when he will attack, but not how. For an indication of his intended technique, observe his posture. There is an excellent training method for this.

An instructor will stand, facing a student, and assume a fighting stance. The student observes the instructor's posture and makes an estimate of his weight distribution. After a moment of observation—the time allowed for this should be gradually reduced until the student can do it in a fraction of a second—the student might say, "sixty-forty," to denote that the instructor has 60 percent of his weight on his front foot and 40 percent on his back foot. Then the instructor shifts to a new stance and they repeat the exercise. (The student's progress will be much faster if the instructor hits him with a stick every time he makes a mistake of more than 10 percent.)

The advantages of developing this ability are readily apparent. An enemy cannot advance rapidly if his weight is too far back. Neither can he kick freely with a foot that is bearing more than half his weight. By being able to discern his balance, you can understand both his intentions and his capabilities.

It is of such things that the myriad strategies of kage are made. You perceive and you conceal. You suppress and shadow. You seek reality while hiding it.

GETSUKAGE NO HEIHO

Getsukage, the "moon-shadow," is often used as a general rule of fencing for beginners. The rule states that, when you do not know what to do, you should copy your opponent. A proper application of this allows a beginner to look like a master, even if he does not have the slightest idea of what is happening. He may not accomplish anything, but at least he will look good doing it. This will conceal his lack of ability from his opponent.

For example, when your opponent raises his sword to cut your head, copy him. This action will have two results. First, because your sword is now covering his intended target, it will suppress his technique. He may be forced to change his strategy in mid-stride. Secondly, if he moves his sword to cut, it will open his head to your own attack. When he realizes this, it will act as an additional suppressant. If he gives up on his original plan and shifts position for a different attack, you will copy him again for similar results.

The obvious difficulty with this strategy, and the thing that makes it a very advanced technique, is the timing. If you raise your sword a fraction of a second too late, your opponent can ignore it and drive straight in. He will then cut both your wrist and your head—you will be helpless because you are still in the act of raising your sword. Beginners get away with using this strategy as often as they do only because they are normally fencing with other beginners. The junior opponent will usually hesitate for a fraction of a second before committing himself to the attack, allowing ample time to copy him.

Getsukage requires that you learn to move in exact synchronization with your enemy. The classical training method for developing this ability is kiri gaeshi, which is discussed in Chapter One.

Although the physical application of getsukage is easy enough, the spiritual aspect is another matter entirely. It necessitates completely suppressing your ego. As long as there is the slightest trace of your individual personality remaining, the strategy will never work the way it is supposed to. This requirement is what makes getsukage almost impossible for a beginner to execute properly. Although his sword work may be quite good, there will invariably be enough of his ego left to cause a slight delay. Although this pause may be so small as to go unnoticed by another beginner, a senior will make devastating use of it.

When it is used properly, getsukage should make your enemy feel that he is fighting himself. To understand this better, press your palm firmly against your partner's hand. No matter how carefully you both try to balance the pressure, there will always be a slightly mushy feeling present. Now press your own hands together. No matter what the pressure, it will feel much stiffer. This is because your left hand can instantly react to any change of pressure from your right hand—both your hands are working with each other. However, when you did this with your partner, you were reacting to him. The tremendous difference between *to* and *with* is readily apparent.

You can use this demonstration as a training method. Practice pressing palms with a partner until it feels the same as when you do it by yourself. You will quickly discover that as long as you retain any awareness of yourself this exercise is impossible.

In business you can use getsukage to foil a corporate take-over. When a competitor starts buying stock in your company, you should do the same to him. You match his purchases proportionally, share for share. If you can do this instantly, and with a vigor that matches his, you will force him from the position of an aggressor into a defensive attitude. You must move fast and strong, for if you delay or act timidly he will suppress your counter.

Another obvious example of this heiho is the modern arms race. By achieving a state of military parity, two countries effectively disarm each other. Neither can fire a missile without receiving exactly as much destruction as it inflicts.

Getsukage is not very well thought of by seniors because it is indecisive. It is, basically, a method of forestalling rather than destroying an enemy. More often than not, both partners will just wind up back where they started. This is why the strategy is so popular among nonwarriors, such as diplomats and politicians. They are more interested in not losing than in winning.

This is a popular strategy in fencing only because there are so few seniors. Also, because so many beginners use it, there are almost as many variations as there are swordsmen. This can be a source of some confusion among the juniors. They see a certain technique labeled as a getsukage and believe the name refers to the physical action. This is usually not the case. As with most strategies, the name refers more to the way you think than the way you move. Getsukage no heiho means that you think like the shadow of the moon. You follow the motions of your enemy and cover his strategy with darkness, suppressing his techniques.

TACHIFUMI NO HEIHO

Tachifumi means "to stomp on a sword." This is a rather poetical way of saying that each time your enemy attempts to cut you, you immediately stem his attack. This is a form of the previously discussed moon-shadow strategy. Another variation, to be discussed later, is *kageosae*, "to hold down a shadow." But, whereas getsukage is indecisive—it is an action of closing the gate on an attack—and kageosae is small, tachifumi is very aggressive and vigorous.

When your opponent raises his sword to cut your head, immediately cut his wrist. If he brings his sword to his side in preparation for a horizontal slash, step in firmly and slam your shoulder into his chest. If he changes his grip to thrust, slap his sword aside. No matter what he attempts, you instantly counter it. You are not countering his technique; you are countering his preparations for the technique. This will keep your opponent in a constant state of imbalance. You throw a dark shadow over his plans, so that even he cannot see what he should do next.

In a karate match, your actions are analogous. When your opponent shifts his weight to his left leg, kick his right leg. If he lowers his shoulder, punch his arm. If he lowers his hips for stability, move away. When he adopts a higher stance for increased mobility, jam in close and force him into a corner. By doing these things you can stem his attacks before they are launched.

The same approach applies to a judo match. Before your opponent can throw you, he must move into position and, simultaneously, break your balance. To foil this, as soon as he starts to move, slam your body into his.

In a battle between armies, you use tachifumi by looking past the front lines and observing the enemy as a whole. If he starts to build an airfield, bomb it. When he attempts to build a bridge, destroy his heavy equipment. If he begins to marshal troops, attack the staging area. Whatever the enemy starts to do, immediately attack the area where he is doing it and disrupt the attack before it is launched.

In business, the proper time to mount a counter advertising campaign is before your competitor starts production; do not wait until he actually has his new product on the market. Although his patent application will prevent you from competing directly, there is nothing to stop you from campaigning against the new product. This can so delay and disturb your competitor that you will have time to develop a competitive product of your own. Then you can halt your negative ads, allow a little time for the public to forget them, and start advertising your own product.

Tachifumi means that you must always study your opponent carefully and in totality. Whether your enemy is a sword or an idea is of no importance. Keeping your weight well forward, you remain constantly poised for attack. Then, the instant you find a target, you leap forward and destroy your opponent's strategy.

The previous strategy, getsukage, suppressed your enemy's technique gently, covering his strategy like the soft-edged shadows of a moonlit night. Tachifumi no heiho is more like the darkness accompanying a great storm. Your opponent will not understand what is happening or what he should do about it as his best-laid plans are blown away at the instant of their conception. The battlefield becomes as dark as midnight and he cannot perceive any possibility of successful action. This will rapidly destroy his kokoro.

This is a superb strategy. Although it was made famous by Musashi in his classic book *Go Rin No Sho* (A Book of Five Rings), it typifies the fundamental thought of such aggressive styles of combat as those of the Itto-ryu heiho and shotokan karate. If you had to restrict your studies to a single strategy, this should be it. More clearly than any other heiho, tachifumi illustrates the value of the most basic rule of combat: attack, ATTACK, *ATTACK!*

KAGEUGOKASHI NO HEIHO

When you cannot discern the intentions of your enemy, you must move the shadow that is in the way. You do this with *misekake,* a feint. (A feint is a technique that looks real but is not fully extended.) By faking an attack, you draw your opponent's technique out of the shadows and then, when you understand his plan, you devise a strategy to defeat him.

It is very, very dangerous to relate to your opponent's inscrutability merely by waiting. Waiting allows your opponent to launch his attack whenever he is ready, and it may be too strong for you to evade. By using a misekake you can force him to move when you want him to, not when he decides the time is right. Then you will be in perfect balance and ready to receive his attack. Also, because he moves at a time of your choosing instead of his own, the power of his attack will be reduced. This makes it even easier to avoid.

For example, suppose you sense that your opponent's strategy may involve a powerful counter of some sort. In this case you should fake a strong attack. Then, under relatively controlled conditions, you can study the nature of his counter. When you understand it, you can devise a new attack to negate its effectiveness.

Using karate as a format for this example, feint with maegeri. If your opponent shows a tendency to dodge to his right, use a *maegeri-mawashigeri* combination. This is a technique which starts as a classical front kick, but halfway through it you snap your hips around to transform it into a circular kick. As your opponent slides to the side in order to evade what appears to be just another linear kick, your foot will circle to follow him.

If your opponent is very aggressive and you feel his strategy may involve an attack, draw him out. Present a target but do not try to counter, just concentrate on evading his technique. This will let you discover his speed and range. Then you can devise a suitable counter.

Whatever the actual method, once you have succeeded in using *kageugokashi,* you should apply the knowledge at once. If you delay, even for a moment, your opponent may have time to change his strategy. Then you will have to start over.

Although it is often used by beginners, this heiho is not well liked by most seniors. The reason is that it can become very negative—overuse tends to lead to too much dancing around and thinking. This, in turn, creates a weak and defensive spirit. Seniors prefer to tighten the belly, empty the mind, and step straight in with a decisive stroke.

In business, not understanding the intentions of a competitor is a common problem. Industrial espionage is the standard solution, but when tight security makes that impossible, kageugokashi should be used.

For example, if your competitor is about to launch a new advertising campaign, and no matter how hard you try, you cannot discover its nature, you should draw him out. You could spread a false rumor that you have seen his new ads and are busily at work preparing a countercampaign. This may force him to release his ads before their scheduled dates. Then, once you have actually seen a few of them, you can get to work on a suitable counter. The fact that your competitor started his campaign a little early may not seem like much of an advantage, but he is now operating on your schedule rather than his own. This may not be much, but it is better than if you had done nothing.

In warfare between armies it is similar. If you sense an impending attack but are not sure where it will occur, do something to force your enemy to change his schedule. One way of doing this is to make a great show of strengthening your defenses. Your enemy may then feel that if his attack is to succeed, it must be now or never. (This last point is that which makes some people very nervous about the present-day arms race.) Because of attacking early, his strength will be slightly reduced.

Simply stated, kageugokashi no heiho is a strategy for forcing your enemy to march to the sound of your own drummer. Generally, the advantage this creates is very marginal. However, in a battle you take everything you can get.

KAGEOSAE NO HEIHO

The strategy of "pressing down the shadow" is used when you have managed to discover the intentions of your enemy. This is a *very* advanced heiho. Do not expect very much success with it for your first twenty years of practice.

The essence of kageosae is to make a small move which

forces your opponent to change his strategy. This in turn forces him to attack with a technique which is lower on his list of favorites. Because he will probably not be quite as proficient with the alternative technique, you will have a better chance of countering it.

When you sense your opponent is going to cut your shoulder, shift your sword to that area and take a small step forward. Because his target area is covered or the distance is not quite right, he will be forced to change his plan and set up for a different attack. If he appears to be preparing for a stroke to your head, lean in sharply as he raises his sword. This will place you a few inches too close, and your opponent will be forced to take a small step back to adjust the maai. As he does that, lean to your rear, again spoiling the maai.[1]

These and similar changes that you make are so small as to be almost invisible. If you apply this strategy with enough subtlety, your opponent may not even be aware of what is happening. It is all a matter of minute adjustments of posture and distance. When you do this constantly, forestalling each of his attacks as it is being prepared, you cast a shadow over his strategy.

Whatever move you use to forestall an attack, it must be perfect. If it is too small, too early, too late, or of any other extreme, it will not work. Your enemy will decide to blast right through the interference, even though he realizes that the results of his attack will be less than optimum. This makes kageosae a tool for only the most senior of strategists.

Timing is important for most strategies; for kageosae it is critical. The proper time for this heiho is the single instant of time between your opponent's decision to use a certain technique and his first physical move to implement it. When you succeed in acting in this instant, it is called *sensente*.[2] Although, at first glance, it may seem that you have to be a mind reader to accomplish this, it is not quite as hard as it seems.

There is a simple exercise you should practice to prepare yourself for kageosae. You and your training partner sit facing each other. You both hold your hands up in a position of preparing to clap. Relax completely and then, when you sense that your partner is about to clap, you try to clap first. If you have any physical or mental tension you will never beat him. If you are too nervous, you will be clapping at random intervals when your partner had no intention of moving. However, if you can relax completely and empty your mind, you will not have too much trouble sensing the subtle changes in your partner that signal his impending motion.

Your training partner should never treat this exercise as a contest. He should attempt to keep his mind a blank and then suddenly think, "clap!" He should definitely not make any attempt to try to fool you. If you clap when he had no intention of doing so, he should shake his head negatively; when you succeed in beating him, he should nod his head in encouragement. By this combination of clean intentions and instant feedback, he will greatly enhance your training.

For a much more advanced form of this exercise, instead of clapping your hands, clap your right hand against your partner's left. This exercise teaches you to predict position as well as timing.

Start by holding your right hand close to the center of your chest. Moving at a random time and toward a random position, your partner will snap his palm forward and then back as fast as he can. Your objective is to clap your palm against his before he returns his hand to the center of his chest. Because he can shoot his palm out to any position within his reach, it is very hard for you to hit it. You should not try to compensate for your inability by leaning forward in an effort to reach his withdrawing hand. Neither should your partner slap at a point in space which is outside your normal range. As in the previous exercise, the secret is complete physical relaxation and mushin.

To achieve some degree of success in an exercise such as this is no great feat. However, to be able to use this ability in the heat of combat is another matter. That will require many years of practice.

You can observe kageosae in action at almost any football game. The offensive team goes into a huddle and the quarterback calls the next play. As the players break from the huddle and assume their positions, you may note a sudden shift in the defense—it has sensed what is going to happen and is modifying its formation to counter it. This forces the offensive quarterback to call an audible: he changes his strategy while his team is lined up. If the defensive team again modifies its formation to foil his plan, he may be forced to change a second time. This can go on until the quarterback has to call for time out and talk with his coach.

To use kageosae in business, you should disrupt your competitor's plans while they are still on the drawing board. For an example of this, consider the automobile industry. If you discover that your competition is designing a small sports car, shift the stress of your advertising to emphasize how safe your large model is in a collision or how much passenger space it has. This may cause your competitor to pause before going into production.

When commanding an army, look beyond the enemy lines and discern his plans. If he marshals troops for an attack on your left flank, quickly shift some of your forces to that area. If he prepares a frontal attack, raid his flank to force him to shift his troops to that area. Whatever he plans, act quickly to stem his attack before it is launched.

When using kageosae, you should endeavor to make your moves as small as possible. If getsukage is the shadow of the moon, kageosae is the shadow of a shadow. Your enemy should not realize what you are doing; he should just become more and more frustrated.

An excellent counter to kageosae would be any technique delivered with the spirit of sekka no heiho. Because you attack from wherever you are with no preparation, you do not allow your opponent a chance to counter. (Obviously, the reverse is also true. The longer you prepare, the more susceptible you are to kageosae.)

SHINKAGE NO HEIHO

Shinkage means "spirit shadow" and it is a method for covering your true intentions. The essence of this strategy is using one technique to distract your opponent while you score with another. The difference between this strategy and a simple feint is that when using shinkage, you maintain the pressure of your original move. A feint will only distract your enemy for a fraction of a second; shinkage can hold his attention considerably longer.

For an example, consider the basic boxing strategy of a jab to the head followed by a hook to the body. You normally do this as two distinct moves—the left jab is withdrawn as your right hand hooks to the body. To apply shinkage to this combination, do not withdraw your left hand. First, jab with your left hand toward your opponent's head. Then, when he blocks, bear down on his blocking arm with your left. As he instinctively resists this pressure, hook to his body with your right fist without relaxing the pressure of your left hand.

Shinkage no heiho is not just a physical distraction. True, you are tying up your opponent's blocking arm, which makes it easier to score with your second technique; but even more important, for a moment you are shifting his mind from offense to defense. For the first instant that you apply pressure, his mind will be drawn from your body to his own arm. He will not be aware of your right hook until it hits him.

You can do a similar thing when fencing by not withdrawing your sword after your cut is blocked. Instead, bear down hard. Then, as your opponent strengthens his block, kick him in the groin.

To apply this strategy with an army, use half of your forces to attack one end of the enemy line. In a battle of this type the flanking troops will expend the most energy because of their large movements. When their resources become depleted, they should attack and stick to the enemy. Then they may be resupplied while their compatriots at the other end of the line are moving about, striking at targets of opportunity.

The objective of shinkage is to trap your opponent's mind. In his normal mode of combat, he will concentrate on hitting you. His mind is focused on the target, your body. When you apply shinkage, however, his attention will momentarily shift

When your opponent attacks with uraken, block with your left hand.

Maintain the pressure of the block to draw his attention toward your left hand and strike his side with your right fist.

from your body to some portion of his own. This makes the rest of his body vulnerable.

Shinkage works best against an opponent who is not very advanced. An experienced opponent, because of his strong mental discipline, will be very hard to distract.

METSUKE NO HEIHO

The *metsuke* is the point at which your eyes are focused. This has many strategic applications.

When you engage another swordsman, you should not look directly at him. Neither should you look at his sword. Adopting an attitude of mushin, defocus your eyes and observe your enemy as if he were very far away—look through him and off into the distance.

Using your eyes like this will greatly increase your peripheral vision. To test this, focus your eyes on a point and then check how far to the side you can see without moving them. Now defocus your eyes and check again. Your field of vision should be considerably broader. You can increase this even further by looking down at a slight angle. This is of tremendous value when engaging more than one opponent—you can see what they are all doing without moving your eyes.

In individual combat, look toward and through your opponent's body, specifically his solar plexus. This allows you to note instantly any motion of either his hands or his feet. More important, you can detect motion of his hips, which will always precede a major attack. This last point is of great importance, because it allows you to determine how far your enemy will advance when he attacks. There is a fine exercise for practicing this, and you should study it well.

Stand facing your training partner, in a natural stance. Adjust the maai so that, by extending his arm, your partner can just touch your chest with his fingertips. Then he should step forward and extend his hand to touch you. As he does this, you step back while maintaining the maai. As you retreat, you match the length of his forward step so that, when all motion stops, his fingertips are barely touching your chest. To make the exercise interesting, your partner will vary the length of his step each time.

If your metsuke is proper, you will find that, by observing his initial hip motion, you can easily predict the length of his step—a large step will always be preceded by a powerful hip rotation. The value of developing an ability to judge this is obvious. If you know how far your opponent will travel, before he completes his attack, you can position yourself for a devastating counterattack. (This is a form of seeing through the shadows.)

When using this method at night, look away from your opponent instead of through him. The center of your eye is crowded with color receptors; the side contains mostly intensity sensors. By observing your opponent from the side of your eyes, you gain increased sensitivity to motion. However, because this technique reduces the total amount of data about the combat area that you can perceive, it should be used with caution.

The two types of sight, seeing and perceiving, are called *ken* and *kan*. There are philosophical as well as physical differences between these two methods.

When you see an opponent with *ken* there will always be a duality: *you* see *him*. This prevents you from remaining objective about the battle—as soon as your eyes focus on the target, so does your mind. You trap yourself just as surely as if you had entered a cage. However, if you perceive instead of seeing, you free your spirit. As you look off into the distance, your opponent becomes just another item in your field of vision, no more important than any other object.

Takuan, a famous Zen master, discussed this in great detail in a series of letters which are well known to all sword students.[3] The essence of his teaching was that a swordsman should never allow his mind to stop on any one point; the mind should flow through the events of combat like wind through a forest.

When you (physically) defocus your eyes and look off into the distance, your mind will also defocus. Because your metsuke is nowhere in particular, your mind is nowhere in particular. In this state, you can flow freely from one task to the next without pausing.

To get a feel for this defocused state, pick two points on your desk which are about two feet apart and two feet away from you. Focus first on the right-hand point and touch it. Then shift your focus to the point on your left and touch it. Do this as fast as you can. This illustrates the wrong way to strike at two targets. No matter how fast you move, you will always use two distinct motions: one-two!

Now that you know the wrong way to hit two targets, try it the right way. Look off into the distance, directing your line of sight midway between the two points—do not allow your gaze to stop at the surface of the desk. Now, without changing your metsuke, touch the two points in succession. You will find that you can do this very smoothly. It should feel like one motion instead of two distinct actions. This is because your mind does not stop on either point.

There are some moral implications to this type of sight. When you do not allow your mind to stop on a target, you become disassociated from it. Such an impersonal attitude is very important for a professional soldier. In a war, if you stop to consider that the stuff splattered all over a wall used to be a person, it becomes very easy for your enemy to turn you also into a splatter. A soldier's spirit should be just as impersonal as the bullets he fires.

The advantages of a proper metsuke are best seen in multiple combat. When your mind does not stop on one target, you can move freely from one enemy to the next. Even if you do this at a comfortable pace, you will still be much faster than your opponents. They may be racing about frantically, but because they allow their minds to stop with each technique, they will always be behind the pace of the battle and trying to catch up.

As you can see, metsuke no heiho gives you a powerful advantage over an enemy. However, to make full use of this strategy, you must also consider the metsuke of your opponent. By controlling the point of his gaze, you can also control his mind and body.

To control the metsuke of your enemy, you must give him something to focus on. Sometimes you can do this with a sudden motion. Then, once you have him looking at something, you can shift his gaze to something else with little difficulty. There are many ways to do this. However, none of them work very well against a senior. Because he has seen everything before, there is little you can do that he will find interesting enough to look at.

Beginners, on the other hand, are very susceptible to metsuke no heiho. They have so little experience that almost anything you do will draw their attention. Be alert for this. If a beginner looks at your sword, kick him. If he looks at your feet, cut him.

Another way to draw a beginner's attention is to shift your feet constantly. If you keep doing this, his attention will be drawn to them. Keep it up even longer, and he will start adjusting his maai relative to your feet instead of your sword. Then you can draw close enough to cut him easily.

You could also cut his hand to focus his attention. Even if this is a very small injury, he will focus on it long enough for you to make a decisive stroke. Again, this will only work with a beginner. A senior can receive a major injury without blinking an eye—he has been hurt so many times before that pain has lost all shock value.

Occasionally a beginner will even focus his own attention, perhaps by trying to grab your sword arm. To grab impersonally requires much practice, so if he tries to seize you, let him. As soon as his hand closes on your arm, his mind will be drawn to that point. Then he becomes an easy victim for almost any technique.

Metsuke is frequently used in a karate match. When you are fighting someone who allows you to get close, extend your left hand toward his face instead of using the standard fighting stance. When his attention is drawn to this, attack with a low kick.

There is an assassination technique using a sword that is another variation on this theme. As you are walking along on the left side of your senior—this is the traditional position for a junior—quietly, with your left hand, strip the scabbard back from your sword. As it falls to the ground behind you, the strange noise will attract the attention of your victim. As he turns to look, draw your sword and cut him.[4]

A similar variation may be seen in the technique of *sodezuki* from the Tenshin-ryu. Standing to the right of your victim, point to something with your left hand. When he looks, draw your short sword with your right hand. The drape of your left kimono sleeve, the *sode,* will conceal this action, allowing you to thrust into his side through your sleeve.

Although such distractions may at first seem childish, they can work with devastating effectiveness. However, as you strive to control your opponent's metsuke, take great care that your metsuke is not also drawn to your actions. When you stomp your foot or raise your hand, it must be as if the hand or foot moves itself. Your mind remains nowhere in particular.

In the most limited sense, the use of metsuke is a giho, a technique. It is a good technique, with many variations, but that is all it is. However, metsuke no heiho is much deeper. To go from giho to heiho, you must think of the point of gaze as a tool and manipulate it constantly. You do this both with your own metsuke and that of your opponent. When you have mastered this, the *shinobi* waza, "techniques of stealth," will be revealed to you.

It is impossible to close a discussion of this nature without a brief comment about looking at your opponent's eyes. According to popular thought, by doing this you can read his intentions. This strategy was created by Hollywood and bears little relation to reality. True, a beginner's eyes will signal his intention to attack, but this information is useless. The problem is that his reactions are very slow. The signal from his eyes is so far ahead of his actual body motion that, if you react to his eyes, he will cut in the wake of your block. On the other hand, the eyes of a senior reveal nothing. It is like looking into a deep pool, and he will cut you to pieces while you are waiting for some change.

NOTES

1. Determining when an attack will occur is easy; discern-

ing its target is hard. Refer to the discussion of haragei in Chapter Seven.

2. *Sente,* the "first hand," is to take the initiative. *Sensente,* "before the first hand," is to wrest the initiative away from your opponent.

3. Takuan Soho (1573–1645) wrote the *Fudō Shinmyō Roku* to Yagyu Tajima No Kami Munenori (1571–1646), the second-generation headmaster of the Yagyu Shinkage-ryu.

4. A Japanese sword has a wooden scabbard, called the *saya.* The sword is worn thrust through your sash, edge up. Drawing this bare blade without cutting yourself after the saya has fallen away will require much practice. There is nothing between a razor edge and your side but the thickness of your kimono.

Chapter Sixteen

Ojite: Responding

In any form of conflict, it is always best to set the pace, forcing your enemy to conform to your actions: you act and he reacts. However, due to the fortunes of war or your own lack of ability, this may not be possible. In such a case, you may be forced into a situation of *ōjite,* responding to your enemy's actions.

Reacting to, instead of with, your opponent is less than ideal. In such a situation you should not plan on winning a decisive victory. Your primary goal should only be to regain control of the battle. Do not ignore an opportunity for victory; just do not plan on it.

Your strategy for responding will frequently involve the execution of two techniques on a single beat. When you are lagging behind the pace of the battle by a half-count, this will move you into the lead by a half-count. The second technique of this combination, which will rarely be decisive, should be immediately followed by a third, stronger technique.

The secret to many of these three-technique combinations lies in your breathing. Typically, you exhale with two stress points while executing the first pair of techniques, inhale, and then exhale strongly for the third technique.

It is the measure of the current state of the arts of combat that the techniques of ojite are the primary focus of attention in many modern schools. This is totally wrong. These techniques should only be called upon as a last resort, when you are in a losing position. Instead of studying how to get out of a losing situation, you should be studying how never to get there in the first place.

NITŌBUN NO HEIHO

Nitōbun is a broken-rhythm attack, which is used against an opponent who is much stronger than you are. Against such an enemy, no matter how strong and fast your attack is, he will be able to block it. Because you cannot seize the advantage directly, you use this strategy to take it indirectly.

To use nitobun, start a technique and then pause for a fraction of a second about halfway through it. This slight delay will disrupt your opponent's timing enough for your original attack to score. It is very important to do this, not with a rhythm of one-two, but with a feeling of "o-ne." If you use a definite two-count rhythm, a strong opponent may recover in time to counter. However, by using only a slight hesitation, you deny even the fastest enemy this recovery time.

Nitobun is an excellent strategy for a karate match. If your opponent is very fast and has blocked each of your attacks, you can shift to this heiho and score at will. For example, start a punch with your hip and shoulder, pause for an instant, and then continue with your shoulder and arm. Your initial surge of motion will trigger your opponent's block. The tiny pause, however, will cause his blocking arm to pass its intended point of impact before your fist gets there—your fist should pass behind his block to strike the target.

The most common problem with this strategy is making the pause too long. This timing may be checked easily in the preceding example. As indicated, your fist should graze the back of your opponent's blocking arm while it is still engaged in the blocking motion. If you graze his arm while it is recoiling from the block, your delay was too long.

A second major problem with nitobun is the difficulty in generating power in the second half of the strike. In most techniques, much of the final power is derived from the initial surge of motion, especially the hip rotation. Because you have checked this initial action, the final power of the technique will be drastically reduced. In fact, it may be so weak as to be useless.

To correct this weakness, you should practice each of your techniques starting from its midpoint. This requires you to apply power, suddenly, at a distance from your body. This is very difficult and requires great strength. For example, consider the basic karate punch. You must train yourself to hit hard without the normal hip rotation. While some systems, such as the Shorin-ryu, do this as a matter of course, for most people it will necessitate many hours of long, hard training.[1]

This strategy is best applied against a man who occupies a strong defensive position: he can neither be lured into an attack, nor can he be forced to retreat. Therefore, you force him to do what he wants to do, defend. But, you make him do this at a time and place of your own choice. To accomplish this, your initial surge of motion must be very strong. It can't just resemble a real attack, it must *be* a real attack. Anything less and your opponent will ignore it and be ready for the final part of the strike.

For best results, apply this strategy in conjunction with ichi no hyoshi no heiho. Attack several times, as fast as you can, in the manner of ikiuchi. Then, when your enemy is locked into a pattern of fast blocks, switch to nitobun. (Using these two strategies in a random pattern is a form of magiri no heiho, and it will confuse your enemy.)

In olden times, an army used this heiho by staging its attack in two waves. If it was properly timed, the second wave would strike the target just as the enemy exhausted its ready supplies of ammunition.

With a sword, aim a strong cut at your opponent's head and then pause. After his block sweeps past the point your sword should have been at, you can easily cut him.

In a judo match, start a foot sweep. Your opponent will

lift his targeted foot above the line of attack. Then, as he starts to put his foot back down, continue your sweep. You might also try a hip throw. Spin in and then, when your opponent stiffens up to resist, wait. When he finds that you are not straining to throw him, he will relax. Then you can continue the throwing action.

The counter for nitobun no heiho is obviously a broken-rhythm defense. This is typified by the *Okinawa-te*[2] technique of *mawashi-uke,* an ancient, double-layered blocking technique that still may be seen in some karate schools. In this block, a middle-level defense is done with both arms, one following the other. If the first block is too fast then the second arm, arriving an instant later, will meet the attack. (If the first block is successful, the second one is converted into a strike.)

Nitobun no heiho is a very elegant strategy. It requires a delicate touch and should not be used in a heavy-handed, one-two manner. If your timing is subtle enough, your opponent may not even realize what you are doing. He will think he is missing blocks because of his own faulty timing. If he happens to be fairly senior, this will have a punishing effect on his spirit.

NAGASHI NO HEIHO

Nagashi means "to flow."[3] This strategy is used against an enemy who is a master of *tai sabaki.*[4] If your opponent consistently evades your attacks by moving about, instead of attacking several times you extend your initial attack and follow his motion with your sword.

To cut with this strategy you attack slowly and, by twisting your shoulders and hips, follow your enemy wherever he goes. Only by cutting slowly can you change the trajectory of your sword enough to do this; if you cut with speed, your blade will have too much momentum to track your opponent as he dodges.

A slow attack creates a problem: the power of a cut is proportional to the speed of the blade. To compensate for the power lost by cutting slowly, you must develop great

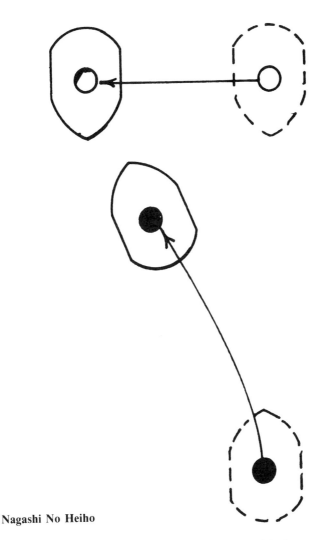

Nagashi No Heiho

strength in your hips. Then, when your blade reaches the target, you can force it through with your body.

The classical exercise for developing strong hip rotation is *shikkō sabaki,* commonly referred to as the samurai walk. (Standard exercises, such as sit-ups, do not work because they do not develop the waist muscles used for turning.) Shikko sabaki is a method of moving smoothly while in a kneeling position—it is used in all traditional dojo. Because it is impossible to use your legs in this position, you are forced to rely on your hips for locomotion. Starting with both knees on the floor and your buttocks resting on your heels, with a snap of your hips you send one knee forward. Then, pressing that knee to the floor, you snap your hips in the other direction to send your opposite knee forward. With a little practice you will develop the ability to move forward, backward, and turn with ease. The disciples of a traditional dojo usually spend their first year training from a kneeling position, specifically to develop this ability. By their second year, when they are allowed to practice standing techniques, they can turn with tremendous speed and strength.

A second training method for nagashi is to tie you and your partner together with a length of light string. Your partner then races about in a random pattern in an effort to break the string. Whatever he does, you must remain close enough to keep a little slack in the cord. Obviously, a strong hip rotation (derived from shikko sabaki) is a prerequisite for this.

Nagashi no heiho is the art of keeping your enemy under constant pressure. You chase him about with your sword, your body, and your spirit, not allowing him an instant to rest. As you track his motion with your sword, you must always remember to cut with hip power. If you use your arms, your body will get stretched out, making it very easy for him to counter.

One great beauty of nagashi is that, even though you are cutting slowly, the total duration of the technique is relatively short. This is because you are only doing one technique—the initial cut is extended. This one slow technique consumes much less time than withdrawing your sword and launching a second attack at your opponent's new position. Consequently, nagashi places your enemy under much greater pressure than a series of simple attacks.

An army may use this strategy to good effect when dealing with a band of guerrillas. It is a common error when attacked by such a group to fight back savagely and then, when they break off, rest and regroup. Although this may win a battle, it will not win the war. To apply nagashi no heiho, maintain contact with your enemy at all costs. When the raiding party attempts to disengage, counterattack and maintain a steady pressure. Do not consider such time-consuming options as calling for an air strike or reinforcements; just attack constantly.

This constant pursuit is not as hard as it might seem because the typical paramilitary band is not equipped for extended engagements. Also, it is difficult for them to fire accurately while they are retreating. Therefore, it is imperative that the pursuing troops maintain a constant pressure. If the retreating force never has a chance to rest, it cannot dig in and resist with any great strength.

You can augment the pursuit by having fresh troops on standby. Then, when the original pursuers begin to tire, new troops can be airlifted in to continue the chase.

If the raiders scatter, so should the pursuers. Then they can run down the individual guerrillas. If the raiders converge on a base camp for support, this offers you the possibility for a major battle. In any event, you are carrying the fight to your enemy and forcing him to fight in your style.

Cutting in the style of nagashi requires the development of a special set of muscles. It is the same when you use an army. Whether pursuing your enemy with a sword or with a company of troops, the principle stays unchanged. Your initial move, augmented by power from your center, is extended to track your enemy as he attempts to evade. You do not use a series of techniques; you use one long, slow cut that never stops until it reaches the target.

Nagashi no heiho is rarely a decisive strategy—no matter how strong your hip power is, you cannot cut very deep with this method. Even so, it tends to have a major effect on your opponent's spirit, an effect which is out of proportion to his actual danger from the strategy. When your enemy finds himself pursued by a seemingly relentless force, his strategy of hit-and-run no longer seems viable. The longer the pursuit lasts, the more his spirit will be crushed.

ZENTAI NO HEIHO

Zentai means "total body." To use this heiho, you cut all

parts of your enemy's body with one stroke of your sword.

Normally, when you attack you aim at a particular target, such as the head, neck, or shoulder. Zentai no heiho means that you take a larger view. When your opponent's defenses are too strong for you to penetrate with a simple attack, view his total body as your target. Cut, with a single stroke, his hands, head, body, and legs. When he blocks your upper-level attack you continue, taking whatever you can get, even to the point of cutting his foot.

This strategy is closely related to nagashi no heiho. The difference is that in nagashi you cut slowly and change directions to follow the target. With zentai, however, you cut strongly and follow through, continuing along the original line of attack. When your original attack has failed, you carry on, driving strongly with your hips, shoulders, and spirit, not really caring what new target may present itself before your blade.

Zentai requires great strength and stamina, and the key to this is breath control. You must breathe only with your abdominal muscles if you hope to have enough air remaining to cut deeply at the end of the stroke. A classical exercise for developing this breath control is *misogi.*[5]

To practice misogi breathing, inhale for a count of five, hold your breath for a count of five, and exhale for a count of ten. As you do this, do not allow your chest to move; inhale by expanding your abdomen and exhale by compressing it. As you inhale, imagine the air is traveling from your nose to the top of your skull. As you hold, imagine the air is slowly settling from your head to your lower abdomen. Then exhale slowly through your mouth.

When you do misogi breathing, the rate of air flow must remain constant from beginning to end. Do not gasp at the first part of the inhalation and then allow the air flow to slow down. The same when you exhale: breathe out steadily and then sharply cut off the flow of air at the end of ten seconds. To help in controlling the flow, concentrate on the sound the air makes as it enters your nose and leaves your mouth. Keep the tone steady.

Once you have mastered misogi with a twenty-second

cycle, gradually increase the time until one breath cycle lasts for at least a minute. Instructors, to maintain their images as heartless beasts, will usually schedule this practice at the worst possible time: the end of a hard training session. Trying to maintain a one-minute breath cycle when every cell in your body is screaming for oxygen requires iron willpower. The fact that the sensei is doing it effortlessly is a lesson in humility. (Most beginners firmly believe the old man has learned to absorb oxygen through his skin.)

Although good breath control is an advantage in any technique, in zentai it is mandatory. You attack strongly with the power of your exhalation matching the power of the cut, and continue this exhalation for the duration of the technique. If you allow your breath to fade, so will your power.

In addition to physical stamina, you will also need spiritual stamina. If you fail to cut some part of your opponent's body, you will be so deeply extended that fast recovery is impossible. This makes zentai an all-or-nothing technique. It is not for the faint of heart.

Although it is applied in a slightly different manner, zentai no heiho has a psychological effect on your enemy that is similar to that of nagashi no heiho. By ignoring his block and continuing your cut, you inject a doubt into his mind—he will begin to wonder about the effectiveness of his defense.

The actual sword stroke used in zentai goes by various names. In the Nitenichi-ryu it is called *en-giri. En* is a circle, denoting totality. In the Tenshin-ryu and the Shinto-ryu, it is called *take-giri,* the "bamboo cut." This indicates that the cut is delivered with a feeling of splitting a length of bamboo from tip to base. Both titles are saying you should cut all of your enemy, not just a piece of him.

A classical strategy in karate is to stand and counter. By blocking without an evasive move, your opponent places himself in a perfect position for a fast and deadly counterattack. When faced with such a man, use zentai. Attack with any technique and then, when it is blocked, do not try to return to your starting position. Continue your original motion and slam into your opponent with your body. This will destroy his counter. It will also force him to start using tai sabaki, which will destroy his strategy.

In a judo match, you can also use this heiho. When you enter for a throw, your opponent may resist, planning to execute a counterthrow when you shift position for a different attack. To foil his plans, continue your original attack, even if it requires remaining frozen in one position for considerable time. By not changing position, you make it very difficult for your opponent to throw you, and sooner or later he will run out of either strength or patience. If he weakens, you may succeed with your original technique. If he gives up and shifts position, you can use another technique. In either case, you do not allow him even a second to recover.

Apply zentai no heiho with a feeling of heaviness. Imagine that your arms are made of lead and your body is as heavy as a mountain. You want to try to drive your opponent into the ground with your weight, not just your strength. A classical analogy, taken from the Chinese art of t'ai chi ch'uan, is that your bones are made of iron and your muscles are cotton. This is very close to the perfect attitude.

MENZUKI NO HEIHO

Menzuki, "to thrust at the face," is a strategy that can be used effectively against an opponent of low to moderate skill. It is applied when you find that you cannot cut your enemy with a decisive stroke. By thrusting at his face, you make him flinch. Then you immediately cut him deeply.

The thrust at the face will rarely result in a large flinching motion, so your follow-up strike must be delivered, literally, in the blink of an eye. In this respect, this strategy is very similar to harai no heiho. Your main attack must be launched along with the menzuki, because if you wait to see if your opponent flinches from the first technique, the second one will always be too late.

As you thrust, never allow yourself to become overextended. That would make a fast follow-up impossible. Push in strongly with your hips, as if you planned on driving the entire length of your sword through your opponent's skull. Then use this same motion to launch your main attack. You will usually thrust at your opponent's face, and then as he flinches, cut his wrist. When you do this do not lift your blade. Cut with the weight of your body, in the style of zentai.

In a karate match, lead with a fast left to your opponent's eyes—this strike is called *mekakushi-uchi*—and follow it with a right to the body. Your left is just a fast, flicking motion to cover your true attack, so concentrate more on speed than power. For the attack to work, both of these techniques must be delivered with a single motion. Push off strongly with your right leg and allow your body to rotate to the left. As your shoulders come around, your left fist will

Uchitachi (white jacket) raises his sword to attack but flinches when shitachi explodes forward with a menzuki.

flash out, followed a fraction of a second later by your right. Because the two different hand techniques are joined by the rotation of your body and delivered in one breath, they become one smooth flow of motion—your right fist starts forward before your left starts to recoil.

In an argument, introduce a totally outrageous statement. Your opponent may be so astounded that his mind will flinch and cease to function logically. Then you can continue your main argument with little intelligent opposition. As when using a sword, the more shocking your initial move is, the better it will work as a distraction.

The classical military application of menzuki is the artillery barrage. (This is different from a bombardment, which is used to destroy an enemy position; a barrage is part of the main attack.) In a barrage (see page 166), the gunners will walk the shells in just ahead of the advancing infantry. The purpose is to make the enemy troops seek shelter while the infantry is moving forward. For this to work, the infantry stays as close to the exploding artillery shells as it possibly can. This lets it arrive at its objective before the enemy troops can recover.

KADO NO HEIHO

Kado-giri, "cutting a corner," is closely related to menzuki. According to this strategy, when you are unable to make a decisive stroke, you should take whatever you can get.

In any action it is best to settle the matter with a single technique. This leaves less room for making a mistake— nobody is perfect, and, if you continue the battle long enough, you will *always* make an error. However, short engagements are not always possible. Kado teaches you not to waste time. If you cannot destroy your opponent immediately, settle for a target of opportunity.

Junior strategists are prone to overuse of this heiho, and beginners should avoid it entirely. This is because, by using too many small techniques, which is very easy to do, they often lose sight of the primary objective. In addition, small techniques create small spirits. To counteract this tendency, lower-level students should force themselves to rely on large techniques and wide, sweeping strategies.

The effects of overuse of kado are easy to see in the sport of kendo. Due to the nature of kendo's point system, kendo students bounce around on their toes and rely on small, fast cuts. You will never learn the Way of Strategy by fencing like this. (An easy way to cure this problem is to require that, for a point to be scored, the shinai must be swung back so far that its tip touches the buttocks prior to the strike. This would eliminate all small techniques.)

Kado no heiho should be used primarily as a recovery from a major attack which has failed. When you strike at a primary target and the cut is blocked, use the remaining energy to hit a secondary target. This will allow you an additional instant to disengage.

On the battlefield, kado is a standard strategy. An aircraft on a ground-support mission will hit its primary target and then, on the same pass, shoot at anything else of interest. The main target may be worth the risk of an expensive aircraft and highly trained pilot, but the secondary ones rarely are. Although these secondary targets would never rate a mission of their own, as long as the plane is there it might as well do something about them. True, one of these minor targets could turn out to be very important—it could be an enemy headquarters or communication center—but this should not be counted on. Mostly you use kado no heiho only for its nuisance value.

This strategy may also be used as a lead-in attack, but only against a beginner. When fencing with a beginner, strike his hand. This will make him flinch, allowing a strong attack to get through to a major target. It is imperative that you learn to judge the grade of your opponent before trying this. You cannot make a senior flinch by hitting his hands. He will use your small attack as an opening for his countercut.

You can also, again only with a beginner, use a continuous series of kado-giri attacks. A mass of small injuries can so weaken your opponent that he will no longer be able to function effectively. The danger in this application of kado is that if you waste too much time with a long series of small cuts, you may make a mistake. This could allow your junior opponent to kill you accidentally.

Kada no heiho is often used to reduce an opponent's offensive capability. This is frequently seen in boxing matches. If your opponent has a very good left jab, make his left arm the target for your punches. Instead of aiming for his head or body, just keep pounding away at this arm. After a few rounds of this, it will get too sore for him to use it effectively.

This same type of strategy can be used in a karate match. Adopt a standard fighting stance and gradually allow your elbows to open out, away from your body. This will open your ribs to attack. Then, when your opponent attacks with mawashi-geri, drop your elbows and tighten your muscles with sanchin. Instead of kicking your side, his instep will slam into the point of your elbow. This will usually dislocate several of his toes and break a few of the small bones in his foot.

In a judo match, when you step in to grab your opponent's jacket, grab his skin also.[6] This sudden pain will make him flinch and destroy his balance. Then he is easy to throw.

KOKOROZUKI NO HEIHO

When your cut has been parried, keep sight of your true objective and thrust at your opponent's heart.

If you think small, there is always an urge to disengage after an attack has failed and then try something else. However, if you fix your mind on destroying your enemy, you may discover that you can continue on from a failure and still win. With a sword this means you should always aim at the heart. Even when you cut at your enemy's head, your focus is on his heart and you try to cut deeply enough to reach it. This is *kokorozuki*.

As mentioned earlier, Wu Ch'i described a battlefield as a "land of standing corpses." Never forget this. It is the destiny of a soldier to die—survival in war is usually more a matter of luck than anything else. Such being the case, your death has little meaning unless you destroy your enemy. Any time that you spend toward survival and not directed toward this goal, is wasted time, and a dying man has precious little time to squander.

The rhythm of attack among beginners is usually one . . . and two . . . and three. Seniors, on the other hand, attack with a count of one-two-three. Wasting not an instant, they go straight for the heart with every move. This is close to the very essence of combat and should be studied deeply.

It is instinctive for a man to protect his heart, so a direct attack may be impossible. This is especially true when you are fencing with a stronger opponent. In such a situation you will have to make your kokorozuki an extension of the main attack. One method of doing this is illustrated in the iaijutsu kata known as *kiritsuke no ken.* This kata begins with a powerful, left-to-right slash of the blade. When your opponent blocks this, quickly drop your right elbow, rotating the edge of your sword to the left. Then, using the sori of your blade to circle past his block, thrust to the heart.

In a battle between armies, as long as the conflict is limited to troops along the line of battle, the war can go on for a long time. Even though casualties may be heavy, it is still an application of kado no heiho. World War I was a good example of this. However, by striking deeply into a nation's heartland, as in World War II, you can destroy its ability to wage war. (There have been several armed conflicts in recent years in which this lesson was not heeded, with predictable results.)

This is one area in which people forget that strategy between individuals is the same as strategy between nations. In single combat, as long as your opponent's heart still beats, he has the potential for becoming dangerous. It is the same for a country. In modern times, it is no longer enough to destroy an army. To win, you must destroy a nation's ability to field an army.

In ancient times when an army won a great victory in battle, they would continue on to destroy the enemy completely. The victor would raze the enemy's city and poison his fields. Modern man is much too civilized to do this.

Instead, he continues to fight the same wars, generation after generation, with the same enemies, at the cost of millions of lives. Genghis Khan would have been appalled at such barbarity.

NOTES

1. The classical Japanese-style karate punch, *seikenzuki,* starts with the fist positioned alongside the hip, palm up. It is propelled forward with a sharp rotation of the waist.

2. The art of Okinawa-te was the source of karate.

3. *Nagashi* is another pronunciation of the same character that is read as *ryu,* as in Itto-ryu.

4. *Tai sabaki* is evasive body motion. Because it is impossible to block a cut from a Japanese sword with only arm strength, swordsmen are the greatest exponents of this art.

5. *Misogi* means "purification," and it is a part of Shinto, the native Japanese religion. This exercise is taught in most of the aikido schools that are related to the Uyeshiba style. Uyeshiba learned it from Deguchi, the head of the Omoto-kyo branch of Shinto.

6. The standard grip for most judo techniques involves seizing the bottom of your opponent's sleeve with one hand and his lapel with the other.

Chapter Seventeen

Osae: Controlling

There are many martial arts, notably the myriad forms of jujutsu, which make a specialty of controlling an enemy. Although originally this was used only as a means to an end, now it is much different. The reality of conflict has become so obscured by public morality that taking an enemy prisoner has come to be seen as a higher goal than merely killing him.

The essential problem of controlling an enemy is this: What happens when you let him go? Police are forced, by law, to deal with this problem on a daily basis. In a civilized society, where the criminals are only a small fraction of the total population, this is a marginal strategy. In war, where 50 percent of the people on the battlefield are trying to kill you, it becomes an impossible one.

The sad fact is that when you hold an enemy, he is also holding you. You cannot immobilize an opponent without immobilizing yourself, and in open combat, this is fatal.

The original purpose of *osae* was to restrict an enemy's motion. Once this was accomplished he could be disposed of properly, with little danger. To keep an enemy hanging around, always a source of potential danger, is a rather bizarre concept when looked at objectively.

You should always view the various strategies for controlling an enemy in their proper contexts. Your final objective is the destruction of your opponent; restricting his motion is merely a means to an end. Once you have successfully restrained him, you must continue on to your objective without releasing the pressure. If you relax, even for an instant, you will have to start over.

MAKURA OSAE NO HEIHO

Makura osae means "holding down a pillow." You use this strategy to control your opponent by restricting the motion of his head. The rather poetical name for this technique might be misleading if one does not know that a Japanese pillow is smaller and harder than a Western one. This heiho should not be viewed as a soft or gentle one. By holding your enemy's head in place as firmly as a Japanese pillow does, you can control his entire body.

In close combat it is impossible to immobilize your opponent's entire body at the same time by normal methods. You cannot simultaneously control his arms, legs, and torso. However, by anchoring his head, you can greatly restrict the motion of the rest of his body.

To illustrate this, strike with your fist at an imaginary target. Put as much power into the blow as you can, using a lot of hip and shoulder motion. Now see how hard you can hit while pressing your head firmly against a wall. Even if your head is in the best possible position for the strike, you will discover that your total power is greatly reduced. This is an example of the basic theory behind makura osae.

When fighting at close range, press upward under your opponent's chin. Once his head is forced back, he will be very weak and unable to move about freely. Because his range and power are now restricted, you can hit or throw him at your leisure.

When fencing, hold down your opponent's head with a series of strikes. Aim a very strong cut at your enemy's head. If he flinches, move in quickly with a continuous barrage of cuts to the same target, forcing him to keep his head down. From that position he can neither attack nor defend with any great power. You can create a similar situation with a series of thrusts toward his eyes.

You can also immobilize a man's head, and thereby his entire body, by fixing his metsuke. Move the tip of your sword around slowly until his eyes are drawn to it, then slowly reduce the motion. When you finally stop moving your sword, his head will also stop. Against a timid enemy, this strategy will freeze him into place.

(This may well have been the original purpose of what is

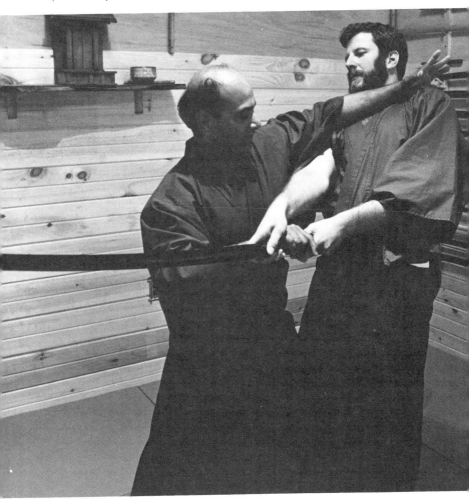

Shitachi slides his left arm up and across the throat of uchitachi, forcing his head back, prior to disarming him.

known as a military posture for troops on parade. It is much easier to control a man when his chin is tucked in than when he is standing in a relaxed manner.)

The head of an army is its commander. Therefore, an attack on an army should be coordinated with a raid on its command post. If the general is forced (literally) to keep his head down, then he cannot freely maneuver his troops to counter your attack. The pressure on the enemy command post should start before the main attack and continue unabated until the army is defeated.

The same strategy can be used in business. A corporate takeover bid should be coordinated with an attack on the personal fortune of the company's president. This will prevent him from devoting his full attention to business matters.

When using makura osae no heiho, you must accept the fact that you can only restrict your opponent's motion. You cannot totally immobilize him. Thus he will still be flopping around a little, and this means that he can still hit you. However, if you have securely anchored his head, the power of these blows will be so slight that they can be safely ignored.

KUZUSHI NO HEIHO

Kuzushi is the action of breaking down the posture of your enemy. You accomplish this by observing the line of his shoulders and forcing it off the horizontal. By doing this, you reduce his strength and restrict his motion.

To see the advantage of this strategy, have your training partner assume a solid stance and then try to move him. If his posture is good, you will find this very hard to do. Now shift the line of his shoulders—have him raise one shoulder an inch above the level of the other. When you try to move him now, you will find it much easier. With very little force, you can drive him around in any direction you choose.

In jujutsu, a throw is always preceded by kuzushi. First you push, pull, or twist your opponent until his shoulders are no longer horizontal, and then you throw him. Trying to execute a throw without this action will, at best, be difficult. Usually it will be impossible.

When fencing, you sometimes execute a feint, a misekake, to open a particular line of attack. When you do this, take care to observe whether or not the misekake actually disturbs the line of your opponent's shoulders. If it was not strong enough to accomplish this, then any follow-up attack will probably fail.

During a karate match, attack with a technique aimed at your opponent's head or groin and observe his shoulders as he blocks. If he raises or lowers his shoulder along with his blocking arm, he is weakening his entire posture. In other words, he is applying kuzushi to himself. Watch his shoulder carefully and attack as soon as it moves.

When you wish to apply kuzushi, you will usually find it difficult to do so directly. Normally it will require a combination of forces. This means that, instead of trying to move your opponent's shoulders with a simple twist or a pull, you should use a twist and a pull simultaneously. When you apply your force along a complex curve in space instead of in a straight line, it becomes much harder for him to resist it.

With an individual, it is easy to observe the line of his shoulders. However, all battles are not fought with individuals.

When studying a business firm, you should consider the major departments to be its shoulders. If you wish to weaken a firm, force it to divert some of its cash flow into expanding its production facilities. Another possibility is to force it to divert cash into more advertising. Either of these actions is the same as twisting the shoulders of an individual.

In an army, there must be a balance between the support forces and the line troops. If the support corps is too large, there will not be enough actual fighting men to mount a major offensive. On the other hand, if the support forces are too small, a major offensive cannot be sustained.

The obvious way to weaken an army is to destroy its combat troops. This is simple but sometimes costly. A more indirect approach would be to encourage an enemy to strengthen an area of its army other than the combat troops. He has only a finite amount of men and money to work with, so to strengthen one area he must weaken another. Simply stated, every man behind a typewriter is one less behind a gun.

Kuzushi no heiho is an excellent example of the proper use of osae. It is used only as a means to an end, to prepare your opponent for your real strategy. This means that your controlling and winning strategies are so tightly welded that they frequently seem to be one event. In fact, in many schools kuzushi is not taught as a separate strategy at all; it is always presented as an integral portion of a technique. This is as it should be.

SHOSOTSU NO HEIHO

An army is composed of *shōsotsu,* an officer and his men. This strategy teaches that if you think of your opponent, not as an enemy, but as if he were one of your own men, you can order him about.

For example, if your opponent raises his fist to strike you, look at him with an annoyed expression on your face and say, "Stop that!" Then, when he pauses for a moment in confusion, quickly hit him several times.

Police officers are very familiar with this strategy. When an officer walks into a dangerous situation and shouts, "everybody up against the wall!" and they do it, he is treating them as if they were his own troops. The police refer to this as command presence, which is just another work for aiki.

When using this strategy, never resort to threats. Never say, "do this or else," for that implies that there is a possibility your enemy will not obey you.

You have probably undergone an experience of being told to do something, doing it, and then wondering, "why in the world did I do that?" You did it because the person who gave the order could not imagine you doing anything else. There is a tremendous difference between saying, "you will do this," because it is an unarguable fact and saying it because you hope it will happen. It is this difference which makes the strategy work.

Commands are not necessarily verbal. When confronted

with an enemy, stand tall and march straight toward him. If you are secure in the knowledge that he is going to retreat, he usually will. In this case you are ordering him with your posture. (This would be a variation of kochiku no heiho.) When you order your opponent with your posture, do not assume any type of fighting stance, especially one of a defensive nature. That would indicate that you think he might not retreat.

From childhood a person is conditioned to accept authority. Shosotsu merely takes advantage of this conditioning. Properly applied, it reaches past your opponent's adult intelligence and affects his emotions. You think of your enemy as being a small child and march straight in, knowing that he would not dare to resist you. Do not ask him to move; order him to do so with your voice and attitude.

This strategy is what holds large armies together. In a small, elite force, the troops attack as a unit due to esprit de corps; a large group attacks as a unit because it is ordered to. In this large force, the men may regard their officer as their enemy. Outnumbered and outgunned, the officer has little to rely on other than shosotsu. He must give an order, especially if it is an unpopular order, without thinking that it might be disobeyed. To do otherwise would invite disaster.

Shosotsu does not work against a well-organized group, because its combined will is much stronger than yours as an individual. To order such a group around, you must first turn it into a mob. Then you can treat this mob as if it were a single individual of very low intelligence.

A well-trained team fights as a unit, and a member of the team rarely has to think about the other men in the group— they have trained together so long that he knows how each man will react to any situation. This allows the individual members to focus their attention on the target. To destroy this cohesion, cause them to think more about each other than about you.

One way to break up the cohesion of a group is to concentrate on one man. Strike him so that he is knocked into one of his teammates. Once this starts happening, the other members will start worrying more about tripping over each other than hitting you. As soon as you sense a lack of coordination in the group, start shouting orders. This will create even more confusion, allowing you to knock down a few more men.

Shosotsu no heiho is the secret of getting good service from any business. If you take the attitude that you cannot imagine receiving anything but the best, you will usually get first-class service. This must be a genuine feeling of quiet self-assurance; if you act obnoxious and overbearing, the staff will assuredly find some way to get even.

This is a strategy that you look forward to. It gets better with age. While a young man may be fast and strong, it is rare to see one with the strength of will required for this heiho.

HISHIGI NO HEIHO

When you engage in combat, you must do so with the desire to crush your enemy totally; just wanting to win is not enough. This does not mean that you must always destroy your enemy. However, each of your techniques must be delivered with this intention. When you step forward to meet your opponent, on the battlefield or in the board-room, form a mental image of him lying at your feet, a pile of shattered bones and torn flesh. Each action you take must have the goal of turning this image into reality.

When you hit someone, you do it with the goal of breaking his bones. The primary maxim of the art of karate is, "One blow, one death." A practitioner of this art believes that if he has to hit a man more than once, he has done something wrong. This is not a matter of secret pressure points; it is pure, raw power. The karateka does not try to inflict pain; he never even thinks about pain. He just concentrates on breaking bones.

Even when you practice in a dojo among friends, you should do so with *hishigi*. Strike with full power and then stop the blow a fraction of an inch short of target. Then spend time breaking boards and bricks. Training in any other way is only a game—it will never teach you the Way of

Strategy. A style of thinking has inertia. You cannot expect to think softly year after year and then suddenly be able to change when you have to. Practice does not make perfect; it makes permanent.

It is the law in many places that, when attacked, you are allowed only to defend yourself. You cannot punish your attacker. You can stop him from hitting you, but you cannot injure him any more than is absolutely necessary in the process. Laws such as this, while morally uplifting, were obviously created by people with no combat experience. There is no room for morality in combat—it is always, in one form or another, an act of knocking down your enemy and stomping on his head until he stops moving. Anyone who tries to fight under a set of rules that is more restrictive than his opponent's is operating at a fatal disadvantage.

A battle, fought with rules, is defined as a sport. This is good as long as you are having fun. When you stop enjoying yourself, it is time to throw away the rule book and concentrate on crushing your enemy.

Actually, approaching an engagement with the strategy of hishigi will stop many fights before they begin. If your opponent is very angry and wants to hurt you, he will probably accept the fact that he may be injured in the process. However, if he senses you want to destroy him completely, that is another matter entirely. Although the thought of injury may not even slow him down, the thought of death may stop him in his tracks.

This strategy is frequently used in no-contact karate matches. In these contests, all killing blows are stopped just short of impact. Although injuries are common, they are accidental. In such an atmosphere, step up to the line radiating an aura of death and destruction. This will seriously discomfit your opponent and immobilize his spirit. He entered the contest to fight for a trophy. Now he is faced with the prospect of fighting for his life. Even though the rational part of his mind tells him that there is no danger and he will be protected by the rules, the more primitive part of his psyche is not so sure. It wants to go home. Because of this, he goes on the defensive before the match begins. No longer thinking about winning, now he wishes only to survive. He will survive, but he will never win with this attitude.

Hishigi no heiho is not a thing; it is an awareness, an awareness of the reality of war. Mercy is something which is granted by the victor. It should never be considered before or during the battle. First you win. Then, and only then, should you consider what to do next.

Chapter Eighteen

Sutemi: Sacrificing

Most people believe that the urge for survival is a natural instinct. Therefore, you may assume that your enemy will expect you to try to survive a battle. If you can sublimate your urge for survival, it can be a fast route to victory. It is very rare for anyone to be able to attack along a path that obviously leads to his own destruction. If you are capable of doing this, you may shock your enemy into immobility long enough for you to win.

SUTEMI NO HEIHO

The strategy of sacrificing is applicable to most kinds of combat. Basically, it requires that you be willing to accept a small injury in order to inflict a larger one to your enemy. A key factor in any *sutemi* is durability—you must be able to endure an injury and still function well enough to damage your opponent.

Your goal in a judo match is to throw your opponent to the mat. He is trying to do the same thing to you, so you must simultaneously struggle against being thrown. In such a situation, you may wish to use a *sutemi-nage,* a sacrifice throw.

When you use a sutemi-nage, you do not throw your opponent; you throw yourself. As you do this, hold your opponent in such a manner that he is forced to fall with you. The fact that you are doing something so unexpected and contrary to the normal strategy of a judo match, which is to throw but not to be thrown, will, in many cases, allow this technique to work where others would not. Also, because you are prepared for the fall while your opponent is not, you will be able to handle the impact better.

There are several judo techniques that come under the general heading of sutemi-nage. The simplest one consists of merely seizing your opponent's lapels and throwing yourself backward at a slight angle. You land on your back and he is yanked, head first, into the mat. (This is why most schools restrict sutemi waza to seniors—they can handle the falls better. A beginner is frequently unable to react fast enough to roll safely out of a sacrifice throw.)

Sutemi is widely used in warfare between nations. The reason for this is that such wars are fought mostly with conscript troops, and such men do not have enough training to be efficient killers. However, because it takes no training at all to die, they are naturals for a sacrifice technique.

When using a sacrifice strategy, a general must weigh all the factors carefully. It is not enough that more damage is done to the enemy; the important thing is that the effects of the damage are greater than the effects of the damage suffered by one's own army. To shoot down two enemy planes for every one of yours that is lost is a good kill ratio, unless the enemy air force is three times as large as yours.

Mental preparation is an important part of any sutemi. If you are ready for pain, it will have less effect on you than if it occurs without warning. This is a good case for keeping area commanders apprised of the estimated casualties of a proposed operation. If a general sends his field commanders in cold, heavy casualties may cause them to pause, disrupting the entire battle plan.

Seniors make extensive use of sutemi no heiho. The primary reason is that they have the mental discipline to bring it off. Secondly, because of their experience, they can make rapid judgments about the dangers of any situation. This allows them to make equally rapid decisions to ignore the dangers and blast straight in with their own attacks. Finally, they have been injured often enough to have lost much of their fear of pain. (For an excellent example of this, consider professional football players. They frequently play with injuries that would put the average man in the hospital.)

Sutemi is another all-or-nothing strategy. If it works, you win; if it does not work, you are usually in such a bad position that there is little you can do to prevent losing. The individuals who can apply this strategy are very, very dangerous men—putting aside all thought of personal safety, they think only about winning. It has been said of many great fighters that "the only way to stop that man is to kill him." If he has mastered the art of sutemi, killing him may not be enough.

AIUCHI NO HEIHO

Aiuchi, the "simultaneous strike," is technically very simple. When your opponent steps forward to cut you down, you do the same to him. As you can see, there is not much to this strategy. However, it does require that the whimpering little animal in your psyche be forced to shut up and be brave. This can present a problem.

Aiuchi means to leap forward to your own death while killing an enemy. You do not just accept death, you lust for it. There is an old dojo tale which illustrates how well this can work.

Once, many years ago, there was a master of the tea ceremony[1] who was challenged to a duel by a wandering swordsman. The tea master knew nothing of swords, so he went to a friend who happened to be a fencing instructor for advice. The sword master explained that, because of the tea master's social position, he could not refuse the duel. Neither could he expect to survive it. However, he offered to give him some basic instruction if the tea master would serve him tea one last time.

The tea master agreed to the request and started the ceremony. The tea ceremony is a thing of great beauty and ritual, requiring intense concentration. As the tea master immersed himself in this ritual, he forgot all about his problems. His body became relaxed and his mind as still as a pool of deep water.

His friend, carefully observing this, suddenly cried out, "There! Just act as you are now. There is no need for practice. When you engage, just raise your sword above your head and pretend you are serving tea. When he attacks, close your eyes and cut down strongly. You will both die, but it will be beautiful."

The next morning the tea master did as he was told. Arriving at the appointed spot, he emptied his mind of all thoughts of survival and calmly began tying his sleeves up.[2] Then he drew his sword and quietly looked off into the distance. The wandering swordsman, observing all this and seeing a completely different man than the one he had challenged, immediately apologized and withdrew from the duel.

This is a beautiful little story, and it has been repeated in fencing schools for centuries. The tea master, although not trained for combat, manifests a key element in the makeup of a dangerous man. A dangerous man is willing to be hurt in order to hurt, and he is willing to be killed in order to kill. This is all a part of kokoro, the mental attitude of a swordsman.

This attitude must be more than just pretense, for a senior opponent can easily tell the difference between reality and pretense. It is all a question of values. If the most important thing in your life is the destruction of your enemy, you are dangerous. If you worry more about personal safety than winning, you are a loser.

The philosophy behind aiuchi is stated in the *Hagakure:*[3] "When you have two options, one which will result in life and the other which will cause your death, immediately choose the path of death." This is not a very easy philosophy for most Westerners to understand, much less accept. It is also the thing that prevents most students of swordsmanship from ever hoping to become swordsmen.

Aiuchi has always been regarded as the ultimate strategy in many ryu. It requires that you launch yourself directly into the teeth of your opponent's attack with an attack of your own. You make no attempt to deflect or avoid his sword—you just concentrate on cutting him down. If his spirit is weak, he will flinch and be cut; if he is brave, you will both be cut. In any event, he will be cut.

A similar action may sometimes be seen in a traditional karate match. There you will see none of the jabbing and maneuvering of the Western boxing match. The two men will square off and quietly study each other. When one man spots a suki, he will launch his attack.[4] It will not be complicated. The typical attack is a linear technique, straight up the middle, and totally committed. The man on the receiving end of this technique will not try to avoid it. As soon as he senses motion, he will launch an even stronger and faster attack of his own.

The result is a war of nerves which lasts only a fraction of a second. If either man flinches, he will lose. If neither man flinches, they will both be carried off. In either case, it is well thought of by the old-timers. (Anytime there is too much blocking and dodging you will hear muttered comments of, "no guts," from these old men.)

A common example of aiuchi in business is the price war. By lowering your prices below the profit point, you hope to drive your competition out of business. Here again, durability is the key. Businessmen who are willing to gamble everything they own in this manner tend to be either big winners or big losers. They cause their more conservative fellow businessmen, who are only willing to gamble with operating capital, to sleep very poorly.

The willingness to die gives a strategist a tremendous advantage in combat. Even a very aggressive opponent will probably only attack with 90 percent of his spirit; the other 10 percent is worrying about his survival. When you have mastered aiuchi no heiho, you hold nothing back—your entire being is totally committed to the attack. Aside from the purely physical advantage of this, it tends to destroy your opponent's fighting spirit. His probable reaction will be to think, "Let me out of here. This guy is nuts!" Once he starts to think in that way, he becomes a walking dead man.

NOTES

1. The Japanese tea ceremony, *cha no yu,* is extremely stylized. Every move is done according to a rigid set of rules. Masters of this art are highly respected for their mental discipline and tranquility.

2. When he had the time, a samurai would tie up the sleeves of his kimono before a fight to keep them out of the way. This action is called *tasuki.* A special length of material was carried in one sleeve for this purpose.

3. The *Hagakure* was written by Yamamoto Tsunetomo (1659-1719) in 1716. Its most famous line is, "I have discovered the heart of bushido: to die!"

4. There was a famous match of many years ago that was called a draw because neither of the men—they were considered the best in Japan—could spot a suki.

Chapter Nineteen

Keikaku: Planning

Combat is usually a matter of instinct—the man who thinks, dies. However, this does not mean there is no place for the mind in the art of war. There are occasions when there may be time, before the battle, to think. The key word here is *before*. This is the time for planning.

If time permits, you should make a careful study of both your enemy and the terrain. Then you can make a logical selection of several strategies that may be appropriate in the coming battle. You should never become fixed on one strategy, for a battle will rarely go according to plan. It is best to choose a variety of heiho of different styles. Then, if the situation demands one of these, it can be instantly and instinctively applied.

As you select various strategies, do not do so with the intention of using them. Just quietly review them in your mind. As you do this, your body will instinctively flex the appropriate muscles, preparing itself for action. The advantage gained from this review may be small, but it may also be the difference between winning and losing.

The moments before a battle are very delicate ones, and if you are not careful during this period, you may lose the fight before it starts. It is imperative that you apply the theory of in-yo every second. Regard your enemy, yourself, and the situation as a single cosmic event. If you allow duality to creep in, it will become easy for your spirit to weaken. And, if this happens, you will start to think more about saving yourself than about destroying your opponent.

In using in-yo, you are not aware of yourself as an individual. Your enemy becomes an extension of your technique, and the battlefield is a stage, not a place of danger. When you see your opponent's face, imagine it adhering to your fist. When you see his body, form a mental image of it surrounding the blade of your sword. When you study the battlefield, picture it as an extension of the soles of your feet—as you move your legs, your body remains motionless and the earth moves. Then, when you select a strategy, choose one that will weld all these elements into a single entity.

Through thinking in such a manner, a battle ceases to be a dreaded thing. Instead of being feared, it is eagerly awaited. How can you be afraid when there is no you there?

DAISHO NO HEIHO

Daishō, "large and small," is a simple name for an important principle of combat. It has two levels of meaning. On a small scale it means that you should not use short-sword techniques for long-sword situations (or vice versa). On the larger scale, it means that you should never become overly concerned with small events.

Until the Meiji Restoration,[1] samurai wore two swords. As explained earlier, the long blade, known as a katana, was the primary weapon and worn only outdoors. The short sword, known as a wakizashi, was for close combat and worn at all times.[2] The combination of these two weapons was known as a daisho.

There are obviously great physical differences between the techniques associated with these two swords. Due to its weight, a katana is wielded in a large and open manner with both hands. (There are a few one-handed techniques for a katana, but they are not well thought of. Because of the weight of the sword, a one-handed cut is not very precise.) The wakizashi, with a blade length of between twelve and twenty inches, is light enough to use with one hand, and the techniques associated with it reflect this.

The physical differences between long and short swords created equally great philosophical differences. Strategies for a katana are associated with a strong and aggressive spirit. Conversely, small-sword techniques are thought to create small, defensive spirits. Because of this, many instructors severely restrict their students' contacts with short-sword techniques for the first ten or twenty years.

Strategically, you use long-sword techniques for large situations and short-sword techniques for small situations. A large situation would be a conflict in which your life is in danger—then you think in a grand manner and your goal is the complete destruction of your enemy. In a smaller situation, such as being harassed by a drunk at a party, you think on a smaller scale—in this case, the situation does not rate the destruction of your opponent.

This may sound so obvious that it needs no explanation. You may even wonder why there is an official strategy for something which is self-evident. After all, everybody knows that you should not kill a guest at a party just because he has had a little too much to drink. Wrong! Every *mind* knows this; you cannot say that about every *body*. The body of a noncombatant is just a body; the body of a warrior is a finely tuned machine. It is a gun—cocked, loaded, with the safety off—and it cares not what manner of man pulls its trigger. A gun does not fire a small bullet at a small opponent and a large bullet at a large enemy; it fires the same bullet at anyone. (This is a major problem for armies. Soldiers who have been on the front lines long enough to become hardened to battle require a cool-down period before they can be released into society.)

Daisho no heiho is a method of bringing this situation under control. By thinking small, a soldier can restrict his automatic reflexes. True, this slows his response to a major situation, but it also limits his response to the more common minor situations. By a conscious act of will, he puts his spirit in a straitjacket in order to live within the rules of society. He becomes a killer who does not kill.

Philosophically, daisho means you must not become confused by these two situations: you recognize the difference between a minor annoyance and a major battle. It also means that you do not become overly involved with minor annoyances. A small matter should never capture more than a tiny fraction of your attention. If it does, you may fail to note a larger situation developing.

An individual with little combat experience is easy to defeat with this strategy. If you quickly tap him on the nose, just hard enough to draw blood, it will capture his attention. It will draw so much of his attention that, even though it is not a life-threatening injury, you are free to do whatever else is necessary with little interference. (This illustrates a major difference between a fighter and a civilian. Injure the civilian and he will become afraid; injure the fighter and he gets mean.)

You can also use daisho in the manner of utsurakashi no heiho and influence your opponent's attitude. Move the tip of your sword around in a small random pattern. Do this lightly and fast. This motion can influence your opponent into adopting a similar style of thought, and he will soon start to move with small, fast steps. He stops thinking big and starts using short-sword techniques. This leaves him vulnerable to a powerful attack.

Businesses are frequent victims of this heiho. To borrow a phrase, the business of business is business. All of a company's activities must be measured against this standard. Customer relations, employee relations, and community relations must all have a positive and measurable effect on the company. Any activity that does not create a profit, either immediate or long-term, must be set aside for one that does. The strength and success of the company must always take precedence over secondary issues, no matter how emotional these may be. Any company that overly concerns itself with small matters is doomed to failure. It may be well loved but it will not be long-lived. Through constant attention to the short sword, the long sword rusts in its sheath.

An army may also fall victim to small thinking. After establishing a beachhead, it can spend so much time consolidating its position that the enemy has time to recover from the shock of the invasion. By being too conservative, the army may dig itself a foxhole too deep to get out of. An army must always differentiate between the time for *dai* and the time for *shō*. The primary job of any military force is killing the enemy. And, during a war, every minute it is not busily engaged in this task is a minute wasted. Once the bugle sounds, the only direction should be forward. A pause in an advance should be viewed as a short-sword strategy in a long-sword situation.

Although large strategies are preferable for spiritual development, there may be occasions when you will wish to use a short sword. This can be of value when you are forced to fight a very strong opponent.

When fencing, discard your long blade and move into a restricted area, such as a grove of trees or a small room. Your opponent's long-sword strategies will then become entangled by his surroundings, giving you the advantage.

In a karate match, when you are faced with a strong opponent, try to maneuver him into a corner. This will restrict his motion and, thereby, reduce the effectiveness of his large techniques. Then you can use your speed and mobility to best advantage.

To apply daisho no heiho in any situation, merely allow your spirit to fill all the available space. This can be a physical space, such as a room, or a philosophical space, such as a war. If your resulting spiritual size is large you will automatically select large strategies. If your spiritual volume is small, you will instinctively use small techniques. In any event, you will precisely fit the situation.

TATEKI NO HEIHO

Tateki means "many enemies." When dealing with multiple opponents, your primary consideration is the order of battle. You will not always attack the closest opponent first. As in the game of billiards, you always work for position. This means that you may be required to take on the most distant man first, or to use a difficult strategy in order to place yourself in an advantageous position.

There is a saying that the intelligence of a mob is equal to that of its dumbest member, divided by the number of people in the group. Although this may sound like humor, it is very close to the truth. It requires long and arduous training to forge a group of individuals into a well-coordinated fighting unit. If the group is without this training, a single individual may overmatch it. This is because the members of an untrained group tend to get in each other's way—one of them will get in the way of his partner's attack.

Defensively, you use tateki by driving your attackers in upon each other until they start colliding. Then, when they become entangled, you treat the group as if it were one large, clumsy individual. There are two standard methods of accomplishing this: the end-around and the through-the-middle methods.

The end-around style—this is often a variation of irimi no heiho—involves a large lateral motion. You attack the person on one end of the enemy force from the outside and drive him into the next man. Keep doing this until you have shoved them all into a large pile.

The through-the-middle method is more dangerous and it is usually reserved for use against larger groups. Race at full speed through the attacking line. As you do this, strike right and left at any targets which may present themselves. Do not pause! If you slow down it will be easy for your enemies to surround you. By repeating this rush through an enemy line several times, you can destroy its cohesion. Then you can push the broken remnants into a pile.

When utilizing either of these methods, try to destroy the strongest enemy first. You are going to have to fight him sooner or later, so you might as well get it over with while you are fresh. This will have a detrimental effect on your other opponents. When they see their strongest member defeated, it will weaken their fighting spirit.

Intelligence in an individual is a function of the degree of communication between the various parts of his brain. In an army, intelligence is a function of the communication between units. Destroying this communication is the same as severing an individual's nerves.

An army may be large and imposing, but with damaged communications, it is incapable of rapid or cohesive action. Planning against this is worth extraordinary attention from the general. He should take great pains to ensure that his lines of communication are well hardened and at least three layers deep. After doing that, he should plan for a worst-case scenario of complete communication failure. He should have a complete set of contingency plans available at the

The strategies in dealing with multiple opponents are frequently the same as for individuals.

local level. Using these, line troops can continue operations until the communication system is repaired.

For example, when an army is advancing, there should be a standing order regulating the speed of advance. Then, in the event of a communication failure, one unit will not advance too far and become cut off. Neither will it advance too slowly and create a gap in the line.

Modern navies are masters of countering the strategy of tateki. They have a long tradition of operating in isolation and have developed a command structure to deal with it. A ship operates first under the naval regulations and then under a specific operation order. This proceeds down, layer after layer, all the way to the captain's night-order book, which tells his officers what to do while he is asleep. With such a command structure, even though a ship may not be doing exactly what the admiral would want, it still adheres to his overall strategy.

A navy-style, layered-operation order is the best way to defeat an opponent who is attempting to use tateki no heiho against you. In such a situation, communications are all-important. Each member of your unit should have a carefully layered plan. He approaches the battle with a specific strategy.[3] If this does not work, he immediately falls back to a more generalized method. If that should also fail, he uses an even more general strategy. By doing this, the group can still continue to operate as a team without outside direction. If they continue long enough, they may still win, in spite of repeated failures.

Modern communications are both a boon and a threat to command strategy. With today's radio networks, a commander can talk to an individual rifleman on the other side of the world. This permits rapid command changes and strategic mobility, but it can also make the troops in the field overly dependent on central authority. If this is carried to the extreme, a modern army could be immobilized by the failure of a ten-cent fuse.

A general guards against overdependency by scheduling exercises to generate self-leadership and initiative. Like the admiral, he teaches his men that they must always reach their objective. If they cannot do this under his personal direction, they should do it any way they can.

The strategist directing a group makes communications his first priority in order to counter tateki no heiho. A strategist wishing to use tateki also makes communications his number-one priority, but in a negative way. His initial efforts are always directed at disrupting enemy communications in order to destroy their cohesiveness. The classical method is to shoot the officers first. However, by whatever method, the strategist turns a well-trained enemy unit into a mob of disorganized individuals.

SHIDAI NO HEIHO

The *shidai* are the circumstances of combat. This strategy is primarily concerned with the selection and utilization of a battlefield. It has always been the mark of a great general that he selects the best possible location and time for a battle. It is the same for individual combat.

To select the proper site is of no avail if you do not make use of it—in wartime a strong point may be bypassed if it is not an active menace. (This was done frequently in the Pacific during World War II.) You must have a proper site from which to launch an attack. Once your attack is launched, you must be prepared to give up your advantageous position and go wherever the tide of battle may carry you.

Tactics are influenced by terrain. By studying the site of a battle, you may discern the strategy of your enemy—you "move the shadow" obscuring his intention by studying the ground. When doing this, you must consider the grade of your opponent. A senior strategist will select terrain to match his tactics. However, a junior may not consider it. In that case, a study of the site may lead you to false assumptions.

When you select your strategy, never try to outbox a boxer or outwrestle a wrestler. If he moves well, pick broken terrain to negate this ability. If he is very strong, fight on flat ground so that you are free to evade his attacks. Always try to place your enemy in a disadvantageous position by your choice of site.

The first kumitachi of Gekken-sho.

You should also be alert to the possibility of modifying the terrain to your advantage. By an act as simple as tossing a chair to one side of your opponent, you will reduce his options considerably. Now he can no longer move freely in that direction—instead of wondering whether he will go right or left, you know from which direction he will attack. An army does the same thing by laying a minefield.

When you modify the terrain, do not try to block your enemy. Just try to control him. This is a mistake often made by armies when they lay their minefields. If you lay a minefield completely surrounding your position, you may feel safe but this is a false security. When your enemy finally attacks, he will have prepared countermeasures for your minefield. This gives you no advanced warning on his proposed line of attack. However, if you set your mines in clearly defined zones, you will make it very tempting for him to attack through one of the gaps. Knowing from which direction he will attack gives you a large advantage.

When caught in a disadvantageous position, try to rectify it before coming to grips with your enemy. If you are on the lower slope of a hill, race along it, perpendicular to the slope. (It is best to go to the right if you are using a sword.) When you have outdistanced your opponent by a few steps, cut up the hill until you are even with him and attack immediately. If you occupy an upper slope, move to your left and attack downhill on a diagonal to the slope, cutting from a low stance. If your enemy occupies a strong defensive position, lure him out with suigetsu no heiho. When he attacks, leave him a path of retreat.[4] When an enemy is cornered, with no hope of escape, he is very dangerous. If you leave him a path of escape, he will think, "if the battle grows too intense, I can always retreat." This will weaken his spirit.

When picking the site of battle, you should also pick the time. When attacking from west to east, do so in the afternoon. Going from east to west, attack at dawn. An individual is weakest after a long march, after a heavy meal, and after being awakened from a deep sleep. Thus, just before lunch is the worst time to attack.

As you can see, there are many different factors involved

in shidai no heiho. This is how the senior strategist earns his wages. He considers the seemingly infinite number of variables involved in a battle and tries to modify each of them to his best advantage. The advantage derived from any of the many decisions may be very small, but when you combine all of them, they can provide a devastating advantage.

Shidai can be utilized with surprising ease. Most men fight only when they have to. The same is true for most armies. This allows you considerable time to maneuver before the engagement. However, this should be done with great caution. Delaying combat, although it may put you in an advantageous position, has a tendency to put you in a disadvantageous state of mind. If you delay the engagement to maneuver, you may also start to look for other reasons to postpone the fight, and your spirit will become too defensive. Remember, to hit well is a good thing but to hit first is better.

KAIMON NO HEIHO

When forced to fight an opponent who occupies a strong defensive position, the final part of your planning is the selection of a strategy that will force him to "open the gate." Although great strength may succeed in battering down the walls of a castle, this is not good strategy. It is much better to have your enemy open the gate to your attack himself. *Kaimon* is the strategy used to accomplish this.

In a karate match, if you attack a target on your opponent's body properly, you can cause him to open that line of attack to your technique. You achieve this by placing your line of attack through his defense instead of around it. This means that you select a point that is hidden behind your opponent's arm as your target. Then, in order to block your punch, he is forced to move his arm to the side and then return it to block. If your timing is perfect, your punch will land before he has a chance to make the return half of this motion. In effect, he has opened the gate to your punch because of his instinctive urge to block all attacks.

In a judo match, when your opponent has a very solid

stance, before a throw you usually use kuzushi to destroy his balance. However, you can use kaimon instead of kuzushi. Attack with a footsweep toward your opponent's nearest foot. When he lifts that foot to avoid your sweep, he will be destroying his own solid stance. Then you can sweep his other foot.

With a sword, kaimon is very easy. Raise your blade, as if you were planning to cut your opponent's head. As he shifts into an upper-level position to counter your move, continue your original motion. Swing your sword in a circle, cutting him from below.

Kaimon no heiho is based upon this manner of thing. You use your opponent's instinctive reactions, moves that he has little control over, to open a line of attack. This all comes from studying the situation. You study your opponent and you study the terrain. Then you use this information to force your enemy to defeat himself.

NOTES

1. During the Meiji Restoration in 1868, the shogun relinquished his military dictatorship and returned power to the emperor. Japan set out on a program of Westernization. As part of this program, in 1876 the samurai class was abolished and wearing swords was outlawed. This was known as the *haitōrei*.

2. Some Western writers have stated that the long sword was for fighting and the short sword was for seppuku, ritual suicide. This is incorrect. True, a wakizashi was occasionally used for seppuku on the battlefield, when in extremis, but the preferred weapon was an ordinary fighting knife. This was mounted in a plain, unfinished wood scabbard and hilt, known as a *shirosaya,* and wrapped in white paper.

3. Note that this is the opposite of the way an individual plans for battle.

4. This was first stated by Sun Tzu (c. 500 B.C.) in his book *The Art of War,* trans. Samuel B. Griffith (New York: Oxford University Press, 1982), pp. 132–3.

Conclusion

There are hundreds of strategies and thousands of techniques—this book only examines a few of the more important ones. Do not try to master them all, just study those that seem to apply to your chosen art and try to understand their essence.

Merely being able to use a strategy should not be enough. You must continue past the point of mastery to the level of understanding, going through the jutsu to realize the do or michi.[1] Then you will no longer be just a person who uses strategy; you will be a strategist.

The world is full of armchair warriors, men who do not understand the reality of combat. To master the Way of Strategy, you must remove the blinders of civilization and see war the way it really is. Then you can appreciate the Four Great Truths of combat:

1. *Violence is a part of life.* You do not have to like it, but you had best be able to deal with it.

2. *Violence hurts.* Even when you win a fight without being touched, you will still have sore knuckles.

3. *Long battles are bad.* When you are forced into a violent situation, it is best to get it over with as soon as possible.

4. *It is better to win than to lose.*

You can win with speed or you can win with strength. You can also win with superior technique. However, all of these methods have physical limits. In the words of some forgotten cowboy: "There ain't never been a horse that couldn't be rode, or a cowboy who couldn't be throwed." No matter how good you are, there is always someone who is better. Even if you make it to the very top and are the best in the world, one day you will grow old. Then, when your strength and speed fail you, you will have nothing left.

Heiho no michi is a way around this dilemma. It is an art of the mind and the spirit, growing stronger with each year. It will not make you invincible; it just makes you better. And, because the strength of the mind far outlasts that of the body, you will be better longer.

Still, even after reading this book, there will be people who continue to say, "violence never solved anything." That is sad. Graveyards are full of good men who have been misled by this fallacy. Violence has *always* been the ultimate argument. That is why countries go to war: to achieve an objective they cannot reach by any other means. Every nation in existence today is here because it stepped away from the negotiating table, picked up the sword, fought, and won the right to exist.

Men also used to have to fight for the privilege of life. The fact that life has come to be viewed as an inalienable right has caused too many people to think it is also free. Life is only free for the lucky ones. Sooner or later, the average man always has to fight and bleed for it. If you have mastered the Way of Strategy, when the time comes for your battle, you may win.

Aside from the pure survival value of studying strategy, there is always the mystique of the warrior. It is this that keeps men studying the profession of arms long after their need for it has passed. This is the fascinating aspect of the Way of Strategy and the reason very many people choose this path. It comes closer than any other art to the heart of the warrior. This is something that is beyond rationality. It is an inner drive, an innate part of being a man. Although most people see this urge as a danger to civilization, it should be honored for its role in making mankind the dominant species—if men had never marched off to war, the human race would still be huddling in caves, trembling at strange noises in the night.

NOTES

1. See the beginning of Chapter Two.

Appendix A

Pronunciation Guide

Japanese is one of the easiest languages in the world to pronounce. There are only five vowels, each of which has but a single pronunciation. (Compare this with the multiple pronunciations of each English vowel.)

The Japanese vowels are pronounced as follows:

a	as in	f*a*ther
i	as in	m*ee*t
o	as in	t*o*w
e	as in	p*e*t
u	as in	t*oo*

Remember, there are no variations. Avoid the common error of pronouncing recurring vowels in the same word differently (e.g., eh-ree-mee for *irimi,* instead of ee-ree-mee).

There are nine consonants. The only one of these that presents any difficulty is *r.* A Japanese *r* is halfway between *r* and *l* in English. Try saying *ram* and *lam* at the same time to approximate this sound.

These consonants are never used alone; each one is always followed by a vowel. The resulting forty-five combinations, plus the five vowels, gave a total of fifty basic sounds. The old name for the Japanese language was "the Fifty Sounds."

Five sounds are no longer used and a nasal *n* has been added, giving a new total of forty-six basic sounds. The nasal *n* is used unvocalized and *only* at the end of a syllable. The basic sounds are usually arranged on a grid, as follows:

-*n*	*wa*	*ra*	*ya*	*ma*	*ha*	*na*	*ta*	*sa*	*ka*	*a*
		ri		*mi*	*hi*	*ni*	*ti*	*si*	*ki*	*i*
		ru	*yu*	*mu*	*hu*	*nu*	*tu*	*su*	*ku*	*u*
		re		*me*	*he*	*ne*	*te*	*se*	*ke*	*e*
	wo	*ro*	*yo*	*mo*	*ho*	*no*	*to*	*so*	*ko*	*o*

This is known as the *kunrei-shiki rōmanji* system for writing Japanese in roman letters. It was introduced by the Japanese government in 1937. The problem with this system is that it does not illustrate certain changes that took place in the spoken language over the centuries. In other words, all the combinations on the chart are not spoken exactly as they are written. Because of this, although the kunrei-shiki romanji is handy for learning to conjugate verbs, it is rarely used for normal translations.

The system in general use today is the *Hebon-shiki rōmanji* system, dating from 1885. Rewriting the chart of basic sounds with Hebon-shiki romanji (this is the Japanese pronunciation of Hepburn-style-roman-characters) makes it look like this:

-*n*	*wa*	*ra*	*ya*	*ma*	*ha*	*na*	*ta*	*sa*	*ka*	*a*
		ri		*mi*	*hi*	*ni*	*chi*	*shi*	*ki*	*i*
		ru	*yu*	*mu*	*fu*	*nu*	*tsu*	*su*	*ku*	*u*
		re		*me*	*he*	*ne*	*te*	*se*	*ke*	*e*
	(w)o	*ro*	*yo*	*mo*	*ho*	*no*	*to*	*so*	*ko*	*o*

In certain combinations, some of the basic sounds are modified into what are known as voiced sounds. This gives a second chart of *daku-on:*

ba	*pa*	*da*	*za*	*ga*
bi	*pi*	*ji*	*zi*	*gi*
bu	*pu*	*zu*	*zu*	*gu*
be	*pe*	*de*	*ze*	*ge*
bo	*po*	*do*	*zo*	*go*
(h-)		*(t-)*	*(s-)*	*(k-)*

Although these daku-on may seem a bit strange, they are quite logical when viewed in context. For example, consider the words *kesa kiri,* meaning a diagonal cut with a sword. If you say them fast, combining them into one word, the second *k* becomes a *g: kesagiri.*

This gives twenty-five new sounds, for a total of seventy-one.

The last group of modified sounds are the *yō-on,* "twisted sounds." These are formed by combining the y-column with the i-row:

rya	*mya*	*hya*	*nya*	*cha*	*sha*	*kya*
ryu	*myu*	*hyu*	*nyu*	*chu*	*shu*	*kyu*
ryo	*myo*	*hyo*	*nyo*	*cho*	*sho*	*kyo*

This gives twenty-one new sounds, for a total of ninety-two.

When you modify these into voiced sounds, you get:

bya	*pya*	*ja*	*gya*
byu	*pyu*	*ju*	*gyu*
byo	*pyo*	*jo*	*gyo*

As you can see, this is a very logical system. There is a total of 104 sounds, and all of them are logical derivations of the basic grid of forty-six.

The only other thing you need for proper pronunciation is an awareness of the long vowels, indicated by a macron. When you see this, make sure to stretch the vowel out for twice its normal length. If you do not, you may be saying an entirely different word. For example: a *koto* is a harp; a *kotō* is an old sword; *kōtō* is a red-light district.

The use of the macron is also part of the standard method of writing Japanese in roman letters. For all practical purposes, there is no other system. However, Westerners still persist in making up their own systems. The most flagrant example of this is the common practice of writing *jūjutsu* as *jujitsu.* That is entirely wrong, no matter where you see it. The only other proper way to write *jūjutsu* is in the kunrei-shiki system: *zyūzyutu.*

One final point: there is no plural tense in Japanese. So, try to avoid adding an *s* to Japanese words—you have one *katana* or ten *katana,* never ten *katanas.*

Appendix B

Future Study

If you desire to continue your study of heiho, you must join a traditional dojo—there is no other way. The vast majority of all information on Japanese strategy is handed down in the form of *kuden,* oral traditions, and there is very little written material on the subject. Also, heiho is something you must experience physically to learn; reading about it is not enough. (The samurai liked to say that a man who read too much smelled like dead leaves.)

Proper dojo are few and far between, so plan on devoting a lot of time to finding one. Almost every small town has some form of martial-arts school or club, but only a fraction of 1 percent of these qualify as traditional dojo. Plan on visiting every school within one hundred miles of your home and observing the classes.

Here are some positive things to look for: an instructor who looks like a cross between a bank president and a marine sergeant major; a school that is spotlessly clean and somewhat stark in appearance; rigid discipline; training uniforms that are immaculate and identical for all students; much silence; lots of noise; exaggerated respect toward seniors; a shrine; real swords; and a spiritual intensity that seems thick enough to feel.

Here are some negative signs to watch out for: a sales pitch from the school manager; students arriving for class who are wearing casual clothes; children; music; friendly instructors; students addressing their seniors by given names; imitation swords; casual attitudes; personalized training uniforms; students sitting tailor fashion, with their legs crossed in front of them; and introductory lessons.

As you visit these schools, there is one important fact you should remember: a good instructor probably does not want to bother with you. It is your job, as a prospective disciple, to convince the sensei to accept you, not the other way around. When you find a place you like, make it a point to talk with a few of the students before requesting an interview with the headmaster. The students will be happy to give you a few tips on how to act. For example, the discussion of money in a dojo is considered terribly vulgar—tuition is placed in an envelope and discreetly left on the instructor's desk, preferably when he is absent. There are many minor points such as this that you should learn before requesting membership.

Appendix C

Famous Battles

There are many lessons, both positive and negative, that can be learned from the past. The study of famous battles, therefore, has always played a major role in the education of a strategist.

Because hindsight is always more accurate than foresight, it is a great temptation for students to pass judgment on how these battles were fought. This should be done with caution, because military history tends to be long on physical detail but short on strategic background—the history books are full of information on *what* a particular general did, but they rarely mention *why* he did it.

Because of this lack of information—information about the *why* of a battle—the examples in this section were selected for clarity of strategy, not importance. A case in point is Operation Overlord, the Allied invasion of Europe in 1944. This is probably the most famous battle of modern times, but there was little strategy involved.

It is an unpleasant fact that there is not much great strategy to be found in these old battles. The more that you study, the more apparent this becomes. The reason for this lack is that, in the past, many officers were quite incompetent. It used to be very common for an officer to purchase his commission. This resulted in generals who were more qualified to host a party than to lead an army. Happily, modern armies have finally begun selecting their officers by ability rather than breeding.

However, despite the unclarity or lack of strategy, there is still much to be learned from history.

THE SOMME (1 July 1916)

After the initial German assault on France, the war settled into a stalemate. This was caused by a new weapon: the machine gun. With this, one squad could pin down a company of infantry. The military commanders were unprepared for this defensive style of war, which led to the catastrophe at the Somme.

If there is a single case that could be said to exemplify the worst strategy in the entire history of war, this is it— just thinking about the battle makes most military men angry. The Allied commander, General Sir Douglas Haig, decided on a frontal assault against the German lines, a war of attrition. There was no strategy and very little technique involved; it was just brute force applied against an immovable object. If the battle plan had been created by a lieutenant instead of a general, he would have been shot for incompetence.

During the first day of the assault on the German lines, there were 57,000 casualties. Although any general can make a mistake, even a disastrous one such as this, there is no excuse to continue it. Although the initial phase of the attack had to be continued because of inadequate communications, Haig seemed to adopt an attitude of, "don't confuse me with facts, my mind is made up." He continued for 140 days! During the month of July, the British lost an average of 10,000 men per day. The estimated total casualties at the end of the battle were 630,000 on the Allied side and 660,000 for the Germans. For this appalling loss of men, Haig managed to push his line forward five miles.

CAMBRAI (20 November 1917)

If the Somme was a disaster, Cambrai was brilliant. The

British massed a force of 381 tanks forty-five miles south of the Somme in total secrecy. Not announcing the attack with a traditional artillery barrage, this force rolled forward through the mists on the morning of November 20.

The tank was a new weapon, and the Germans were terrified. At a cost of only 1,500 casualties, the British accounted for 10,000 Germans. They punched a four-mile-wide hole through the German lines and drove in for ten miles.

Strategically, this was an excellent example of kime. By using the armor as a unit, instead of spreading it out in support of the infantry, its total power was focused on a small segment of the enemy line. Launching the attack in secret was an example of kage—the sudden appearance of these monstrous new weapons had a much greater effect on enemy morale than if they had been used as part of a traditional attack.

Tragically, General Haig did not take advantage of this victory. What should have been a German rout and the turning point of the war became an inconclusive engagement. Cambrai should have been used as a harai no heiho. However, since the Allies did not instantly follow up on the armored victory, the Germans had time to regroup and eventually regain their lost ground.

This is perhaps a worse condemnation of Haig's lack of ability than the disaster at the Somme. It is the mark of any good strategist that he always stands ready to make use of any advantage. Even if the suki comes without warning, he is ready to seize it.

(One wonders what a Patton or a Rommel would have accomplished with a few hundred tanks and half a million lives to spend.)

AUSTERLITZ (25 September 1805)

It is not the main battle, but the opening phase at Ulm that is so interesting.

Napoleon, with a series of provocative cavalry raids, lured the Austrian army to the east. This was nobashi no heiho. Then, with a perfect example of irimi no heiho, he surrounded them at Ulm. To use such a large force (200,000 men) in this manner was brilliant. (Napoleon was a great believer in the use of mobility as a weapon.)

EL ALAMEIN (23 October 1942)

This was a case of General Sir Douglas Montgomery at his best. While not the cowboy type—daring was never a word used to describe him—he was a great planner. At El Alamein, in North Africa, he was finally allowed time to think and he made a good job of it.

Montgomery's selection of the battlefield was brilliant. With the sea at his left and cliffs on the right, Rommel's mobility was greatly reduced. This application of shidai no heiho was to Montgomery's advantage, because Rommel was considered to be the world's leading master of tank warfare.

The actual attack was made in the manner of shinkage no heiho. Montgomery led with an attack to the southern end of the German line, then hooked with his armor toward its northern end. The steady pressure in the south prevented Rommel from shifting troops north, immobilizing him even further.

Overall, El Alamein was a case of good keikaku and clear heiho. Montgomery took advantage of every opportunity he was presented with. Combining good planning and strategy with solid technique, he achieved a major victory.

GETTYSBURG (1 July 1863)

This is a battle that Lee should have won. He was a brilliant strategist, and if he had not had a cavalry commander as independent as Stuart, the war might have had a different conclusion.

General Robert E. Lee started the battle pinned down by Northern troops in the South. With a superb example of hanashi no heiho, he disengaged his entire army from the line, shifted to the west, and raced north into enemy territory. The objective was kokorozuki no heiho, a thrust at the enemy heart.

However, General James E. B. Stuart started an independent raid on June 25. Stuart paralleled Lee's line of advance, but far to the east.

The primary job of the cavalry in a strategy such as Lee's is providing intelligence. Because Stuart was so far away, Lee was forced to operate blind. He was not aware of the pursuit by Union troops, or of their strength, until it was too late. Even after the battle had begun, Lee was still unsure of his opponent's strength and distribution.

Stuart's raid is a good example of forgetting daisho no heiho. Although his raid hurt the enemy, his failure to provide intelligence to Lee cost the South the war.

PEARL HARBOR (7 December 1941)

The Japanese attack on Pearl Harbor was pure ichi no hyoshi no heiho. For all practical purposes, it destroyed the United States as a naval power in the Pacific. If the Japanese had managed to catch the American carriers in port, the results would have been catastrophic instead of merely disastrous.

The standard question about Japan in World War II is, "If strategy is so good, and if the Japanese are masters of it, why didn't they win?" The answer is twofold. First, after the Meiji Restoration, the samurai class was no longer in power and the military was taken over by commoners, men not well versed in heiho. True, there were some great strategists in the upper levels of the military, but these men were often restrained by civilians in uniform. Decisions were often based on politics instead of practicality.

The second reason for the Japanese defeat was physical. Japan is a very small nation. It is so small that, even if it had defeated the United States, it could not have done anything with the victory. There simply were not enough people in Japan to provide an occupation force. The knowledge that they had taken on a giant colored all aspects of Japanese strategy. They became much too conservative, and no war was ever won with defensive thinking.

Conservative strategy was manifested by the Japanese

failure to carry through when they had an advantage. This was seen throughout the war, starting with Pearl Harbor.

After the initial Japanese attack, the Pearl Harbor defenses were destroyed. If the Japanese had wished, they could have occupied the islands. Even a follow-up attack would have allowed them to destroy the submarine base, which was untouched in the first raid. However, their fears of counterattack—they did not know where the American aircraft carriers were—caused the Japanese fleet to withdraw. This withdrawal was an example of menzuki no heiho without a proper follow-through.

BLITZKRIEG (9 May 1940)

Although it was not very enjoyable on the receiving end, this is an example of war at its best. Sweeping around the northern end of French defenses, the Germans destroyed all opposition in less than a month. The line of attack was in the style of irimi no heiho, avoiding the Maginot Line with its fortified French artillery.

Germany's attack on France was a modification of the Schlieffen Plan, which had been around since the turn of the century. It was augmented by use of armor and air support as a unified striking force. In other words, kime. The fact that this plan worked is a monument to the inertia of military thought—the French were expecting World War II to be a replay of the previous war. By the time they found out that the strategies of the previous generation were no longer viable, it was too late.

The only problem with the German attack on France was that it was too successful. With the army advancing faster than Hitler had dreamed possible, he grew timid and held them back so he could study the situation. By the time he decided that it was not a trap and he really was winning, the British had evacuated its troops from the beaches of Dunkirk.

Hitler's failure to take advantage of the situation is a clear example of not using makuraosae no heiho. He violated the prime rule of combat: when you are winning, don't stop!

If he had not paused, he could have continued his attack all the way to London. The American people were still strong isolationists and wanted no part of a European war. If presented with a fait accompli, the United States might never have entered the war.

Appendix D

Glossary

Aiki. The principle of dominating an opponent with your spirit.

Aikidō. A modern form of aikijujutsu; the ultimate reality of aikijutsu.

Aikijūjutsu. The jujutsu of the Daito-ryu; jujutsu techniques applied with aiki.

Aikijutsu. The art of using aiki.

Aiuchi. Simultaneous strikes; the act of hitting an opponent at the same time as he hits you.

Bokken. A wooden sword. The standard length is forty-one inches, and the usual material is oak or ebony.

Budō. Lit., "the Way of War"; the ultimate reality of war.

Bujutsu. The science of war.

Chikama. A close combat interval; the range at which you can strike your enemy without taking a step.

Chikara. Strength.

Chūden. Middle-level teachings.

Chūshin. The center.

Daishō. Lit., "large and small"; the combination of long and short swords worn by a samurai.

Daitō-ryu. The original school of aikijutsu.

Deshi. A disciple.

Dōjō. A training center for Japanese martial arts.

Dori. *See* tori.

Engetsu. Lit., "full-moon"; a large circular motion with a sword.

Fudōshin. An immovable spirit.

Fudōtai. An immovable body.

Fukurami. Combining form of *fukuramu,* "to expand."

Fumikomi. An attack step.

Geri. *See* keri.

Getsukage. Lit., "moon-shadow"; to reflect your opponent's physical or spiritual action.

Gihō. A technique.

Giri. *See* kiri.

Go Rin No Sho. A famous book on strategy, written by Miyamoto Musashi.

Gohō. A hard-style method of combat; a technique applied directly against your opponent's line of motion.

Hanashi. Combining form of *hanasu,* "to let go of, to separate from."

Han'on. A half step.

Haragei. Intuitive thought.

Harai. Combining form of *harau,* "to sweep aside."

Heihō. Strategy.

Henka. A variation on a technique.

Hiden. Secret teachings.

Hijiki. Reflex action; to spring (away from).

Hishigi. Combining form of *hishigu,* "to crush."

Hito e mi. Lit., "action toward unity"; to blend with an opponent's action.

Hyōshi. Rhythm.

Iaijutsu. A method of drawing a sword and cutting in one motion.

In. The negative force of nature; negative, dark, female.

Ippon. One point.

Irimi. The action of entering; moving toward your opponent's rear corner; a leaping turn.

Itten. A spot about two inches below the navel; the center of balance of a human body.

Ittō-ryu. A famous sword school.

Jūdō. A modern sport derived from jujutsu; the ultimate reality of jujutsu.

Jūhō. A soft-style method of combat; a technique applied in the same direction as your opponent's line of motion.

Jūjutsu. A combat art based on the principle of juho. Its techniques include throws, joint-locks, chokes, and strikes, both with and without weapons.

Jutsu. A suffix denoting science or art.

Ka. A suffix denoting a student (i.e., a karateka is a student of karate).

Kado. A corner.

Kage. A shadow.

Kaimon. An open gate.

Karate. A modern combat art, derived from the art of Okinawa-te.

Kata. A prearranged series of techniques; the shoulder; one (of a pair).

Katana. A long sword, worn thrust through the belt with the edge up.

Katsuri. Lit., "method of winning"; to win by changing speeds.

Kawari. Combining form of *kawaru,* "to change."

Keikaku. Planning.

Ken. A sword.

Kendō. Lit., "the Way of the Sword"; a modern sport derived from kenjutsu; the ultimate reality of kenjutsu.

Kenjutsu. Japanese swordsmanship.

Keri. Combining form of *keru,* "to kick."

Ki. The life force.

Kiai. Intense ki.

Kime. Focus.

Kimono. A Japanese robe. For a man, the normal color was black with white crest insignia. The classical costume for a samurai was: *fundoshi,* a loincloth; *juban,* an under-kimono; *obi,* a sash, approximately four inches wide by ten feet long; *tabi,* socks with a separate section for the big toe; *zori,* straw sandals; *hakama,* a divided skirt; and kimono.

Kiri. Combining form of *kiru,* "to cut."

Kirigaeshi. A sword exercise.

Kissaki. The tip of a sword.

Kōchiku. A tall bamboo stem.

Kokoro. Heart; mental attitude.

Kokyu chikara. Strength applied while inhaling.

Kokyū dōsa. A breathing exercise.

Kuzushi. Combining form of *kuzusu,* "to break down."

Maai. The combative engagement distance.

Magiri. Combining form of *magiru,* "to stir up."

Makura. A pillow.

Mawashi. Combining form of *mawasu,* "to turn, to rotate."

Meiji. The emperor of Japan from 1868–1912.

Mekakushi uchi. A strike used to temporarily blind an opponent.

Men. The face.

Metsuke. Focal point.

Michi. The Way; *dō* in compound words.

Minari. Appearance.

Misekake. A feint.

Momiji. Lit., "red-leaf"; to fall as softly as an autumn leaf.

Munen. To have no plan.

Mushin. To have no thoughts.

Musō. To have no thoughts.

Nagashi. Combining form of *nagasu,* "to flow."

Nage. Combining form of *nageru,* "to throw."

Nebari. Combining form of *nebaru,* "to stick to."

Nippon. Japan. (Note: The name *Japan* is a mispronunciation of a Portuguese mispronunciation of a Chinese word.)

Nitenichi-ryu. The school of fencing created by Musashi.

Nitōbun. Broken rhythm.

No. Possessive particle. Read it *of,* from right to left (e.g., "two *no* one" is read "one of two.")

Nobashi. Combining form of *nobasu,* "to stretch."

Nyūnanshin. To be ready to accept new knowledge.

Obiyakashi. To threaten.

Ōjite. To respond to.

Okinawa-te. A form of hand-to-hand combat indigenous to the islands of Okinawa.

Okuden. Hidden teachings; the advanced techniques of a ryu.

Omote. The front; techniques of a ryu which are revealed to the public.

Osae. Combining form of *osaeru,* "to press down, to control."

Renshu. Training.

Ryōte. Both hands.

Ryu. A traditional style of combat; a school or system.

Ryuchō. Lit., "flow-bounce"; two methods of connecting techniques.

Sabaki. Motion.

Samurai. A member of the ruling caste of Japan in the seventeenth to nineteenth centuries.

Sanchin. A method of hardening the body to withstand an attack.

Sankai. Lit., "mountain-sea"; opposites.

Seiza. A sitting posture akin to kneeling.

Sekka. A spark.

Sensei. A teacher; a title of respect for a person having advanced knowledge.

Sente. To take the initiative.

Seppuku. Ritual suicide.

Shibui. Elegant.

Shibumi. Elegance.

Shidai. Circumstances.

Shikko sabaki. A method of moving while in a kneeling position.

Shikkotai. To stand close to.

Shinkage. To hide the spirit.

Shinken. A real sword.

Shintō. Native Japanese religion.

Shintō-ryu. An ancient school of swordsmanship.

Shinza. A shrine.

Shoden. The basic teachings of a ryu.

Shōgun. A military dictator.

Shorin-ryu. A system of karate.

Shoshinsha. A beginner.

Shōsotsu. Lit., "officers and men"; to order.

Shotokan. A system of karate.

Shukotai. To stand a little closer than normal.

Sori. The curvature of a sword.

Sudori. Combining form of *sudoru,* "to pass."

Suigetsu. Lit., "moon-in-water"; to draw an attack and then evade it.

Suki. A momentary gap in concentration.

Suriage. To slide upward.

Sutemi. To sacrifice.

Tachi. A long sword worn slung from the belt, edge down (pre-sixteenth century).

Tachifumi. To prevent your enemy from cutting.

Tai sabaki. Body motion.

Tateki. Several opponents.

Tenshin-ryu. A style of swordsmanship derived from the Itto-ryu and Shinto-ryu.

Tokoshi. To cross a great distance.

Tori. Combining form of *toru,* "to take."

Tsuki. Combining form of *tsuku,* "to thrust."

Uchikomi. An attack step.

Uchima. Standard fighting interval.

Ugokashi. Combining form of *ugokasu,* "to move."

Undō. An exercise.

Ushiro. Back; to the rear.

Utsurakashi. To transfer an emotion.

Waza. A technique.

Yagyu-ryu. A famous fencing school.

Yamate-ryu. A school of aikijutsu.

Yō. The positive force of nature; positive, male, light.

Zanshin. The involuntary pause after a technique.

Zazen. Seated meditation.

Zentai. Total.

Zuki. *See* tsuki.